D1172855

**Here's What Industry Leaders Are Saying about** *Corporate Universities,* **Revised and Updated Edition:**

*Jeanne Meister's book detailing the growth of corporate universities raises critical strategic and operating issues for training executives and for the leaders of U.S. higher education. It's on a 'must read' list for anyone who wants to understand trends that will help shape the future of post-secondary education.*

Charles Hickman
Director of Projects and Services
AACSB—The International Association for Management Education

*Every organization has to do a thorough analysis of its own development needs. But it's critical to continuously scan the environment for new, fresh ideas and approaches. Jeanne Meister's book is an invaluable reference for what is happening in the field of 'university'-style programs. If you're a practitioner in this field—or want to be—you can't afford* not *to read this book.*

Steven P. Kirn, Ph.D.
Vice President, Education and Development
Sears, Roebuck and Co.

Corporate Universities: Lessons in Building a World-Class Work Force *stimulated creative thinking on how Mutual of Omaha can develop a high-performance work force for the twenty-first century.*

Robert Bogart
Executive Vice President of Human Resources
Mutual of Omaha

*Jeanne Meister's* Corporate Universities *was the cornerstone of thinking that prompted Anheuser-Busch to launch the Busch Learning Center. Jeanne's vision for the emerging role of the corporate university concept provided us with a practical approach to build the vision, mission, and infrastructure of the Busch Learning Center.*

David Vaughn
Director, The Busch Learning Center
Anheuser-Busch Inc.

*In the increasingly competitive global business environment, Jeanne Meister's extremely useful and easy-to-read book on corporate universities will help European managers learn from their U.S. counterparts the best practices of corporate learning centers. We found useful tools for best practice sharing and helped answer the core questions: Where are we today? Where do we want to be? How will we get there?*

Bernadette Conraths
Director General
European Foundation for Management Development

*I found Jeanne Meister's excellent book on* Corporate Universities *a rich source of ideas. It served as the inspiration for our own initiative. You will find in this book a clear, up-to-date definition and description of what it takes to support the development of a world-class global work force.*

David Owens
Vice-President, Worldwide Professional Development
Unisys Corporation

*In 1993, Southern California Water Company (SCWC) facilitated the paradigm shift toward a* learning organization *by introducing the corporate university concept. Jeanne Meister's book on* Corporate Universities *was indispensable for planning and launching our university model.*

Diane Rentfrow, NCC, CT
Corporate Dean, Employee Development University
Southern California Water Company

*Jeanne Meister's book provided Conoco University with some excellent insights as we developed our direction and approach for launching a corporate university. Jeanne's exploration into corporate university best practices provides a useful source of key learnings and practices.*

David J. Nelson
Manager, Organization Development, Human Resources
Conoco

# CORPORATE UNIVERSITIES
## Lessons in Building a World-Class Work Force

# CORPORATE UNIVERSITIES

## Lessons in Building a World-Class Work Force

### Revised and Updated Edition

*Jeanne C. Meister*

**McGraw-Hill, Inc.**

New York  St. Louis  San Francisco  Auckland  Bogotá
Caracas  Hamburg  Lisbon  London  Madrid
Mexico  Milan  Montreal  New Delhi  Paris
San Juan  São Paulo  Singapore
Sydney  Tokyo  Toronto

**Library of Congress Cataloging-in-Publication Data**

**Meister, Jeanne C.**
    Corporate universities : lessons in building a world-class work
force / Jeanne C. Meister. — Rev. and Updated ed.
        p.   cm.
    Rev. ed. of author's: Corporate quality universities.
    ISBN 0-7863-0787-0
    1. Employer-supported education—United States.   2. Employees-
-Training of—United States.   I. Meister, Jeanne C.   Corporate
quality universities.   II. Title.
    HF5549.5.T7M423   1998
    658.3'124—dc21                                                      97-32842
                                                                              CIP

# McGraw-Hill

*A Division of The McGraw·Hill Companies*

1   2   3   4   5   6   7   8   9   DOC/DOC   9   0   2   1   0   9   8   7

ISBN 0-7863-0787-0


*The editor for this book was Patrick Muller,  the editing supervisor was John M.
Morriss, and the production supervisor was Suzanne W. B. Rapcavage. This book
was set in Palatino. It was composed by Digitype, and production supervision by
Progressive Publishing Alternatives.*

*Printed and bound by R. R. Donnelley & Sons Company.*

For more information about other McGraw-Hill materials, call
1-800-2-MCGRAW in the United States. In other countries, call your
nearest McGraw-Hill office.

*To Bob and Danielle*
*for your love and support*

# Preface

*A time of turbulence is a dangerous time but its greatest danger is the temptation to deny reality.*

Peter Drucker

While corporate universities have been around for the last 40 years with the launch of General Electric's Crotonville in 1955, the real surge of interest in launching a corporate university as a strategic umbrella for managing an organization's employee learning and development began in the late 1980s. The last ten years has seen the number of corporate universities grow from 400 to over 1,000. During this period, many companies witnessed a radically shortened shelf-life of knowledge, and began to determine that they could no longer rely on institutions of higher education to re-tool their work force. Instead, they set out to create their own "corporate universities" with the goal of achieving tighter control and ownership over the learning process by more closely linking learning programs to real business goals and strategies.

The unprecedented growth of corporate universities suggests just how acute the need is for corporations to re-tool their work forces. Increasingly corporations are entering the business of education in order to ensure their own future survival. As corporate universities lead the way in experimenting with distance learning, forming collaborations with local and international universities and creating electronic storefronts for learning at the desk-top, they are providing models of market-driven educational systems. These systems not only better serve the needs of working adults but they also bring efficiency to the process of designing, developing and deploying learning programs worldwide. Corporations ranging from Silicon Valley's Sun Microsystems and Wall Street's First Union Corporation to General Motors are using their corporate universities as an umbrella for cost effective management of a worldwide education function.

This book continues my previous work in *Corporate Quality Universities* by providing an updated, in-depth and behind the scenes look at how fifty corporations are using the corporate university model to manage their investment in employee education. What is distinctive about these firms as a group is that they are taking a proactive role in developing educational systems and cooperative partnerships with academia to create a work force that can operate successfully in a knowledge economy.

While the word university conjures up thoughts of a physical campus, deans and tenured faculty, the corporate version is remotely different and refreshingly innovative. In fact, many of the corporate universities profiled here, lack any distinctive physical site. Instead, these corporate universities are a process where all levels of employees are involved in continuous life long learning to improve their performance on the job. Even as some corporate universities do build physical campuses, they utilize these buildings not as places of learning but as a nexus for sharing best practices globally. The corporate universities profiled here have become more than "dressed up training departments with a new name," rather they represent a best-in-class effort to develop all levels of employees in the skills, knowledge and competencies needed to be successful in their current jobs and capable of adapting to future job requirements.

Companies steering their resources into creating these corporate universities fervently believe that the key to their success and competitive advantage in the marketplace will be giving employees greater access to updating their knowledge and skills. *Corporate Universities* presents an in-depth examination of the types of learning solutions the best of the breed are developing for their own employees as well as for their customers and suppliers to ensure that all the members of their value chain have the skills needed for success. This revised edition offers a ringside look at innovative corporate university programs at world class companies known for their long history of investing in employee learning and development such as General Electric, Motorola and Xerox. This book also looks at corporate university initiatives launched at smaller privately held companies like Lord Corporation, a diversified, technology-based firm employing 1,800 workers and reaching $336 million in sales in 1996.

Taken together, the learning and development programs profiled here are evidence of a movement that is both an opportunity and a threat to traditional institutions of higher education. Traditionally, learning was performed by academic institutions, schools, colleges and universities. But as more learning becomes a function of work, the private sector under the umbrella of a corporate university is increasingly taking on the role of educator.

What is surprising though is just how much student volume flows through corporate universities. Corporate University Xchange, Inc. conducts an Annual Survey of 100 corporate universities, known as *Corporate University Future Directions*. The body of students represented by these 100 corporate universities is roughly equal to 125 Universities of Michigan (based upon the 1996 total enrollment of 36,000 students). Increasingly, the job of educating these 4 million plus workers is being handled by a combination of corporate universities and their learning partners which includes both traditional training firms, accredited universities as well as the rapidly growing segment of for-profit education firms.

The entrance of the private sector into the learning business is placing severe pressure for transformation on America's 3,632 institutions of higher education. These institutions need to reinvent themselves for the knowledge economy. This re-invention involves both updating the content as well as altering the delivery system. Learning must be relevant to the skills needed for success in the knowledge economy as well as accessible and convenient to how adults learn, that is, on-the-job and from co-workers.

While there are signs of change and progress, much of the experimentation learning is taking place in corporations rather than in universities. Consider that corporations responding to our *Annual Survey of Corporate University Future Directions* predict that by the year 2000 up to 50% of all learning will be delivered via technology.

This book presents a detailed look at why and how corporations are leading the innovations in education. So, whether you are the president of an institution of higher learning, a chief executive officer of a company, or operate in the learning and development arena as a chief learning officer, chief information officer or human resource director, you'll find a number of basic guidelines that can assist you in evaluating and reinventing your organization's ap-

*courses on financial by*
*by H.H.*

*courses by CFO*
*J. Marchese*
*B. Burke*

proach to learning. Some examples of the guidelines revealed in this book include:

**Senior level management support and active involvement is crucial to the evolution of learning.** Chief executive officers must consider training to be a lever for cultural change rather than an "executive perk." Enlightened CEOs at companies ranging from General Electric, Saturn and Bank of Montreal are in fact playing the role of chief learning officer by spending significant amounts of their time facilitating learning, building educational partnerships with academia and publicly stating the importance of learning as a competitive advantage to the corporation. Consider the fact that our Annual Survey of Corporate University Future Directions found 15 percent of our sample of 100 firms to have a CEO that spends up to three days per month facilitating learning and sharing best practices. What's more, many of these firms have put into place recognition and reward systems so that employees are rewarded for their commitment to learning not just for meeting the numbers.

**Effective learning is carefully tied to the strategic needs of the business through a network of learning councils and advisory boards.** Key business leaders and general managers must be involved in creating the vision and charter of the corporate university and be accountable for measuring its overall effectiveness. In other words, the interest, excitement and involvement in employee learning and development must be transferred from the training department to become the concern of every business manager. How does this transformation occur? By creating a system of governance where business leaders share their key challenges as well as the specific type of skills needed for their employees to be successful in the marketplace.

*IMPORTANT SM!*

**World-class learning solutions are the result of forming collaborative partnerships with a myriad of innovative firms.** In order to create a truly market-driven educational system, corporate universities must form alliances with an array of learning partners which include local universities, nationally known uni-

versities, international universities, community colleges, technical
institutes, training firms, consulting companies and for-profit educational companies offering web-based accredited learning
courses. In order to offer accessible, convenient and portable
learning credentials, corporations must enter into partnerships
with both traditional and non-traditional suppliers of learning.
Vendor selection and management becomes a key competency for
corporations to develop and nurture as the job of managing outsourced learning partnerships becomes much more complex.

**Technology must be aggressively utilized to accelerate
employee learning.** Major innovations in support systems, improved delivery technologies and global reach are transforming
the face of learning at breakneck speed. The ability to disseminate
new material within the company overnight is now the expected
norm. With technology-based learning, employees can complete
courses just-in-time of needing the knowledge." In a market-
driven economy where business conditions change so fast, this is
crucial to obtaining a competitive advantage in a global marketplace.

**The audience for learning now extends beyond the cor-
poration to include key participants in an organization's value
chain.** Companies frequently train their customers but usually
this training revolves around the features and benefits of using
their products. World-class companies profiled here are experimenting with revamping their entire customer education department so it becomes both a vehicle for brand preference as well as a
profit center for the corporation. Companies that will be successful
in creating learning organizations realize that everyone—including dealers, distributors, wholesalers, suppliers and customers—
must understand the company's shared vision and, more importantly, how to realize this vision in the marketplace. Creating an
enhanced customer education service is becoming vitally important to sustaining competitive advantage in this decade and the
next.

This book concludes with an appendix which lists the names
and addresses of the fifty corporations who have adopted the cor-

porate university model. This can serve as a useful guide for readers to network and benchmark with practitioners in identifying ways to enhance their organization's learning and development programs. While reading this book, it's important to remember that the corporate university is a "work in progress." Given the rate of change, what seems state-of-the-art today, will be hopelessly archaic tomorrow. The very form and structure of a corporate university survives only with constant adaptation and change, so these best practices need continual updating by you—the reader. I encourage you to visit our website at www.corpu.com and join our international network of leaders of learning so we can keep these best practices current and "on-target."

Regards,

**Jeanne C. Meister**
jcm@corpu.com

# Acknowledgements

I want to acknowledge the many people who have patiently cooperated with me over the past three years to write *Corporate Universities*. They have generously given their time to discuss the future of higher education and specifically the blurring of corporate universities with institutions of higher education. Thank you for your insight and contributions. I hope you are proud of what is conveyed here.

I am of course deeply indebted to the team at McGraw-Hill including Patrick Muller, Development Editor, for the commitment he brought to ensuring this book became a reality and to Jeffrey A. Krames, Publisher, for his continual vision and perspective. Finally, I owe a special debt to Adam Eisenstat, and Linda Thornburg, for contributing to the final shape and scope of this book.

Writing and consulting on the topic of corporate universities has taken me across the world, interviewing, visiting and meeting with scores of wonderfully talented individuals who manage the learning functions at the fifty corporate universities presented here. I also have examined the impact of corporate universities on higher education and I am indebted to the following organizations for their guidance, wisdom and sponsorship: American Council on Education, AACSB—The International Association for Management Education, European Foundation for Management Development, Council on Adult and Experiential Learning, Distance Education and Training Council, and National University Continuing Education Association. I came away from this journey with an appreciation for the fast-changing landscape of higher education both in the United States as well as abroad.

And thanks beyond words to the staff of Corporate University Xchange, Inc., especially Gilbert Tang and Yevgeniy ("Gene") Ostrinsky for their research, fact-checking and endless hours of revising until we were all pleased with the end product.

Finally, a special thanks to my support system at home which makes all of this possible; Bob Meister, for patiently listening, and Danielle Meister, for her inspirational artwork, which helped to motivate me.

**J. C. M.**
November, 1997

# Contents

*Preface, ix*
*Acknowledgements, xv*

*Chapter One*
CHANGES IN THE WORKPLACE                                         1
The Corporation of the Twenty-first Century, 1
   The Emergence of the Flat, Flexible Organization, 1
   The Knowledge Economy: From Brawn to Brains, 7
   The Shorter Shelf Life of Knowledge, 9
   Lifetime Employability Becomes the
   Corporate Mantra, 9
   Corporations Become Educators, 10
New Workplace Competencies
Employers Require, 12
Corporate Universities Emerge, 19
The Mission, Scope, and Nature of Corporate
Learning Expands, 19
New Findings from the Annual Survey
of Corporate University Future Directions, 24
   Management Commitment, 24
   Learning Alliances Grow in Importance, 25
   Surge of Interest in Using Technology
   to Create a Virtual Corporate University, 26
   Corporate Universities Operate as a Business, 26

*Chapter Two*
HOW THE CORPORATE UNIVERSITY
MODEL WORKS                                                     29
Key Principles of the Corporate
University Model, 29

Provide Learning in Support of the
Business Goals, 31

Consider the Corporate University Model
a Process, Not Necessarily a Place, 33

Design a Core Curriculum Around the
Three Cs, 39

Train the Value Chain, 42

Move from Instructor-Led to Multiple Formats
of Delivering Learning, 47

Encourage Leaders to be Involved with and
Facilitate Learning, 49

Move from Corporate Allocation to
Self-Funding, 51

Assume a Global Focus in Developing
Learning Programs, 53

Create a Measurement System to Evaluate Outputs
as well as Inputs, 55

Utilize the Corporate University for Competitive
Advantage and Entry into New Markets, 57

*Chapter Three*
DESIGNING A CORPORATE UNIVERSITY                    59
The Corporate University Design Process, 59
Top Management Is the Driving Force
Behind a Corporate University, 61
Ten Building Blocks in Designing a
Corporate University, 65

Form a Governance System, 65

Create a Vision, 68

Recommend the Scope and Funding Strategy, 69

Create an Organization, 71

Identify Stakeholders, 73

Create Products and Services, 74

Select Learning Partners, 75

Draft a Technology Strategy, 76

Create a Measurement System, 77

Communicate . . . Communicate . . .
Communicate, 80

The Chief Learning Officer as Leader of the
Corporate University, 85

*Chapter Four*
LEARNING PROGRAMS AT BEST PRACTICE
CORPORATE UNIVERSITIES                                           88
The Corporate University Curriculum, 88
  The Three Cs of the Core Curriculum, 89

Corporate Citizenship, 93
  Training in the Values, Vision, and Culture of
  the Organization, 93
  Metaphors Teach the Corporate Values, Culture,
  Big Picture, and Traditions of the Organization, 94

Contextual Framework, 98
  Know the Company's Big Picture: Customers,
  Competitors, Industry Trends, and Best Practices
  of Others, 98
  Know and Practice Core
  Workplace Competencies, 104

Core Workplace Competencies, 105
  Learning to Learn, 105
  Communication and Collaboration, 108
  Creative Thinking and Problem-Solving, 110
  Technological Literacy, 112
  Global Business Literacy, 114
  Leadership Development, 119
  Career Self-Management, 122

Employee Self-Development Linked
to Compensation, 126
Themes of Formal and Informal
Learning Programs, 128

*Chapter Five*
CORPORATE UNIVERSITIES BECOME
LEARNING LABORATORIES                                          130
Technology Transforms Learning, 130
The First Step: Establish Criteria for
Media Selection, 134

Satellite-Based Learning, 136

Multimedia-Based Learning, 142

Collaborative Learning Technologies, 144

Knowledge Databases on the Intranet, 148

Web-Based Learning, 150

Virtual Campus, 162

Technology-Assisted Learning: Exploding
into the Twenty-First Century, 165

*Chapter Six*
OUTREACH: FORGING PARTNERSHIPS
WITH SUPPLIERS, CUSTOMERS, AND
INSTITUTIONS OF HIGHER EDUCATION                           168
Why Partner with Value Chain
Participants?, 168

Partnering with Suppliers, 172

Extending Customer Training to Dealers
and Wholesalers, 174

Building Alliances with Institutions of
Higher Education, 181

A Framework for Building a Corporate/College
Partnership, 182

Customize Executive Educational Programs, 186

Launch a New Accredited Degree Program, 190

Create a Corporate University Consortium, 197

Consider Accreditation of Your
Corporate University, 201

Training the Value Chain Becomes a Strategic
Goal for Corporate Universities, 205

*Chapter Seven*
CORPORATE UNIVERSITIES: OPPORTUNITY
OR THREAT TO HIGHER EDUCATION?                             207
The Metamorphosis of the Education
Market, 207

Emergence of the Non-Traditional Student
as a Consumer of Education, 208

Rapid Advancement of Technology, 211

Need for Life-long Learning, 212

Introduction of Distance Education, 213

Higher Education's Dilemma, 215

New Entrants to the Education Market, 215

Externally Focused Corporate Universities, 216

Consortiums, 218

Virtual Universities, 221

For-Profit Education Firms, 226

The Future: A Market-Driven
Education System, 231


*Chapter Eight*
TWELVE LESSONS IN BUILDING A
WORLD-CLASS WORK FORCE                                      233

Twelve Lessons in Building a World-Class
Work Force, 236

1. Tie the Goals of Education and Development to
   the Strategic Needs of the Organization, 236

2. Involve Leaders as Learners and Faculty, 237

3. Select a Chief Learning Officer to Set the Strategic
   Direction for Corporate Education, 238

4. Consider Employee Orientation an On-Going
   Strategic Process, Rather Than a One-Time
   Event, 239

5. Design a Core Curriculum to Stress the Three Cs:
   Corporate Citizenship, Contextual Framework,
   and Core Competencies, 240

6. Link What Employees Earn to What They
   Learn, 243

7. Experiment with Technology to Measure, Track,
   and Accelerate Learning, 244

8. Extend the Corporate University Beyond
   Internal Employees to Key Members of the
   Customer/Supply Chain, 245

9. Operate the Corporate University as a Line of
   Business Within the Organization, 247

10. Develop a Range of Innovative Alliances
    with Higher Education, 249

11. Demonstrate the Value of the Corporate
    University Learning Infrastructure, 250

12. Develop the Corporate University as a Branded
    Competitive Advantage and Profit Center, 252


*Appendix, 255*

*Benchmarking Best Practices Among Corporate
Universities, 263*

*Fifteen Frequently Asked Questions About Corporate
Universities, 267*

*Notes, 273*

*Bibliography, 279*

*Index, 285*

*Chapter One*

# Changes in the Workplace

*For training to be effective, it has to maintain a reliable, consistent presence. Employees should be able to count on something systematic, not a rescue effort summoned to solve the problem of the moment. In other words, training should be a continuous process rather than a one-time event.*

— Andrew S. Grove, chairman and CEO Intel Corporation

## THE CORPORATION OF THE TWENTY-FIRST CENTURY

The corporate university is emerging into the twenty-first century as the fastest growing sector of higher education. Companies such as Motorola, Sun Microsystems, and Bank of Montreal are transferring their successful business models of service, accessibility, and state-of-the-art technology to corporate education.

To understand the significance of these corporate universities as both a state-of-the-art model for higher education and, in a larger sense, a key instrument for cultural change, it is necessary to understand the broad forces that have supported this phenomenon. Essentially, there are five: the emergence of the flat, flexible organization; the transformation of the economy into a "knowledge economy"; the shortened shelf life of knowledge; the new focus on lifetime employability rather than lifetime employment; and a fundamental shift in the global education marketplace. These broad trends point to a new key vehicle for creating a sustained competitive advantage—the company's commitment to employee education and development.

### *The Emergence of the Flat, Flexible Organization*

The workplace is undergoing change at an accelerating rate. Having restructured and re-engineered themselves during the 1980s

1

and 1990s, American corporations face increasing competition in global markets in the years ahead. Today's corporation is leaner, flatter, and less hierarchical than it was 10 or 15 years ago. According to *U.S. News & World Report*, American businesses announced the elimination of over 516,000 jobs during 1995 alone, almost as many as in the recession years of 1991 to 1992.[1]

One of the most far-reaching changes of this revolution of American business is that the corporation of the twenty-first century is fundamentally very different from that which dominated the American business landscape during the 1950s and 1960s. Compared to the corporate hierarchy of past decades, the emerging organization is distinguished by ambiguity, fewer boundaries, and more rapid communication between the company and its employees (including union members), product suppliers, educational suppliers (the universities that supply the organization with its human talent), and customers.

The corporate hierarchy, once stable and slow-moving, with the "thinkers" at the top of the pyramid and the "do-ers" at the base, is poorly suited to the fast-moving, competitive environment of today. Instead, corporations are opting for a flat, flexible organization, characterized by decentralized decision making. Organizations are struggling to compete and, in the process, putting a premium on speed and efficiency. The new organization often structures itself as a loosely knit confederation of entrepreneurial units and relies on teams to create value and profit. This twenty-first century organization values teamwork over individualism, seeks global markets over domestic ones, and focuses on customer needs, rather than short-term profits. Hence, it views cycle time, rather than costs, as the key competitive advantage.

As Figure 1–1 shows, the corporation of the twenty-first century exists in an economy where more and more added value will be created by human capital. This paradigm shift in management thought—from success based on efficiency and economies of scale to success rooted in a culturally diverse work force of knowledge workers—is the essence of the twenty-first century organization. Here work and learning are essentially the same thing, with the emphasis on developing the individual's capacity to learn. Thriving in this ever-changing global environment requires a new kind of organization, where a shared mind-set among all employees is critical to long-term success.

**FIGURE 1–1**

## The Corporation In Transition

| Old Model | Organization | 21st Century Prototype |
|---|---|---|
| Hierarchy | **Organization** | Network of Partnerships & Alliances |
| Support Today's Way of Doing Business | **Mission** | Create Value-Added Change |
| Autocratic | **Leadership** | Inspirational |
| Domestic | **Markets** | Global |
| Cost | **Advantage** | Time |
| Tools to Support the Mind | **Technology** | Tools to Support Collaboration |
| Homogeneous | **Work Force** | Diverse |
| Separate Work Functions | **Work Process** | Cross-Functional Work Teams |
| Security | **Worker Expectations** | Personal Development |
| Job of Institutions of Higher Education | **Education & Training** | Corporate America Plus an Array of For-Profit Educational Firms |

© 1997 Corporate University Xchange, Inc.

All of these changes put entirely new demands on workers and require that they master entirely new roles and skill sets.

**Xerox.** Consider the transformation of Xerox within the last decade. A 1993 restructuring reduced management from 18 pay levels down to just 3, while eliminating 9,500 Xerox jobs.[2] Although 9,500 jobs were eliminated, the number of middle managers showed a modest decline, but far less than the media reports of middle manager slaughter. The reality is that many more employees are in a decision-making mode and thus elevated to a management category.[3] So if one's job remains, it often changes quite substantially.

The job of a Xerox sales manager has enlarged now in terms of both the sales territory and the specific job duties. This restructuring also altered the jobs of sales representatives reporting to the sales manager. Now these representatives have authority to decide pricing and other sales terms without seeking the sales manager's authority. This results in more employees with manager-like responsibilities, all in need of training and development to cope with broader roles and responsibilities.

The transformation of Xerox, as well as countless other organizations, has had profound implications for employees at all levels within the organization. There are far fewer managers to oversee workers, and there is a new corporate emphasis on speed, flexibility, and competitiveness. As a result, employees in various organizations and industries are seeing their work processes examined to eliminate waste and redundancy, and in the process, broadening their roles and responsibilities.

**Chrysler.** In the traditionally organized company, assembly line workers usually performed a set of narrowly defined and routine tasks under close supervision; but in many plants today, assembly line workers must not only be able to perform their own jobs, but also understand a range of additional assembly functions to maximize a team's flexibility. In a sense, Detroit has become a microcosm of work force changes. Once high-paying, low-skill manufacturing jobs like those in the auto industry were the linchpin of the economy, setting wage standards for the middle class, most of whom were high school graduates. With the trend toward high skills manufacturing that became standard in the mid-1980s, the rote skill of the assembly line worker is being replaced with an industrial vision that requires skilled and nimble workers to think while they work.

In the 1990s, what was once the industrial avant garde has become the mainstream as high-skill/high-wage practices have spread across the manufacturing sector. Figure 1–2 shows that the share of U.S. factory workers with a year or two of college has jumped to 25 percent from 17 percent in 1985, according to the Bureau of Labor Statistics.[4] However, this investment in education and training carries a none-too-subtle message for manufacturing workers: hone your skills or risk being left behind.

**FIGURE 1–2**

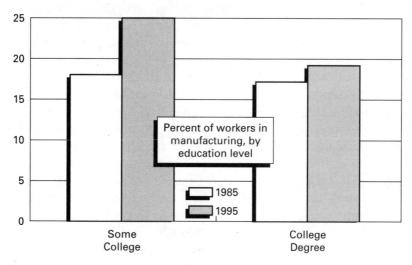

**Factories Are Hiring Better-Educated Workers**

Percent of workers in manufacturing, by education level

☐ 1985
■ 1995

Some College

College Degree

Data: Bureau of Labor Statistics, Business Week

Chrysler's plant in Windsor, Ontario is just across the river from downtown Detroit. Today, 26 percent of the workers on all the plant's shifts have college degrees; five years ago the percentage was in the single digits.[5] Indeed, the old formula of company loyalty, brawn, and showing up on time no longer guarantees job security. Today, industrial workers will thrive only if they use their brains and keep adding to their skill base.

**Chase Manhattan Bank.** When Chase Manhattan Bank cannot reach one of its delinquent credit card customers, it does not send a threatening letter or even have one of its credit card collection agents place numerous phone calls. Instead, it sends a videotape with a comforting message: "Even though you're in collection, you're still our customer," says the commentator. "You're still Number One with us. Just call us and together we can work things out for you."[6]

The stakes are high. Of Chase's $9.7 billion in credit card loans, about 5.6 percent or $543 million are more than 60 days past due.

What's behind this new approach? Has Chase Manhattan Bank gone soft with delinquent customers? "Just the opposite," says Donald Kramer, partner in Kramer & Frank, a law firm specializing in collections, "Chase Manhattan Bank recognizes that people would rather do business with a company that understands their needs rather than one which harasses them with frequent letters and phone calls."

This significant change in how Chase deals with its delinquent credit card customers has profound effects on the role, responsibility, and skill base of a credit card collection agent. Once hired for their aggressive style, these credit card collection agents must now  learn new skills, such as relationship building, active listening, and creative problem solving. The company mantra has become "relationship-based selling," and Chase's collectors must demonstrate warmth and caring in dealing with delinquent customers. For example, collection agents are trained to probe with questions like: "You've never been in collection before, has anything changed in your life now? Is there anything we can do to help you?"

All these changes point to a much broader set of skills, knowledge, and competencies required of collection agents to carry out this relationship-based strategy.

**Epsilon.** Epsilon, a $100 million subsidiary of American Express, is a full-service database marketing company headquartered in the Boston area. Epsilon has about 700 employees, and in the recent past the job of project manager has changed dramatically. Information technology jobs at Epsilon are in transition as new work roles are permeating the workplace. Increasingly the company is requiring project managers to not only recommend technical solutions but to understand the customer's business and propose value-added business solutions. This new role is both high value and high risk because the project manager must demonstrate not only technical knowledge, but also a breadth of skills in the areas of communication, negotiation, and general business literacy.

Tim O'Leary, vice president of open systems at Epsilon, notes that project managers were traditionally called on to provide a single technical solution. Now, customers are much more savvy about information technology solutions, and the project managers must *skills* be able to call on a whole new set of skills: strategic thinking, creativity, negotiation, conflict management, and above all, the ability to form a partnership with the user and mutually come to terms with how the project will be measured to provide a value-added business result. Given that these project managers will continue to play an increasingly important role in formulating business strategy and interacting with senior business managers, they must have broader skills and be rewarded for demonstrating them.

As the preceding examples show, there is a pronounced difference between workers' relatively limited roles in the past and the considerably more ambitious and demanding scope of many workers' daily jobs today. What this means to the average worker is an urgent need to be able to draw on a much broader complement of skills than was deemed sufficient in the traditional organization. The link between workers' skills and an organization's competitiveness was brought home by Lester Thurow, dean of MIT's Sloan School of Management, when he said:

> The education and skills of the work force will be the key competitive weapon in the twenty-first century. The reason: there is a whole set of technologies coming along that will demand that the average office or production worker have skills that have not been required in the past. These skills go beyond the narrow duties of doing one's job to a broad skill set to adapt to new technologies and change in the marketplace.[7]

To keep its footing in a fast-moving global marketplace, therefore, an organization must proactively embrace change. The ability to adjust and improve systems and processes becomes a survival issue. In such an environment, learning skills rank high in importance because an organization's power to introduce change successfully depends on its workers' abilities to learn new roles, processes, and skills. This ability to tap employee intelligence, ingenuity, and energy has never been more important than in today's knowledge economy.

## The Knowledge Economy: From Brawn to Brains

The knowledge economy may sound like an abstract concept, but it is essentially how we manage information in our jobs. Professor Stephen R. Barley, professor of industrial engineering and industrial management at Stanford University, tells us that an ever increasing percentage of workers are "knowledge workers." Consider that the share of the American labor force whose jobs involve working with things (farmworkers, laborers, craft people) or delivering nonprofessional services (hotel and restaurant workers, distribution workers, etc.) will have fallen by more than half by the year 2000, from 83 percent in 1900 to 41 percent now; those who work chiefly with information (sales, professional, and technical jobs), 17 percent of the work force in 1900, will be 59 percent by the year 2000.[8] In fact, knowledge-intensive companies—those that have 40 percent or more knowledge workers—account for 28 percent of total U.S. employment, but in the last half decade they produced 43 percent of new employment growth.[9]

Not only do more people do knowledge work, but the intellectual component of many jobs has also increased. According to Kiichi Machizuki, a former executive of a Japanese steel company, "When you talk about skill, the word 'skill' is wrong: It implies manual dexterity to carve wood. Now skill is mental rather than manual."[10] Witness the factory workers at the U.S. Bureau of Engraving and Printing, the only authorized printer of U.S. currency and securities, selling mainly to the 12 Federal Reserve Banks and the primary supplier of stamps for the U.S. Postal Service. Although the Bureau is part of the federal government, it is a public sector manufacturing firm. Timothy Vigotsky, associate director of management operations, explains the transformation of the Bureau of Engraving and Printing manufacturing this way, "Our production requirements will total 12 billion currency notes by 1999, or a 70 percent increase over 1990. While we read about the inroads of digital cash, in fact, currency production has increased by over 100 percent in the past decade, while full time employment went up by only 3 percent."

Essentially, the Bureau of Engraving and Printing has been able to accommodate this growth by the introduction of new technology into the manufacturing process. In fact, many currency manufacturing jobs require workers to know such concepts as statistical process control, pareto charts, and other tools of statistical analysis to recommend how to cut time and waste out of the currency manufacturing process. In fact, BEP University was created to address these explosive changes in the currency manufacturing process.

## The Shorter Shelf Life of Knowledge

Because this knowledge economy requires continuous learning to develop broader skills, the private sector is increasing its commitment to learning and education. As Louis Ross, Ford Motor Company's Chief Technical Officer, said to a group of engineering students, "In your career, knowledge is becoming like a carton of milk. It has a shelf life stamped right on it. The shelf life of a college degree is less than two years. So, if you're not replacing everything you know every three years, then your career is going to turn sour, just like that carton of milk."[11]

Jim Moore, director of SunU (the corporate university of Sun Microsystems, an $8 billion firm based in Mountain View, California), believes the shelf life of knowledge at his firm is as short as one to two years. In fact, to illustrate this point, Moore estimates that over 75% of Sun Microsystems revenue in 1996 was generated from products in the market less than two years.

Thinking about the shelf life of knowledge, one need only look at the evolution of the Internet. Consider how we used to communicate with each other just five years ago when the Internet barely existed for most of us. Now, according to the Internet Society, which measures traffic, there were about 100,000 hosts in 1989; one million by 1992; and close to 10 million by the end of 1995. This number is projected to grow to more than 20 million by the year 2000.[12] It is no wonder that we have come to rely on the Internet as a research and communications tool in both our jobs and personal lives.

## Lifetime Employability Becomes the Corporate Mantra

The old implied social contract—you work hard and we will give you a job for as long as you want—does not exist. Job security no longer comes from sticking with a single company but from maintaining a portfolio of job-related skills. This shift signals a "new psychological contract" between employer and employee. Under the terms of this new contract, employers provide learning in place of job security. The skills and knowledge acquired promotes each worker's continued employability—the ability to find a meaningful job inside or outside the company. In other words, employers are giving individual employees the opportunity to develop enhanced employability in exchange for better productivity and some degree of commitment to company mission for as long as the employee works there. The result is what consultant Robert Waterman calls a career resilient work force, one that possesses the skills needed for the company to remain competitive in the global marketplace.[13]

A by-product of this new contract is the transfer of responsibility for learning from the training department to the individual employee and his or her business unit manager. From the employee's perspective, developing a commitment to learning comes from being able to answer such questions as:

- What am I supposed to do for the organization?
- Do I consider this meaningful work?
- Am I participating in the "right" types of learning programs to be successful in this job?
- How will my successful completion of these learning programs be recognized and rewarded by the organization?
- How will my compensation relate to completion of learning programs; i.e., will what I earn be based on what I learn?

Each company may differ in its answers to these questions, but increasingly they are being asked and the answers have become the very essence of an organization's learning philosophy.

### Corporations Become Educators

The American education marketplace is undergoing a tremendous shift, moving from a government-run monopoly with little accountability, to a market-driven system that competes on price and quality. Businesses complain that they cannot employ the "product" coming out of our nation's schools. In fact, 31 percent of our nation's children do not graduate from high school on time and 10 percent drop out of school entirely. International comparisons show American students finish near the bottom in math and science, yet the United States spends 9.8 percent of its gross domestic product on education—a total of $619 billion dollars, of which $60 billion is targeted to workplace training. (See Figure 1–3.) Amazingly, this is second only to health-care spending, which totals 14 percent of our gross national product.[14]

Education no longer stops when workers graduate from tradi-

FIGURE 1-3

---

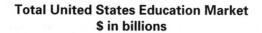

**Total United States Education Market**
**$ in billions**

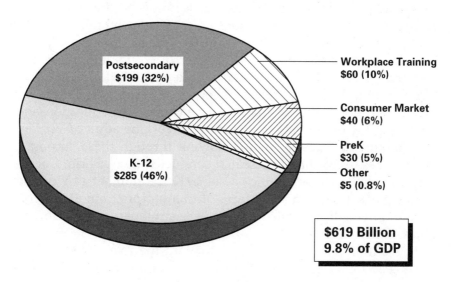

Sources: U.S. Dept. of Education. EduVentures. *The Education Industry Report*™. Training Industry Report October 1993 Issue. Lehman Brothers, and American Society for Training and Development.

Courtesy of Lehman Brothers

tional schools. In the old economy, one's life was divided into the period one went to school and the period after one graduated and worked. Now workers must expect to build their knowledge base throughout their life. For a moment, think about your own job and the new skills you have needed to learn over the last two years. Work and learning are overlapping in industries as diverse as computer software, health care, utilities, telecommunications, and even training and development. This means there is really no such thing as graduation. Our knowledge and skills are really only adequate for a period as short as 12 to 18 months, and then we must replenish them to compete in the global knowledge economy.

Therefore, many American businesses intent on becoming leaders in the global economy have launched corporate universities as a vehicle to gain competitive advantage in the marketplace. Corporate universities are essentially the "in-house" training and education facilities that have sprung up because of the frustration of businesses with the quality and content of post-secondary education on the one hand; and the need for life-long learning on the other. They have evolved at many corporations into strategic umbrellas for educating not only employees, but also customers and suppliers.

In just eight short years, the number of corporate universities has grown from 400 to over 1,000, while some 200 colleges have closed down. With the growth of corporate universities, firms are creating a more efficient market-driven model of education and becoming the predominant educators of working adults. Consider the amount of student volume flowing through these corporate universities. According to research conducted by our firm, Corporate University Xchange, Inc., as of 1997 the number of working adults participating in some form of training program at 100 corporate universities equaled the student enrollment at 125 Universities of Michigan, assuming a 1996 total enrollment of 36,500.

This entrance of the private sector into the role of educator is placing serious pressure for transformation on America's 3,632 institutions of higher education. These institutions need to re-invent themselves for the knowledge economy, or face competition not only from corporate universities but also from such for-profit educational firms as University of Phoenix, which has grown from 3,000 students to over 40,000 in the last decade. The growth in the number of options in the higher education landscape requires change in how institutions of higher education design, develop, and deliver their product.

## NEW WORKPLACE COMPETENCIES EMPLOYERS REQUIRE

These trends set the stage for understanding the seven core workplace competencies identified by the companies in this book. These competencies are defined as the sum of skills, knowledge, and implicit know-how needed to outperform the competition. They form the foundation of individual employability and are further explored in Chapter 4. They include:

1. Learning to learn.
2. Communication and collaboration.
3. Creative thinking and problem-solving.
4. Technological literacy.
5. Global business literacy.
6. Leadership development.
7. Career self-management.

**Learning to learn.**   Today's workers are expected to give constructive input on everything from how to ensure the quality of raw materials used to make the product to how to improve processes used to deliver and install the product. This requires that they be able to draw on a set of skills, which includes being able to analyze situations, ask questions, seek clarification of what they do not understand, and think creatively to generate options. These employees must be able to apply existing knowledge to new situations; experiment with learning from a variety of sources such as co-workers, customers, suppliers, and educational institutions; and build this learning into their everyday lives.

The goal is to have learning to learn become a natural part of how employees think and behave on the job. Former Secretary of Labor Robert Reich has noted, "Forty years ago we considered labor to be a cost on the balance sheet. Now we think of labor as an asset, hopefully able to identify problems and then solve them."[15]

**Communication and collaboration.**   When good job performance meant doing a set of prescribed and repetitive tasks to satisfaction, the technical skill associated with each particular job was the most important element. With teams moving to the fore as the vehicles of performance within flexible organizations, individual effectiveness is increasingly linked to well-developed communication and collaboration skills. These include not only the traditional interpersonal skills of listening and communicating effectively with co-workers but also such skills as knowing how to work in groups, collaborating with team members to openly share best practices across the organization, and networking with customers, suppliers, and key members of the value chain.

**Creative thinking and problem-solving.**   In the past, a paternal management took on the responsibility of developing ways to increase worker productivity. Today lower echelon employees are expected to figure out for themselves how to improve and streamline their work. This requires that they think creatively, develop problem-solving skills, and be able to: analyze situations, ask questions, seek clarification of what they do not understand, and suggest improvements. Such an environment requires employees to go well beyond the surface data to create innovative solutions to unexpected problems.

Also, because the fast and flexible organization must be able to respond quickly far from home-office supervision, employees must increasingly make decisions at the point of production or at the point of sale. They need to develop critical thinking and problem-solving skills to handle situations effectively without direction.

**Technological literacy.**   In the workplace of the recent past, technological literacy meant knowing how to operate your personal computer for word processing or financial analysis. Now the emphasis is on using an information appliance that connects you to your team members around the globe. Much of the collaboration employees will do in the twenty-first century will require them to use the personal computer not only for job-related tasks but also for networking with professionals around the world, sharing best practices, and recommending improvements in their work processes.

In this connected world, corporations are developing courses to train employees in virtual reality, groupware, and the Internet to make global team collaboration a reality. These technologies will change the shape of knowledge by extending the scope of anywhere/anytime business practices.

**Global business literacy.**   It probably goes without saying that leaders must have exceptional business acumen and technical skills. However, what is different today is the realization that managers must be trained in a "new" set of business/technical skills that take into account the competitive global environment where they cannot predict with any certainty what the future holds for their industry or organization. In this volatile environment, the ability of management to understand the "global big picture" of how the business operates is fast becoming a necessity in adding value to the organization.

Specifically, business literacy implies training select individual contributors and managers in the economics and strategic implications of running a global business enterprise. Here the corporate university becomes the vehicle to train employees in a core set of business literacy skills such as finance, strategic planning, and marketing, with a specific focus on the emerging competitive markets the organization is targeting for the future. This global business literacy curriculum includes courses on how to do business in China, Mexico, or South America and also business simulations based on real global issues that an internationally expanding organization faces on a day-to-day basis.

**Leadership development.**    In the workplace of the past, the key skill was managing. Directives for the company emanated from the top and work was managed (i.e., administered and controlled) down through the ranks where it was translated into action. In the twenty-first century organization, inspirational leadership is eclipsing managing as the key to developing a shared mind-set and moving the organization in one direction. In such an organization, all employees are encouraged to be active change agents rather than passive recipients of instructions. Employees at all levels need to develop abilities to envision an improvement or a new direction and elicit the active commitment of others to realize the organization's shared vision.

The new imperative is now on leadership development, which focuses on identifying and developing exceptional people capable of moving the organization into the twenty-first century. The best practice organizations profiled in this book view leadership development as the opportunity to provide top managers with the tools they need to build organizational competitiveness.

Rather than simply sending high potential managers to external executive education programs, these organizations are developing focused large-scale customized action-learning programs with measurable results. These hands-on, application-driven programs are based on actual business challenges facing an organization and give participants an opportunity to actively discuss, diagnose, and recommend solutions to real-life business challenges.

**Career self-management.** Finally, self-development and self-management skills teach employees to take charge of their careers and manage their own development. As the skills needed for the workplace continue to evolve and change, employees at all levels must become committed to ensuring that they have the requisite skills, knowledge, and competencies for both their current and future jobs. The ability to manage one's professional life is now considered a learned competence necessary for all the other workplace competencies. In turn, corporate universities are helping employees manage their own careers by developing virtual career development centers so employees can learn the skills they need for a current or future position within the company.

These seven workplace competencies differ from those listed in the 1994 edition of *Corporate Quality Universities.* First, the basics of reading, writing, computation, and cognitive reasoning have been elevated to a higher level. Employers require basic skills more than ever, but what has changed is that the bar has been raised in this twenty-first century organization. High performance workplaces now require employees to have not only the basic skills of reading, writing, and cognitive reasoning, but also the abilities to use the latest software, make a succinct presentation, organize information, and draw conclusions. The emphasis has shifted to these "higher order basic skills" of creative problem-solving, collaboration, and communication.

Another change from the 1994 edition in what are considered core workplace competencies is the vastly increased emphasis on building global business literacy skills. As detailed earlier, senior managers are struggling to adapt themselves and their organizations to the twenty-first century business world where geographic boundaries will be less important than they are today. Breakthroughs in digital electronics will come from such places as Malaysia and China. Business opportunities will explode and management know-how must include having a core set of global business literacy skills in such areas as competitive analysis, marketing, finance, and planning new market entry strategies.

While these global business literacy skills start with learning the language and culture required to do business in such countries as China, Korea, Russia, Argentina, or Brazil, of paramount importance is the need to provide a forum for discussing a global market entry strategy. For example, while Motorola University offers a course in doing business in China, its most significant contribution has been to offer small groups of Motorola executives the opportunity to meet and discuss how to do business in China with the emergence of a China entry strategy. Global business literacy skills encompass both competence-based courses as well as strategy-based initiatives where top managers discuss how they can become more effective global players.

Finally, perhaps one of the most significant changes to the set of core workplace competencies is the way they fit into an emerging, hybrid skill I have coined the z-shaped skill. As illustrated in Figure 1–4, z-shaped skills encompass deep expertise in one discipline along with enough breadth to see connections with other disciplines.

Project managers in an organization's information technology area are an interesting example of the need to develop these hybrid z-shaped skills. Increasingly, project managers are required to not only have depth of skill in client server, systems integration, and systems analysis, but also to be proficient in marketing, communications, strategic planning, and client relationship-building skills so they can interact with clients to offer value-added business solutions rather than technical answers to client requests. Dave Muntz, director of IT training at Presbyterian Healthcare, describes the need to cross train IT professionals in the following manner when he says, "We no longer hire 'star' IT professionals. Instead, we look to develop and nurture employees who not only have superior technical skills, but also know how to work with our customers. Consequently, our IT curriculum includes topics in netware usage and UNIX training as well as the delivery of high quality customer service."

The need for these z-shaped skills surfaces anywhere the organization requires problem solving across different deep functional knowledge bases. People possessing z-shaped skills are able to shape their knowledge to fit the problem at hand rather than insist the problem appear in a particular form. Best practice organizations understand not only what they are good at—their core competencies—but also the need to develop employees who have hybrid skills so they can put their insights into practice on cross-functional teams. What is striking about a number of these core workplace competencies is how closely they resemble what companies traditionally regarded as management-type skills.

Essentially, what is happening is that new, flexible, decentralized organizational structures are pushing responsibility and authority

FIGURE 1–4

## Z Shaped Skills

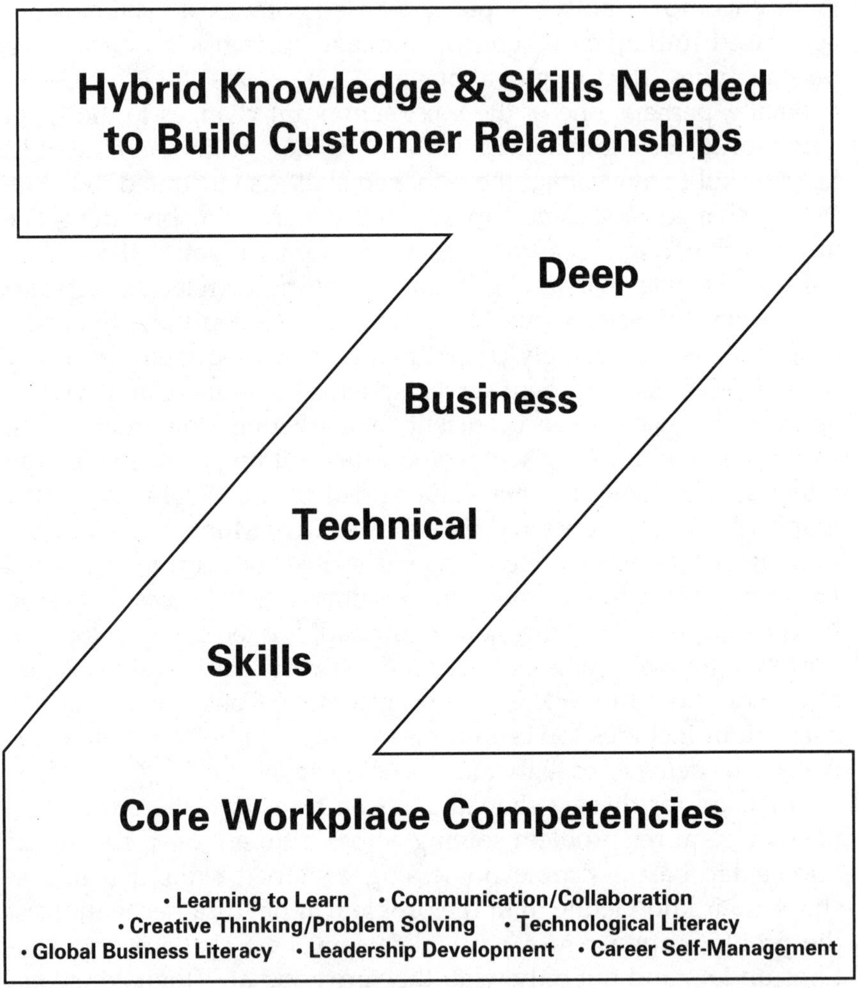

**Hybrid Knowledge & Skills Needed to Build Customer Relationships**

**Deep**

**Business**

**Technical**

**Skills**

**Core Workplace Competencies**

• Learning to Learn   • Communication/Collaboration
• Creative Thinking/Problem Solving   • Technological Literacy
• Global Business Literacy   • Leadership Development   • Career Self-Management

© 1997 Corporate University Xchange, Inc.

downward in the organization, from managers and staff engineers to the rank-and-file workers. Now more employees need to think and act as managers. These workers must now know how to interpret information, apply it to their work, and make a business decision. As the workplace flattens and the gap narrows between those in leadership positions and those responsible for producing and delivering the product or service, the role of the individual employee is becoming increasingly managerial in nature.

This dramatic transformation of roles and skill requirements throughout the organization affects the kind of education and training employees need. Indeed, in the 1990s and beyond, the issue is not simply training employees to learn more skills but rather introducing them to an entirely new way of thinking and working so they can perform broader roles in the workplace.

## CORPORATE UNIVERSITIES EMERGE

Thus, as we have seen, some of America's most visionary companies are meeting the challenge of creating continuous learning infrastructures head-on. The companies profiled in this book share a common goal: to sustain competitive advantage by inspiring lifelong learning and exceptional performance.

These companies are transforming their corporate classrooms into virtual corporate learning infrastructures where the objective is to focus on how to leverage new opportunities, enter new global markets, develop deeper customer relationships, and propel the organization to a new future.

While the corporate university of the past decade existed primarily as a campus, today the corporate university consists of a process rather than a physical place. Some corporate universities profiled in this book do have an elaborate physical setting, such as Bank of Montreal's $50 million residential facility or Motorola's campuses in Schaumburg, Illinois; Phoenix, Arizona; Austin, Texas; Yokohama, Japan; Singapore, Beijing; and Tianjin, China, but regardless of the existence of a physical building, the focus has shifted from the classroom to developing a learning process where networking the entire organization's knowledge becomes the priority.

## THE MISSION, SCOPE, AND NATURE OF CORPORATE LEARNING EXPANDS

Traditionally, American companies have focused their employee training on upgrading the skills and expertise of professional employees. During the 1950s, 1960s, and 1970s, large and small companies set up classrooms to teach professional workers how to do their jobs better. These educational infrastructures within corporations proliferated across the United States and became known as corporate universities, institutes, or colleges. The goal was, in most cases, to keep professionals abreast of developments or, better, ahead of them.

The most sophisticated programs evolved in companies with large technology investments. As Charles DeCarlo and Ormsbee Robinson stated in their book, *Education in Business and Industry,* "The most advanced corporate education programs are found in those industries which have the highest investment in R&D and where new R&D processes created the need for training and retraining of professional workers."[16]

These corporate universities spread across industries. Nell Eurich, in her 1985 groundbreaking book, *Corporate Classrooms,* estimated that by that date there were at least 400 businesses with a building or campus labeled "college, university, institute, or education center."[17] As noted previously, there are now more than 1,000 corporate universities.

These corporate university programs often included a cafeteria curriculum of hundreds of courses in management, marketing, and financial practices and principles. In a sense, companies put a rich smorgasbord on the table for professional managers to choose the courses that "were right for them." Often, these focused on upgrading technical skills within the company's professional and managerial ranks.

The implicit assumption was that if the company gave professional workers enough insight and knowledge through clever teaching methodologies in the classroom, they could acquire new skills to do their jobs better. Somewhere in this process, the thinking goes, these workers become transformed into more productive and committed employees. Sounds like magic today, but the underlying assumption was that with enough of the "right" training culminating in a management certificate, almost anyone could change his or her fundamental behaviors and emerge from the classroom to solve the business problem at hand.

Gradually, as more companies experimented with empowering their workers through high-performance work teams, they recognized the need for excellence *across* the work force, not only in the professional managerial ranks. The theme coming out of a handful of companies in the mid- to late-1980s was that increasing productivity is every worker's goal, not just the challenge of professional managers or expert consultants.

A growing number of companies have begun to perceive a need to shift the focus of their training and corporate education efforts from one-time training events in a classroom that builds individual skills to creating a continuous learning culture where employees learn from each other and share innovations and best practices with an eye toward solving real business issues.

Figure 1–5 shows this paradigm shift where the focus of training moves beyond the individual employee to the organization developing its capacity for learning. Where individual participants attended classes, now intact work teams collaborate on how to become a community of learners. And the "raw material" to help this community of learners is no longer a Harvard Business School case but a business issue the team faces in their day-to-day jobs.

For example, in General Electric's Business Manager course, executives learn about doing business in other countries by forming teams and spending a week in another country, interviewing country business and political leaders, and creating a GE strategy for doing business in the country. In recent years, participants in this course have created mock strategies for doing business in India, Mexico, Vietnam, and China. Through these learning experiences, the participants return with recommendations of how to put global strategies into action.[18]

Additionally, the individual faculty members have changed rather dramatically from the Harvard Ph.D. to senior business managers who use "training" to not only teach concepts they use every day in their business life but also to model these concepts for the participants. At the Tennessee Valley Authority, mid- to senior-level managers are required to be course instructors at TVA University. There are several benefits, says Lynn Hodges, manager, external programs. The managers understand "a certain educational component extremely well, because they deliver it and they teach it. Secondly, it begins to demonstrate what we feel is an appropriate role as managers, as leaders, and as teachers. And thirdly, it has economic advantages. Rather than going out and hiring professional facilitators to come in, we use our own work force."

## FIGURE 1–5

---

### Paradigm Shift from Training to Learning

| Old Training Paradigm | | 21st Century Learning Paradigm |
|---|---|---|
| Building | **Place** | On Demand Learning—Anywhere, Any place |
| Upgrade Technical Skills | **Content** | Build Core Workplace Competencies |
| Learn by Listening | **Methodology** | Action Learning |
| Individual Internal Employees | **Audience** | Intact Teams of Employees, Customers, and Product Suppliers |
| External University Professors/ Consultants | **Faculty** | Internal Senior Managers and a Consortium of University Professors and Consultants |
| One Time Event | **Frequency** | Continuous Learning Process |
| Build Individual's Inventory of Skills | **Goal** | Solve Real Business Issues and Improve Performance on the Job |

© 1997 Corporate University Xchange, Inc.

The Bank of Montreal Institute for Learning holds open forums, such as Forum 1995. Diane Blair, Manager of Meta Learning at the Institute, says, "The goal of Productivity Forum 1995 was to design a rich learning environment where informal learning is the norm. To achieve this, the open forum is void of what one normally thinks of as 'formal training.' There are no lectures, no speeches, no presentations, and no predetermined agendas. Instead the vision is to create the 'ultimate watercooler' where participants discuss common issues and begin to resolve problems through collective learning."

In this scenario, the desired outcome is no longer completing a formal course but rather learning while doing; developing one's capacity to learn and continuing this process back on the job. Indeed, this realization of training transformed into continuous learning extends from the actual participants throughout the entire learning function. Traditionally, many training departments have operated as "order-takers," whereby clients put in orders for training and the training department either found or created courses to fill these orders. Often there was little interaction regarding outcomes. Now, with the emergence of corporate universities, organizations are restructuring their corporate learning environments to be proactive, centralized, targeted, and truly strategic in nature. One very significant shift here is how the owner of the learning process moves from the training department to live business managers. Figure 1–6 illustrates key components of this shift to performance-based learning.

**FIGURE 1–6**

| Training Department | | Corporate University |
|---|---|---|
| Reactive | **Focus** | Proactive |
| Fragmented & Decentralized | **Organization** | Cohesive & Centralized |
| Tactical | **Scope** | Strategic |
| Little/None | **Buy-In** | Management and Employee |
| Instructor-Led | **Delivery** | Experience with Various Technologies |
| Training Director | **Owner** | Business Unit Managers |
| Wide Audience/Limited Depth | **Audience** | Customized Curricula for Job Families |
| Open Enrollment | **Enrollment** | Just-In-Time Learning |
| Increase in Job Skills | **Outcome** | Increase in Performance On-the-Job |
| Operates as a Staff Function | **Operation** | Operates as a Business Unit |
| "Go Get Trained" | **Image** | "University as Metaphor for Learning" |
| Trainer Dictated | **Marketing** | Consultative Selling |

© 1997 Corporate University Xchange, Inc.

## NEW FINDINGS FROM THE ANNUAL SURVEY OF CORPORATE UNIVERSITY FUTURE DIRECTIONS

Corporate University Xchange, Inc., our New York City-based corporate education consulting firm, conducted a survey of 100 corporate university deans to identify and codify their best demonstrated practices and provide a framework for exploring how corporate universities will emerge in the twenty-first century. The primary tools used to identify the best practices included an extensive questionnaire, as well as a literature search and review of course catalogues and organization charts.

We identified several key elements in the design, launch, and management of a corporate university that are likely to become ever more important, such as the need for management commitment, the importance of establishing an array of learning partners, the move toward technology in creating a virtual university, and the need to operate the corporate university as a business.

### Management Commitment

The past few years have seen an important shift in the strategic direction of corporate universities. This shift is driven by the changing role of the CEO and the greater importance of a high level of management commitment in the operations, direction, and strategies of the corporate university. These CEOs are not only publicly supporting an investment in employee education, but they are also facilitating, learning, and building educational partnerships throughout the organization.

Many directors of corporate universities that have the best practices—Motorola, Bank of Montreal, General Electric, *et al.*—have said the single most critical success factor in launching and operating a corporate university is the passionate involvement of the CEO. CEOs at companies with world class universities spend a considerable amount of time cultivating and managing the personal intellectual capital of their organization. At the companies we surveyed, they spend an average of one full day per month personally facilitating learning in their organizations. At 15 percent of the companies surveyed, the CEOs spend three or more days per month doing so. They know that to be successful, the organization must leverage knowledge to boost employee productivity.

This role is supported by a governance structure that provides key business units with a direct link to the university. Corporate university governing bodies help to support the movement to collective, organizational intelligence, with a shared vision and effective coordination of different parts of the organization with the university. They provide a structure for transferring the lessons learned from individual experience into the corporate knowledge base. Almost three-quarters (72 percent) of responding corporate universities have some form of formal governing body.

Governance systems and reporting relationships vary considerably. They range from chairman-led policy boards with line, area, and corporate staff representation to steering committees drawing representation from labor, management, and employees. Reporting relationships vary from direct relationships with the chairman/CEO to direct relationships with the vice president of human resources. Those corporate universities with the largest scope usually report directly to the chairman and have very explicit governing boards composed of senior line and corporate staff executives. Some very large multinational corporations also have regional university boards throughout the world.

## *Learning Alliances Grow in Importance*

Our *Annual Survey of Corporate University Future Directions* found that nearly half of all corporate universities currently have some type of alliance with an accredited educational institution. While the higher education model has traditionally catered to the needs of the 18- to 22-year-old residential student, the corporate university model of education is being shaped by the requirements of the nontraditional working adult. Hence, the biggest growth areas for establishing learning alliances are with such nontraditional learning partners as on-line universities and satellite-based educational programs.

Additionally, our survey found that four in ten corporate universities expect to start granting an accredited degree program jointly with an institution of higher education. These degree programs range from an associate degree in retail management, health care, and computer science to a master of business administration. Some corporate universities are also forming an elaborate web of local alliances to grant a new customized degree program. The Bell Atlantic NEXT STEP alliance with 23 colleges in the State University New York (SUNY) and City University New York (CUNY) system provide an innovative model to offer an associate degree in telecommunications technology. This alliance is distinctive in that it is the first time union employees have had the opportunity to acquire an associate degree at outside schools on company time.

It is not inconceivable that the day might come when a company with a reputation for excellence in a certain area such as customer service, total quality, or high technology might offer its own accredited degree that could become more valuable than a degree from a recognized institution of higher education.

### Surge of Interest in Using Technology to Create a Virtual Corporate University

Technology has taken education out of the classroom. Corporations are now setting the pace for experimenting with various delivery modes to train more workers more cost effectively. While corporations have traditionally sent their workers off to "go get trained," in the 1970s and 1980s, the 1990s have seen a tremendous growth in using technology to deliver education.

Our annual survey of 100 corporate universities found that while only 18 percent of training is currently delivered via new technology, half of all training is expected to be delivered in this manner by the year 2000. There has also been a dramatic change in the mix of technologies used by corporate universities. In addition to traditional technologies such as videotape and audiotape, the technologies making the greatest inroads in the virtual corporate classroom include the intranet, Internet, satellite-based programming, and interactive desktop videoconferencing.

### Corporate Universities Operate as a Business

Leading corporate universities are charged with operating themselves as business units. Increasingly, they focus on understanding and serving the needs of their customers (whether employees, suppliers, or external customers). They market themselves, their scope and their role *within* the organization as well as *outside* the organization. They create business-driven measurements tied to the company's strategic issues, and they are moving toward a self-funded, pay-for-services model. More than half of the corporate universities surveyed receive direct funding from business units rather than being funded totally through corporate allocations. In fact, SunU of Sun Microsystems has the goal of being 100 percent funded from business units by the year 2000!

Part of corporate universities' move toward operating as business units is their leaning toward being organized as *shared internal services,* a mode currently popular in Information Services circles but now spreading to other functions within organizations. Shared services entered the corporate lexicon in the early 1990s as large decentralized companies sought to combine basic transactional processes such as payroll, purchasing, and accounts payable, and sell these services at cost to the individual business units. The shared services concept—also known as *insourcing*—is designed to capture the economies of scale of centralization and keep support functions focused out to the business units, much like independent businesses. Tim Longnecker, partner in Deloitte & Touche Consulting Group's Detroit office describes shared services as "commonization rather than centralization." The difference, according to Longnecker, is that a centralized organization answers to corporate dictates, whereas a shared services organization answers to internal business units, who often have the corporate blessing to shop elsewhere if the shared services unit cannot deliver the goods better or cheaper than an external provider.

This shared services mind-set is finding its way into organizations that have a corporate university. Under such a model, a corporate university is run as a business, meaning it is not assured a fixed budget, only whatever fees it charges internal customers for services they are willing to pay for.

This emphasis on running the corporate university as a cost-effective business unit is driving many CEOs to examine the lessons of a shared services model from information systems and apply these to corporate education. In essence, the corporate university of the year 2000 and beyond is becoming the strategic hub for the organization with an eye toward providing cost-effective, high quality learning solutions. The means to this end varies across organizations, but the common themes of linking learning to business strategies, emphasizing improvements in perform- ance, developing alliances with external learning partners, and de- livering these learning solutions through an array of distance learning programs are what brings this group of world-class orga- nizations together. This emphasis on promoting a spirit of contin- uous lifelong learning makes corporate universities vastly differ- ent from the traditional corporate classrooms of the past.

Increasingly, the companies examined in the book are moving away from thinking about training as something done "to or for employees." Rather, training must become a continuous process where all the critical links of a company's employee/customer/ supply chain develop a coherent view of the company's vision and values. As more companies think of their employees as hu- man capital worthy of development and their customers and sup- pliers as key contributors also needing learning and development, the corporate universities profiled here will become models for scores of other companies to learn from and then adapt to fit to their particular businesses.

*Chapter Two*

# How the Corporate University Model Works

*Our vision is to be one company worldwide. That means more than just selling or operating globally. It means building business processes that assure the transfer of best practices, taking advantage of similarities, and fostering teamwork across regions of the world. This has become the major driver behind Brandywine Performance Centre: to be the vehicle for translating this vision of "one company" into reality.*

—David Whitwam, chairman of the board,
Whirlpool Corporation

## KEY PRINCIPLES OF THE CORPORATE UNIVERSITY MODEL

At the heart of each corporate university profiled in this book is a basic tenet that defines the corporate university as: The strategic umbrella for developing and educating employees, customers, and suppliers in order to meet an organization's business strategies.

Corporate universities come in many shapes and sizes. Some, such as Motorola University, have campus locations around the globe. Others, such as Dell University, Sun U, and Verifone University have no campus at all. These companies have committed to the virtual university model as an expression of their learning philosophy and commitment to continuous learning.

As a group, corporate universities provide a state-of-the-art learning environment for their own employees and, in many cases, for select members of their customer/supply chain: customers, suppliers, distributors, dealers, and even the educational institutions that supply the company with its human talent.

29

To build a top-flight work force, companies profiled in this book have adopted the corporate university model as a way to systematize and streamline their learning and development efforts. Just as each state relies on some form of the traditional university model to systematize higher education and avoid unnecessary duplication, companies with corporate universities employ the university model to organize their learning and developmental experiences into one cohesive, purposeful whole.

The corporate universities profiled here are in various stages of development and maturity. Some, such as Motorola University, General Electric Crotonville, and Disney University, are several decades old and are widely regarded as models for the corporate university approach. In fact, all three—Motorola University, Disney University, and General Electric Crotonville—have become so highly regarded that they now offer a range of training programs to customers and suppliers for a fee. Others, such as the Bank of Montreal Institute for Learning, Whirlpool Brandywine Creek Performance Centre, and Tennessee Valley Authority University are more recent arrivals, having been launched by their respective organizations within the last five years. Finally in 1997, General Motors Corporation announced the launch of General Motors University (GMU) as a vehicle to shape the future leaders of the Detroit-based global automotive giant.

While corporate universities differ in many surface aspects, they tend to organize themselves around similar principles and goals in pursuit of their overall objective—to become a lifelong learning institution. Ten clear-cut goals and principles lie at the heart of the corporate university's power to galvanize employees into the kind of first-rate work force needed for success in the global marketplace. These goals are:

1. Provide learning opportunities that support the organization's critical business issues.
2. Consider the corporate university model a process rather than a place of learning.
3. Design a curriculum to incorporate the three Cs: Corporate citizenship, Contextual framework, and Core competencies.
4. Train the value chain, including customers, distributors, product suppliers, and the universities that provide tomorrow's workers.

5. Move from instructor-led training to multiple formats of delivering learning.
6. Encourage leaders to be involved with and facilitate learning.
7. Move from a corporate allocation funding model to one "self-funded" by the business units.
8. Assume a global focus in developing learning solutions.
9. Create a measurement system to evaluate outputs as well as inputs.
10. Utilize the corporate university for competitive advantage and entry into new markets.

Now, let's take a close look at these principles in action.

### Provide Learning in Support of the Business Goals

The university model is competency based and links learning to the business' strategic needs.

Dave Ulrich, in *Human Resource Champions: The Next Agenda for Adding Value and Delivering Results* poses the following challenges to business leaders: "In this ever changing, global, technologically demanding business environment, sourcing and retaining talent will become the competitive battleground. Just as sports teams recruit aggressively for the best athletes, business organizations in the future will compete aggressively for the best talent. Successful firms will be those that are the most adept at attracting, developing, and retaining individuals with the skills, perspective, and experience necessary to drive a global business."[1]

The Bank of Montreal Institute for Learning offers an example of how an organization focuses on linking employee skills to business goals. "Our starting point for creating a new learning program is always a business issue or opportunity," says Jim Rush, senior vice president and executive director of Bank of Montreal Institute for Learning. "We sit down with our internal customers and ask, 'What's the difference between where you are now and where you want to be? What are the gaps?' The gap may be a problem they're working on or an opportunity they've identified in their business plan. Whatever the case, we work back from that and say, 'OK, if that's the performance gap, what's the skill or knowledge component of this gap?' Then we develop learning solutions to address these performance gaps and assist the business in meeting their strategic goals."

One initiative that exemplifies how the Institute for Learning links its programs to the bank's strategic direction is a self-paced learning program known as Learning for Success, which grew out of Chairman Matthew Barrett's conversations with employees and customers. Employees expressed an eagerness to acquire more and better skills training, but also advance their careers. In addition, customer expectations of service were also changing. Customers were demanding more than just a friendly greeting; they wanted a bank that was willing to take the time to help them identify individual financial needs and provide them with customized solutions. The employee and customer needs analysis pointed to the importance of training in relationship selling or uncovering customer needs and matching them with the "right" Bank of Montreal product and service.

Learning for Success came to life as a performance-based learning system that links learning to successful performance against job-specific technical capabilities and a set of specific behavioral effectiveness competencies. The segment of the system designed for tellers and customer service representatives is organized into five phases of learning illustrated in Figure 2–1. Each phase of learning includes reading assignments, a practice component, peer coaching, a number of computer-based training interventions, and culminating in a test to ensure technical proficiency; all targeted against a set of detailed performance objectives which, when successfully demonstrated, result in job accreditation.

The concept behind Learning for Success is to build the required technical skills and product/service knowledge one step at a time. Each step culminates in a learning milestone called accreditation which validates that all of the minimum performance objectives for a particular job have been met. One of the unique design attributes of Learning for Success is the integration of a personal development assessment and planning guide for each job that Learning for Success supports. This guide incorporates a number of assessment and development tools that support the technical capabilities and behavioral competencies a learner needs to meet job expectations and achieve accreditation. Specifically, the guide includes: an assessment tool that both identifies job requirements and allows learners to target their individual development needs;

**FIGURE 2-1**

---

## The Five-Phase Learning Process

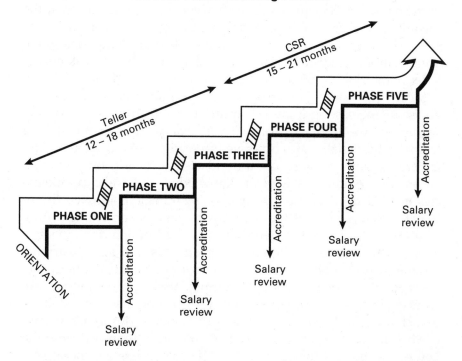

Courtesy of Bank of Montreal

a mapping tool that helps a learner to identify and prioritize their developmental needs; and a planning tool that encourages learners to incorporate learning interventions that best suit their individual learning style. Recognizing the pace of change within the banking industry and the need for roles to evolve and change rapidly, Learning for Success ensures that employees possess and demonstrate the skills and knowledge needed to improve customer service and increase market share.

### Consider the Corporate University Model a Process, Not Necessarily a Place

While some corporate universities may start as a bricks-and-mortar facility, the ultimate focus is on building a process for learning.

"Sometimes I think our classes are an excuse for our people to get together," echoes James Rush, executive director of the Bank of Montreal's Institute for Learning. That institute brings together 250 of the bank's 35,000 employees each week, selected from across the organization's line of businesses, hierarchy, and 1,000-employee sites. The corporate university facilitates team-building across the organization. "It's 'Switzerland' for us," Rush says. "We ask people to leave their SBUs (Strategic Business Units) at the door."[2]

Most corporate universities aspire to the Institute for Learning's goals: to increase employees' aptitude for learning by instilling within each employee a *commitment and accessibility* to lifelong learning. Essentially, the corporate university embodies the organization's learning philosophy, a mindset that focuses on providing all levels of employees with the knowledge, skills, and competencies needed to meet the organization's strategic objectives. Traditional training looks at the learning process as something with a beginning and an end: deliver X amount of training and the job is over. In this approach the student graduates and stops learning, but the corporate university encourages employees to continuously strive to learn new skills and competencies during their entire working lives and to be accountable for learning these new skills.

Richard Skip LeFauve, president of General Motors University (GMU) and former chairman of Saturn Corporation describes the key driver behind the launch of GMU as "assisting General Motors to become leaner, faster and more global as a corporation." LeFauve gives an example of this mindset when he shares a new initiative of GMU-Discovery Centers. "At GMU we want to do more than just share tribal knowledge and best practices around the organization. Instead, we want to reach out and discover new knowledge outside the corporation, bring it into the corporation and distribute it around the network. For example, we are inviting several automotive reporters from the media to have them come in and teach media relations from their perspective. The idea here is to seek out new knowledge and insights and use GMU as a vehicle to leverage these perspectives through the global network."

Why be so bold as to call this a "university?" The companies that have packaged their learning and development programs under the corporate university model have decided the university approach conjured up the sort of expectations that matched their objectives. They wanted a strategic umbrella to systematize the training effort, centralize its design, development and administration, apply consistent measures, become a "new product laboratory" for experimenting with new ways for employees to learn, and reap the cost efficiencies of a shared services model of delivering education. More importantly, they wanted the university metaphor to provide the image for the grand intent of the initiative: promising participants and their sponsors that the corporate university will prepare them for success in their current job and future career.

The university metaphor is easily understandable and in fact lends a certain cachet to the corporate training effort that is attractive to employees. James Chestnutt, general manager of Eaton's School of Retailing, shares some interesting facts about Canadian retailing that propelled the T. Eaton Company into the business of education. "As of 1995, there were approximately 65,000 retail businesses in Canada, and 80 percent of these—or 52,000—had fewer than 20 employees. While Canada's retail sector accounted for 30 percent of the Gross National Product, or $22.2 billion dollars, there was not a single university-level degree program in retailing."[3]

The Canadian retailing establishment, however, faced such challenges as intensified global competition, rapidly changing consumer behaviors, and the entrance of new technologies at the point of sale. The solution: become a leader in the field of retail education by providing state-of-the-art training to both Eaton's employees and the entire retail sector in Canada. The result was the creation of the Eaton's School of Retailing, in partnership with Toronto-based Ryerson Polytechnic University and Bell Canada. The school created by the three partners focuses on the needs of adult learners who work in the retail industry.

The courses within the Eaton School of Retailing are offered at Eaton locations, at Ryerson University, and now, with the addition of Bell Canada, throughout Canada. The term "university" has helped give the program the cachet it needed to get off the ground. The curriculum started with a certificate program and evolved into an accredited degree in retail management. For the adult learners, the prospect of graduating from the Eaton School of Retailing with either a certificate or degree has created a phenomenal excitement for learning. Chestnutt is fond of saying, "The true yardstick of success for the Eaton School of Retailing will be the growth and betterment of our retail employees in Canada."

While corporate universities have many of the accoutrements of a traditional university—a course catalog (frequently found on-line), a distinctive logo, graduation certificates, and even an alumni group—they have become much more than a way to package corporate training. Rather, they have become an impor-tant vehicle to link learning to an organization's business goals and deliver learning in an accessible, cost-effective manner.

The name "university" creates an ideal avenue for corporations to communicate with institutions of higher education. In fact, many of the most innovative alliances are at the K-12 levels. Ed Bales, retired Motorola University director of Educational Al-liances has been instrumental in developing a systems approach to working with K-12 educators. Bales says, "We want to align the in-dividual school district's curriculum with the skills, knowledge, and competencies required by our business segments. Essentially we are trying to take a vertical slice of the entire school system—including the superintendent, board president, parent, and key teachers—and impact the curriculum so that competencies such as creative thinking, teaming, problem-solving, and leadership are included in these K-12 school systems."

Bales illustrates Motorola University's commitment to system-wide innovation by pointing to the learning pyramid (Figure 2–2) as an example. Says Bales, "We, as adult learners, concentrate our learning at the top of the pyramid, spending time in lectures and reading rather than in the bottom of the pyramid where we practice by doing or teach others. Motorola University is currently experi-menting with local school systems to create change by impacting the bottom of the pyramid—practice by doing and teaching others."

While the emphasis remains on creating the process of continu-ous learning linked to business strategies, over time a number of corporate universities have come to believe in the importance of creating a physical facility for learning. As Bill Wiggenhorn, presi-dent of Motorola University, explains, "When I came here I didn't think it was important to have a physical facility. In fact, I was op-posed to it because I did not want to be evaluated on filling the bedroom space. But five years into the development of Motorola University I realized the importance of bringing all our employees from around the world together to one place to share best prac-tices, and transfer knowledge, not just from teacher to student, but also from student to student and from student to teacher. So we now have several places of learning, but the emphasis is on the process of learning not the physical space. In fact, we have no bedrooms, rather we have developed arrangements with local hotels to house our employees during their attendance at Motorola University learning programs."[4] Vincent J. Serritella, Motorola University's director of Planning, Quality, and Joint-Venture Development, describes Motorola University's physical presence this way, "We try to balance 15 minutes at the desktop with a place for employees to go and dialogue for two days."

**FIGURE 2–2**

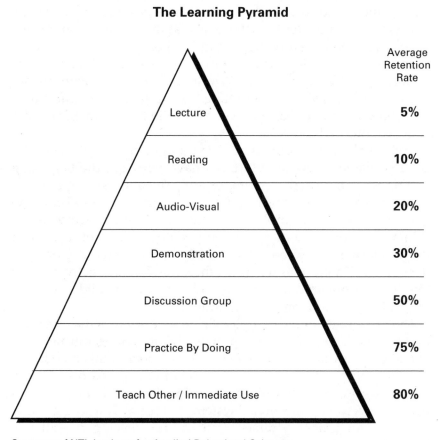

**The Learning Pyramid**

| | Average Retention Rate |
|---|---|
| Lecture | 5% |
| Reading | 10% |
| Audio-Visual | 20% |
| Demonstration | 30% |
| Discussion Group | 50% |
| Practice By Doing | 75% |
| Teach Other / Immediate Use | 80% |

Courtesy of NTL Institute for Applied Behavioral Sciences

Some corporate universities, such as Whirlpool's Brandywine Performance Creek Centre, are making a commitment to bricks and mortar, but this includes building both a state-of-the-art place of learning as well as innovative on-line learning processes. Kent Price, director of Training and Education for Whirlpool, says that one of the forces for creating a place of learning was the changing nature of Whirlpool's business. In 1988, the company manufactured its products in four countries and had 5,822 employees (25 percent of the work force) outside the United States. Today Whirlpool manufactures in 12 countries, has more than 20,000 employees (45 percent of the work force) outside the United States, and does business in 140 markets.[5]

Whirlpool's management felt the need to bring executives from around the world to a single place to share best practices, acquire new skills, and transfer knowledge across the organization. As one of the Whirlpool faculty, Dr. Anjan Thakor, professor of finance from University of Michigan Business School, says, "Brandywine Performance Centre provides Whirlpool executives with an opportunity to realize how everything fits together. Specifically, they learn how Whirlpool has become a leader in North America, Latin America, Europe, and Asia."

Price explains the commitment to building a state-of-the-art facility by saying, "We at Whirlpool have felt from the beginning that bricks and mortar were important. We have a strong philosophy of learning and we want to share this with our 45,435 employees. We believe our employees value going to a place to learn. While our people say they want 30 minute modules of training at the desktop, they also have told us they want to take two or three days to go to a place to reflect on their mission and network with their peers from around the world. Our goal is to build a community of learners both on-site and on-line."

The corporate university umbrella, in a nutshell, is the organization's attempt to promote the same spirit of lifelong learning that one finds in an exceptional university. The goal of this model was summarized by William Esrey, chairman of the board of Sprint, when he said, "Sprint University of Excellence$^{SM}$ is more than a place or even an educational system. Rather, it is a living entity composed of trainers, trainees, curriculum developers—all role models committed to the continuous process of learning and lifelong development. Employees cycle through courses, exercises, and updates created by the University of Excellence as a means of fulfilling their commitment to self-development."[6]

## Design a Core Curriculum Around the Three Cs

The core curriculum of corporate universities is remarkably similar in its focus on the three Cs—developing Corporate citizenship, providing a Contextual framework to the company, and building Core workplace competencies among employees.

One of the most striking features of the corporate university model is the increased emphasis on formally training all levels of employees in the corporation's values, beliefs, and culture. AT&T Universal Card University has "Passport to Excellence"; Motorola University has "Culture Class"; and Tennessee Valley Authority University has "TVA: A New Business Era." Regardless of the name or how the course is designed or delivered, the goal is similar in many of these organizations: to inculcate everyone from the clerical assistant to the top executive in the culture and values that make the organization unique and special and to define behaviors that enable employees to "live the values."

The Southern Company, the Atlanta, Georgia-based utility, provides an excellent example of how values can provide a central focus not only for training, but also for an entire organization's performance and reward system. Allen Franklin, chief executive officer of Georgia Power Company unit, describes the importance of Southern Company College: "Uncertainty in the future of the electric industry is bringing with it greater demands on management and a need to develop among our employees an understanding of our shared vision and the leadership and business knowledge required for success in our rapidly competitive business environment."[7]

The following lists key Southern Company values. These include demonstrating ethical behavior, putting the customer first, respecting shareholder value, making Southern Company a great place to work, valuing teamwork, taking personal responsibility for success, and being committed to the community and to the environment. Southern Company's definition of success entails meeting business goals while adhering to these values. The company trains employees in these values and asks them to assess themselves with regard to each value on a five point scale:

| Value | Self-Assessment | | | | |
|---|---|---|---|---|---|
| Performance Issue | Still Learning | Fully Effective | Consensus Strength | Role Model |
| Ethical Behavior | | | | |
| Customer First | | | | |
| Shareholder Value | | | | |
| Great Place to Work | | | | |
| Teamwork | | | | |
| Superior Performance | | | | |
| Citizenship | | | | |

Training in these values is just the beginning for Southern Company employees. The values have become the lifeblood, the very soul, of the company. As Al Martin, dean of Southern Company College says, "Many companies introduce employees to the corporate values in a day-long orientation program which also covers the corporate benefits, policies, and procedures. Often, this may be the last time the employee hears about the values of the company. But this is not the case at the Southern Company. We make a conscious effort to build the values into the fabric of the company, by stating in detail the behaviors that produce performance in line with Southern Company's values—behaviors the company encourages its employees to build into their day-to-day way of thinking and acting on the job."

For example, "Respects Shareholder Value" is one value. The behaviors tied to this include:

1. *Acts like an owner*—increases stockholder value. Takes personal initiative to do what is best for shareholders, customers, employees, and the community; balances the priorities of different constituencies.
2. *Creates a shared vision*—champions a vision for being America's Best Diversified Utility; maintains a balance between a long-term, big-picture view and near-term results; achieves profitability and maximizes growth potential in business opportunities; encourages entrepreneurial thinking; translates strategies into operational plans.
3. *Is a student of the business*—has a broad understanding of their company's functions and financial structure; knows what it takes to be successful in this industry; understands

the industry's history and trends; understands the market, competition, and regulation.[8]

Southern Company's performance review system makes innovative and effective use of its values. When a Southern Company manager writes a performance review on an employee, he or she measures the employee's behaviors against these values. The company's ongoing performance management system continually reinforces these values and employee behaviors.

The reason to inculcate employees in the vision, values, and culture of a company is simple—to develop a shared mindset among all employees.

Catherine Hammon, general manager of Tennessee Valley Authority University and a key member of the team that spearheaded the launch of TVA University in 1994, stresses values training: "TVA University exists because of our organization-wide commitment to continuous learning. All TVA employees must know TVA's direction; hold a shared vision of our future and possess the skills and knowledge necessary to create the future." A significant way employees learn about our future is by completing a core curricula known as Pathways to Excellence. One learning module in this program is called "TVA: A New Business Era." Hammon continues, "As TVA employees learn more about TVA's values, traditions, culture, and, its vision for the rest of the decade, they report a much deeper sense of organizational issues."

Developing corporate citizenship, which is at the heart of what Southern Company and Tennessee Valley Authority are doing, is modeled after practices at many successful Japanese companies. In Japan, many production workers go through a one-week, off-the-job motivational program to learn the company's values, beliefs, and traditions, often directly from the founder. The purpose of this motivational program is to build employee pride and bonding between the employee and the company. The focus of such training is more than a means of career advancement; it is targeted to building an employee population that *wants* to meet the company's strategic business objectives, rather than mechanically follow a set of instructions and formulas.

Companies build another important objective into their corporate university's curricula—to provide workers with an understanding of the context in which the company operates. Companies are designing courses that explain to employees how the company makes money; who the customers, suppliers, and competitors are; the best practices of other companies; how the features and benefits of the company's products differ from competitive offerings; and how the employee's job fits into the corporate mission. This contextual reference provides employees with a big picture framework so they can understand how important their roles are in meeting the company's business objectives and profit goals.

One course that provides this contextual framework is the Southern Company College's "Student of the Business Fundamentals." During this three-day workshop participants learn the basics of the electric utility business: power generation, transmission and distribution, customers and markets, rates and regulatory issues, and finance. All of this sets the stage for finally introducing critical external forces that influence the Southern Company business: globalization, competition, and The Energy Policy Act of 1992.

Finally, corporate university curricula provide employees with training in a number of core workplace competencies that support and help define the company's competitive advantage. These core competencies combine learning-to-learn skills, communication and collaboration skills, creative thinking/problem-solving skills, technological literacy, global business literacy, leadership development, career self-management, and of course, technical know-how to function successfully in the organization. Chapter 4 provides more details of these programs with examples from leading corporate universities.

### Train the Value Chain

Effective training is system-wide training, that is, it addresses not only employees, but also key members of the company's customer/supply chain, which can include customers, product suppliers, and local schools (K-12 school systems, as well as colleges and universities).

"System-wide training" may sound like another grandiose slogan for the 1990s, but the concept behind the idea is powerful. A system-wide approach involves proactively training and educating key participants in the company's value chain—suppliers at one end and customers at the other. The reasoning behind this is that if all the critical members of the chain understand the company's vision, values, mission, and quality goals, as well as the individual competencies supporting its competitive advantage, the company is better able to meet its business objectives.

This system-wide approach is continuous and open-ended. In other words, rather than offering X amount of training and then regarding the job as finished, companies that adopt this approach develop an integrated learning system that enables employees, customers, suppliers, and key universities to engage in learning and development opportunities continuously.

The combination of an internal and an external focus inherent in the corporate university philosophy often changes the relationships between a company and its product suppliers, customers, and educational suppliers. For example, the traditional view of product or material suppliers regards them as adversaries rather than partners, a view that can create mistrust, fear, and frustration on both sides and impede long-term improvements. Supplier training programs address a fundamental fact: often many of a company's quality problems are really specification and design issues that the partners can alleviate by bringing suppliers into the development process at an earlier stage and offering them training to understand the company's quality imperatives.

Companies with corporate universities have recognized that the success of their suppliers and their customers is critical to their own success. Instead of treating suppliers as adversaries—or, worse, like disposable diapers to be discarded when their function is accomplished—enlightened companies are taking the view that they need to build partnerships with key links in their business channel.

Motorola University has become a vehicle to establish a dialogue with suppliers, learning from them and teaching them the corporation's quality initiative of Six Sigma.* Bob Galvin, chairman of the executive committee of Motorola, uses the example of a plastic supplier to make a point about the need for such dialogues. A Motorola designer, he argues, will know what the plastics part must do, but the plastics manufacturer will have ideas on how to make it more efficient, more reliable, and less expensive because that's his or her

---

*Six sigma refers to six standard deviations from a statistical performance average. In plain English, Six sigma translates into 3.4 defects per million opportunities, or a goal of 99.99966 percent error-free transactions—be it on the production line or in the legal department. In effect, the Six-Sigma process means changing the way people do things so that products and services are virtually perfect.

business.[9] Motorola University sponsors forums in which in-house personnel listen to suppliers as the experts in their fields and gain new ideas from them regarding issues ranging from new-product development to cost-reduction opportunities. In addition, this supplier training also provides a source of revenue for Motorola University through licensing arrangements.

Corporate universities also target for training those on the other side of the customer/supply chain: the company's customers and intermediaries who sell the products to end-users. Corporate universities have become the focal point for building partnerships with dealers, distributors, wholesalers, and retailers and designing programs aimed at helping them to become more successful in their businesses. The belief behind such training is that, as more products meet similar standards, the competitive advantage will go to those companies that have the best-trained work force—whether they are the company's own customer contact people or the sales forces of its customers, distributors, dealers, or wholesalers.

The Busch Learning Center, the corporate university of Anheuser-Busch, is an example of this commitment. The Busch Learning Center targets the 950 Anheuser-Busch wholesalers. David Vaughn, director of the Busch Learning Center, says that the goal is to "lead Anheuser-Busch and its business partners into the future by investing in people, processes, and technology through training, education, consulting, and tools to improve skills, knowledge, and performance."

The reason for creating the Busch Learning Center was simple: to provide the Anheuser-Busch wholesaler network with a competitive edge in the marketplace. While Anheuser-Busch had always offered wholesaler training, it was primarily "classroom-based and not linked to the business goals of Anheuser-Busch. Now the goal is to provide these Anheuser-Busch wholesalers with a fully integrated learning system that meets the needs of a more complex and competitive marketplace."

Vaughn describes the beer market as much more unstable than it was, say, ten years ago. Many new competitors in the micro brewery category have meant that wholesalers and their employees must have much broader skills to be successful. For example, according to Vaughn, past wholesaler training had been primarily instructor-led and focused on selling skills. Now the scope is much broader and includes strategic planning, financial management, and inventory control. What's more, learning includes CD-ROM, intranet, and a Busch Satellite Network (BSN). This satellite network provides programming that runs approximately five hours per week, ranging from sharing best practices among regions to training modules in selling, leadership, and merchandising. What's next? The Busch Satellite Network hopes to offer accredited degree programs so wholesaler employees can continue their education on-site.

This emphasis on customer training is not limited to companies the size of Anheuser-Busch. The Iams Company, a $300 million privately held company serving the premium pet food market, has developed Iams University specifically to provide training to business channel members, including pet store owners, distributors, veterinarians, and breeders. In fact the Iams Company devotes 20 percent of its training budget to train these independent distributors who supply Iams brands to pet specialty retailers worldwide. Jack Tootson, director of Iams University, says, "One reason we make such a generous investment in our distributors' success is simple—their performance is one of the keys to our continued growth and success."

The cornerstone of Iams University distributor training is the Distributor Executive Development Institute, known as DEDI. Modeled on a similar program at the Wharton School of Business, DEDI is aimed at the 30 owners of regional distributorships who now represent the Iams Company on an exclusive basis. The curriculum includes an intensive week of instruction and a best practices sharing forum focusing on such areas as warehousing and customer service. During the DEDI program, these distributors and their managers of customer service and warehousing get the opportunity to benchmark their operation and operating data against other Iams distributors. According to Tootson, "These best practices sharing forums are structured learning experiences, complete with homework and class discussions to share procedures and philosophies that distributors have found successful in lowering operating costs. For example, in our warehousing workshops, distributors are learning from each other the best way to unload and store our product and how to best transport our product to the customer."

"These workshops are then captured both on videotape and through meeting notes, and all the participants take these materials back to their operation for future reference." Finally, Tootson notes that the results of running these workshops have led to 10 percent savings in operating costs for many of the participants. These workshops illustrate an important Iams principle: What is good for the distributors is good for Iams and what is good for the company is also good for the distributors.

This notion of creating alliances with customers, suppliers, and dealers is borrowed from the Japanese who call it *keiritsu*. In Japan, keiritsu refers to multi-company groups tied together by cross-shareholdings. (In the United States, companies are not going so far as developing these cross-shareholdings, but they are building alliances with customers and suppliers to ensure their overall success.) Such an emphasis on teamwork between companies and their suppliers and customer-control links in the marketplace will over time lead to innovation, better quality, and greater productivity.

Perhaps one of the most far-reaching examples of value chain training is the alliance between General Electric and Columbia/ HCA Healthcare Corporation. For years GE sold CAT scanners, magnetic resonance imagers, and other medical imaging equipment to the 300 plus hospitals run by Columbia/HCA Healthcare Corporation. As of March 1996, GE has provided Columbia/HCA with training in how to conduct "workouts" (town meetings at which a cross-section of employees meet together to discuss ways to improve the business) and seminars on supply-chain management targeted with boosting Columbia's productivity.[10]

This deeper relationship is more than simply "training the value chain"; it is a sign of a profound shift at GE. As the firm faces slower domestic growth and cut-throat pricing abroad, Chairman Jack Welch is now committed to enter the customer's business as a consultant in addition to selling equipment. John Trani, CEO of GE Medical Systems says, "Our goal is to create a business by teaching our customers how to take costs out of their operations."[11]

In addition to using an organization's expertise in education and development to enter a new line of business, companies with corporate universities are targeting the educational institutions that supply them with their recruits each year. Why this increased emphasis on forging alliances with institutions of higher education? American companies engaged in global competition are discovering that they compete not only against a better-trained work force abroad, but one that has a stronger tradition of lifelong learning.

Consider the latest Motorola University initiative. For the past decade Motorola University has been committed to establishing a network of academic alliances of universities and community colleges in regions where the company has a major corporate presence, but in September 1996 Motorola tried something even more far-reaching: establishing alliances in regions of the country where the company *anticipates* building a new chip-making plant. The newest collaboration is between Motorola University and J. Sargent Reynolds Community College in Richmond, Virginia. This alliance spells out a range of Motorola University courses—Six Sigma, Customer Satisfaction, Manufacturability—that Motorola University faculty will teach at J. Sargent Reynolds Community College. The goal is to not only train a future work force, but to use the alliance as a recruiting technique for both prospective employees and instructors who wish to become certified to teach Motorola University courses.

Motorola is essentially considering the local educational system as a supplier—similar to product suppliers—and taking steps to manage the quality of the end product, in this case the students. It is creating alliances to develop an awareness among local school systems and prospective employees of the range of skills, knowledge, and competencies Motorola requires. As Chapter 1 pointed out, reading, math and writing are merely the foundation of learning. It is increasingly critical that workers develop higher-order skills and competencies such as creative problem-solving and knowing how to learn.

This commitment to lifelong learning is at the heart of retraining and job redefinition programs. Because learning skills are best developed early in life, companies are developing extensive partnership programs with select community colleges and four-year universities whose graduates will fill their ranks. They want to ensure that these academic institutions teach not only what students will need for tomorrow's jobs but also how to learn and adapt to changes not yet foreseen in new technologies and job functions.

### Move from Instructor-Led to Multiple Formats of Delivering Learning

While corporate universities have extensive programs to train all levels of employees in skills, knowledge, and competencies, their real emphasis is on becoming a learning laboratory for the entire customer/employee/supply chain. These universities promote learning both formally, with training programs delivered in a class-room or distributed through various media, and informally with programs targeted to employees, customers, suppliers, and even the universities that supply the company with its new recruits.

Chapter 5 explores in depth how these universities experiment with new ways of learning. At the heart of this experimentation is the belief that training is much more than passing along new in-formation. Training also encompasses learning how others have taken action and improved productivity, either inside the corpora-tion or in the best practices of innovative companies. The compa-nies profiled in this book share a devotion to experimenting with learning from a variety of sources in order to build a spirit of con-tinuous learning into the organization's fabric.

This passion for experimenting with new ways to learn con-trasts significantly with the emphasis of training in the past, which has been focused on designing and delivering mostly instructor-led, classroom-based training programs. Now the emphasis is on individualized learning using state-of-the-art delivery methods to achieve improvements on the job. This focus on using multiple formats such as the intranet, satellite, and multimedia, points to the enlarged mission and scope of learning: to identify ways the entire organization can continuously learn or, as Peter Senge says in his book, *The Fifth Discipline: The Art and Practice of the Learning Organization,* "to continually expand the capacity of the organiza-tion to create its future."[12]

Companies must therefore go beyond creating *opportunities* for learning in the classroom or even at the computer. Instead, organi-zations committed to learning must help both individuals and em-ployee teams develop the *capacity* to learn. This means being com-mitted to experiment with tools and techniques outside of the traditional trainer's toolkit.

Bank of Montreal Institute for Learning uses Learning Map™ il-lustrations, four-by-six foot graphics designed to produce conversa-tions and reflections around a set of targeted issues or business processes. This tool is used to convey the changing context of the fi-nancial services industry. For example, the Learning Maps* cover the entrance of new players, the bank's reaction to this new competitive environment, the "big picture" of what actually happens to a deposit

---

*A trademark owned solely by Root Learning, Inc.

as it winds its way through the banking process, and research reporting the changing needs of the bank's customers. The bank presents Learning Maps™ to employees in groups of five to seven, facilitated by "guides" who are not professional trainers. The goal is to provide employees with a visual overview of the financial services industry and to use it as a stimulus to create new ideas, share best practices, and propose new solutions. Chapter 5 presents how another company, Sears, uses Learning Maps™ in the retail industry.

Companies with corporate universities are also experimenting with ways to reinforce learning on the job. For example, Frank Hayden, Group Training and Development Director at Rover Group, England, has created an organization within his corporate university to research the transfer of learning to the job. Hayden's group addresses such questions as:

- Are managers briefing and debriefing associates before and after a learning activity?
- Are managers and team leaders ensuring that their team members are getting the opportunity to practice new skills?
- Does Rover Group have the appropriate administrative and tracking system to record the learning undertaken by every associate?
- Does Rover Group have an adequate intranet so associates can input and access information and best practices?

Finally, Rover Group invested in Open Learning Centres at the plant site, so associates can use a myriad of learning modalities—from audio and video to computer-based—to be responsible for their own learning.

As more companies like Bank of Montreal and Rover Group use their corporate university to experiment with learning at the work-site, the workplace is evolving into a university—complete with learning labs, libraries, and laptops, so employees can continue learning on their own time.

### Encourage Leaders to be Involved with and Facilitate Learning

Traditional training utilizes faculty who can present cases and concepts in the classroom to internal employees. These teachers fly in, impart their wisdom, and leave. David Ulrich, consultant and professor of the University of Michigan School of Business, calls this phenomenon the "sea gull" faculty. Many corporate universities have shifted the focus of facilitating learning from external experts to internal leaders.

TVA University's methods are representative of what scores of other corporate universities are doing. At TVA about 700 TVA middle and senior managers participate in a rigorous certification process to become an instructor. These TVA managers deliver approximately 150 hours of classroom instruction within a 12-month period of time. Their participation serves as a role model and, more importantly, as a developmental experience for them as well as means of improving their facilitation and group management skills, and helping them to develop a breadth and depth of knowledge about TVA's businesses. In turn, TVA participants learn from seasoned TVA managers who pepper each workshop with real-world examples.

For those organizations asking how it can possibly obtain a time commitment like this from its managers—150 hours or almost four weeks off the job—the secret lies in the TVA performance management system, which counts the time spent facilitating a TVA workshop as a developmental assignment. Instituting this type of integrated human resource system is critical to having senior business leaders serve as learning facilitators.

Many of the companies profiled in this book are taking the role-modeling concept and expanding upon it to include bringing senior executives into the learning experience to inspire and motivate employees. In our *Annual Survey of Corporate University Future Directions* we found that the average CEO spends one day a month facilitating learning in his or her organization. This commitment to cultivating and managing the firm's intellectual capital was viewed as the single most important role for the CEO—that as chief learning officer. This involvement with employees in the learning process spans participating in workout sessions, orienting new hires to the organization's values and vision, and facilitating senior manager leadership programs.

Role-modeling of this nature promotes a culture of continuous learning and helps to transform the organization. Lawrence Bossidy, CEO of Allied Signal, the automotive and aerospace manufacturer headquartered in Morristown, New Jersey, used to be second-in-command to Jack Welch at General Electric. "The only way to bridge the gap between where we are and where we want to go is education," Bossidy told *Harvard Business Review* in a 1995 interview. "We put every one of our 80,000 people through total quality training. This includes all our business leaders, including me. And I make it a point to visit as many classes as I can whenever I'm on location. We want people on the factory floor to feel as good about training as top level managers do."[13]

Jack Welch calls his involvement in Crotonville Management Development Institute a "two-way radio station" where what he hears is equally as important as the knowledge, culture, and stories he imparts to the Crotonville participants. In fact, Welch has even taken over the teaching chores of a three-and-a-half hour leadership class offered five times a year. Now, according to Steven Kerr, vice president of leadership development at Crotonville, Welch is encouraging other GE executives to begin teaching at Crotonville.[14]

Jack Smith, chairman, CEO and president of General Motors has committed to become actively involved in facilitating learning at General Motors University. Richard Skip LeFauve, President of General Motors University relates how GMU will involve leaders as learners, "We are committed to design various case studies which revolve around lessons General Motors has learned in quality, leadership and union management. These case studies will be tools and support materials for our leaders to use as stimulus materials to facilitate learning programs and share best practices around the global network."

Bossidy, Welch, and Smith are excellent examples of the value of being actively involved in cultivating and promoting organizational learning. These CEOs practice continuous learning themselves by getting feedback from employees at all levels of the organization. This emphasis on role-modeling has the effect of encouraging employees to proactively explore and innovate on the job. Ultimately, the goal here is to have employees make continuous improvements in their work environment.

## Move from Corporate Allocation to Self-Funding

A growing number of senior business managers are committed to a funding model that demands corporate universities reflect a market-driven link between services rendered and customer needs. This "pay for services" funding strategy requires business units to pay for corporate university services rather than allocating payment to corporate overhead. According to our *Annual Survey of Corporate University Future Directions*, the typical corporate university funding model is moving from the current 54 percent corporate allocation to only 30 percent.

It is important to remember here that a "pay for services" funding strategy evolves as a corporate university matures. Corporate universities seldom are launched with a pay for services funding model because few of their "customers" realize just how valuable their services can be. As a corporate university proves its value, pay for services becomes the natural evolution of a customer-focused business. For example, when Motorola launched its university in 1981, corporate overhead covered the entire cost. By 1996, corporate overhead contributed 37 percent of the cost. Essentially this amount was the company's strategic investment in overall corporate change agent initiatives. The remainder of the budget for Motorola University comes from internal business unit customers paying for services delivered (47 percent) and outside sources licensing Motorola University training programs to customers and suppliers (16 percent).

Vince Serritella, director of Planning, Quality, and Joint Venture Development at Motorola University, says this funding model forces Motorola University to demonstrate its value, because over 60 percent of the budget has to be covered by the business units or outside customers. Serritella says, "Essentially this pay for services funding model creates an open market system, placing the competitive pressures of the marketplace on us and driving us to meet or exceed customer needs. We'd like to get the corporate investment down to about 25 percent of our budget and grow the market in other ways, such as more aggressively licensing our training to customers, suppliers, and community colleges."

SunU of Sun Microsystems is betting on creating the ultimate funding model—100 percent pay for services, or a self-funded model where the entire funding comes from customers using the services. SunU's funding has evolved over time; customers contributed 40 percent to the overall SunU budget in 1995, 75 percent in 1996, and Jim Moore, director of SunU, proposes 100 percent by the year 2000. Why the drastic change and what are the advantages of this type of funding model?

First, Moore believes adopting a totally self-funded model requires that a corporate university's customers drive the training agenda and vote with their dollars. A 100 percent self-funded model means the corporate university implements and sustains only those programs and courses that solve real business problems. Second, the corporate university reduces its course offerings because it eliminates courses that are nice but not central to business unit needs. SunU eliminated about 40 percent of the courses it offered in 1995 because they were not addressing the strategic needs of Sun employees. Finally, the implementation of a self-funded business model avoids the danger of becoming isolated from customers and reduces the need to construct elaborate return on investment (ROI) models to justify one's existence within the corporation.

While measurement is certainly important, SunU customers who vote with their dollars will simply stop paying for a training program that does not add value to their business. This aggressive funding model is consistent with the "rightsizing culture" at Sun Microsystems, which cut its manufacturing cycle time from 274 days to 139 days in 1995. This emphasis on efficiency means that SunU corporate education must practice what it preaches as a business unit and strive to maintain this "rightsizing" mindset in its own business operation.

The decision to adopt a particular funding model is really a decision about whether or not a corporate university wants to create an open market for training and education. Those that do embrace a funding model in which most of the budget comes from customer tuition are positioning themselves as the preferred partner for employee education and development.

### Assume a Global Focus in Developing Learning Programs

Motorola University and General Electric's Crotonville, two mature corporate universities, have been instrumental in driving a global perspective among its managers. As a transnational corporation, Motorola has taken the lead in developing workshops where Motorola's senior executives analyze select Asian countries as potential markets and determine how Motorola can successfully compete there. According to Wiggenhorn, Motorola's leadership developed a new perspective from these early workshops: "We began to understand that the sophistication of the customer was in many cases higher outside the U.S. than inside the U.S. If we were going to be *the* benchmark institution we had to understand the needs of the most sophisticated customer and match or exceed those expectations."[15]

Motorola University's globalization workshops have evolved over time to now include field trips where executives see local market developments firsthand and then help teach other managers what they learned and what they think the company's responses should be. Motorola routinely follows these benchmarking field trips by sending teams of production workers, engineers, and staff support workers overseas to capture best practices and incorporate them into their corporate functions back home. Motorola now offers many of these programs to the company's suppliers and customers, as well as to governments in countries in which the company does business.

Wiggenhorn views a large part of his function as that of a "roving ambassador for corporate education," seeking out and importing best practices around the world. He discovered that in Korea, for example, Samsung and L. G. Group (i.e., Goldstar) invest two to three times as much in the development of new hires as many corporations in North America. In Europe, Wiggenhorn discovered that leading firms, such as Mercedes Benz and Dutch Aerospace Group, aggressively prepare work teams to function in cross-cultural environments. At Motorola University these practices are having an influence on its evolution.

Crotonville, General Electric's "corporate university," was launched in 1955 primarily to serve the needs of high potential GE managers. Originally crafted as a 13-week Executive Development Program of three one-month courses spread over the managerial portion of a GE employee's career, Crotonville has evolved to become an agent of corporate change and a vehicle for deepening the bond with its customers.

The China Management Training Program represents GE's commitment to help teach top-level Chinese managers Western management practices. Since 1986, four groups of Chinese managers have completed the program. Six GE businesses currently represented in China each select a group of 25 Chinese managers viewed as future leaders. Following nine months in an intensive English language program conducted in Beijing, these Chinese managers spend one month at Crotonville where they are introduced to the concepts and business practices of a free market economy. Participants then visit various GE businesses and corporate staff functions and conclude the program with an additional week at Crotonville where they address a key question: "How can GE work more effectively with my enterprise?" The program ends with each presenting an analysis of GE's market position in China relative to GE's competitors and making suggestions for improving GE's performance.

### Create a Measurement System to Evaluate Outputs as well as Inputs

One of the primary cost efficiencies of the corporate university is to centralize operations such as design, development, registration, vendor management, and measurement. Much of the emphasis on measurement has been on manipulating training measures defined by Donald Kirkpatrick (covered in detail in Chapter 3). While these measures offer a useful starting point for evaluating an investment in employee education, the real opportunity is to move from measuring the inputs—number of student days or hours—to measuring the outputs—the contribution an education investment has had on achieving a business strategy. As we noted earlier, when customers vote with their dollars and pay for education services, there is less of a tendency to construct elaborate return on investment (ROI) charts and more emphasis on uncovering the value that training has had on moving the business forward. Hence, corporate university managers should ask themselves three key questions as they begin to develop a measurement system:

1. What impact have we had on our human capital in terms of employee retention, satisfaction, and innovation?
2. What impact have we had on our customers, internal and external, in terms of retention, satisfaction, and achievement of business goals?
3. What impact have we had on meeting our business goals and strategies?

These three questions demand that a corporate university manager take a longitudinal view of his/her contribution to the business. This view requires more than conducting surveys six to nine months after training. It means tracking individual employees for up to five years and understanding what contribution they have made to the organization. The goal is to measure the "output" of the learning experience.

Figure 2–3 illustrates an interesting model of how one company, Skandia, the largest insurance and financial services company in Scandinavia, released the world's first public Intellectual Capital (IC) Annual report as a supplement to their financial report in 1995. At the heart of the Skandia IC model is the idea that the real value of a company's performance lies in its ability to cre-

**FIGURE 2–3**

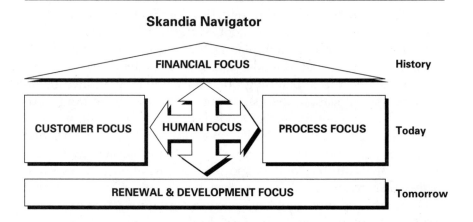

### Skandia Navigator

FINANCIAL FOCUS — History

CUSTOMER FOCUS — HUMAN FOCUS — PROCESS FOCUS — Today

RENEWAL & DEVELOPMENT FOCUS — Tomorrow

**Sample of Key Indicators in Skandia Navigator:**

**Financial Focus**
1. Total Assets
2. Total Assets/Employee
3. Revenues from New Business
4. Revenues/Employee

**Customer Focus**
1. Market Share
2. Annual Sales/Customer
3. Average Duration of Customer Relationship
4. Satisfied Customer Index

**Process Focus**
1. Administrative Expense/ Total revenues
2. Contacts Filed Without Error
3. Administrative Expense/Employee
4. Corporate Quality Goal

**Renewal & Development Focus**
1. Satisfied Employee Index
2. Training Expense/Employee
3. Training Expense/ Administrative Expense
4. Educational Investment Customer

**Human Focus**
1. Employee Turnover
2. Average Years of Service With Company
3. Time in Training (Days/Year)
4. IT Literacy of Staff

ate sustainable value by pursuing a business vision and resulting strategy. From this strategy one can then determine certain success factors that can then be grouped into five distinct areas of focus: Financial; Customer; Process; Renewal and Development, and Human. The Skandia Navigator attempts to pull together into one overall format these key success factors. In a sense, this is a map of the value of an overall enterprise.

This map depicted in Figure 2–3 is in the shape of a house, Skandia's metaphor for the organization. The triangle atop the rectangle, the attic, is the financial focus, including the Balance Sheet of the organization. The Financial Focus is essentially a historical picture of the firm. As you move down the house, you enter the present—the Customer and Process Focus. Finally, the bottom of this house is a look into the future of the organization—the Renewal and Development Focus. The center of the house is the Human Focus—the competence and capabilities of the employees and the commitment of the organization to keep these competencies regularly tuned and updated. According to Leif Edvinsson, vice president and corporate director of Intellectual Capital at Skandia, "We believe that value growth for our shareholders is increasingly dependent on the company's capability to create, sustain, and capitalize this intellectual capital. Hence our commitment to visually depicting this for our shareholders."[16] Increasingly, more companies will experiment with drawing their own pictures of these types of measures as the movement to report the intellectual capital of an organization intensifies.

### Utilize the Corporate University for Competitive Advantage and Entry into New Markets

The final organizing principle in the creation and management of a corporate university is the use of the corporate university for external competitive advantage. Motorola's Vincent Serritella says, "By the end of this decade, our intent is that Motorola University will be a unique competitive advantage. By this I mean that we will assist the company in penetrating markets that would be closed if it was just based on our ability to have the technical answer. Secondly, we believe that Motorola University will give us the ability to listen and to see with a multiple set of eyes and ears what's going on around the world and to feed this back into the organization."

Motorola University is not alone in its desire to become a competitive advantage for the organization. Perhaps the most impressive experiment in using an organization's commitment to education for competitive advantage is General Electric's move to enter the consulting business with its customers. As Jack Welch says, "The product you sell is only one component of your business."[17]

To that end, General Electric is using the techniques developed in Crotonville, such as workouts and seminars on supply-chain management, to position itself as a productivity consultant to its customers. This commitment to using education as an entry into new customers and markets is being implemented because many of General Electric's manufacturing markets are rumbling along with just single-digit growth. As product life cycles shorten and technology becomes easy to emulate, companies must participate in more of the value chain. That means transforming themselves into consultants and advising customers on areas ranging from quality and employee education to productivity and innovation.

The companies applying the principles inherent in a corporate university are creating a continuous learning system where the entire organization is learning and tinkering with new processes and new solutions. This "tinkering" is what Peter Senge calls the ability to run experiments in the margin. Senge cites a study Shell Oil commissioned that examined the changes in the firms appearing on the Fortune 500 list. One-third of the companies listed on the Fortune 500 list in 1970 had vanished by 1983. In fact, the study estimated that the lifetime of the largest industrial firm was less than half the average lifetime of a person in an industrial society. The bright spot uncovered by this study was that those firms that survived for 75 years or longer made a point of continually experimenting and exploring new businesses and creating new sources of growth.[18]

Companies applying the principles evident in corporate universities are looking beyond employee education programs for one target population—internal employees—and building learning systems that bring together the customer, employee, and supply chain in the pursuit of continuous improvement. The challenge is to create a learning environment where every employee and every element of the company's business system understand the importance of continuous learning linked to business goals.

# Chapter Three

# Designing a Corporate University

*One of the things that distinguishes the best companies is the ability to produce a surplus of leaders. The best organizations in the world are net exporters of leadership talent and the rest are importers of leadership talent. Our goal in creating McDonnell Douglas Learning Center is to increase our company's value to its customers and shareholders by strengthening the capacities of our people . . . to learn . . . to work together and most importantly to lead.*

—Harry Stonecipher, president and chief executive officer,
McDonnell Douglas Corporation

## THE CORPORATE UNIVERSITY
## DESIGN PROCESS

Over the past five years, scores of companies and federal agencies have decided to launch corporate universities. They include large organizations (McDonnell Douglas Corporation) and small ones (Lord Corporation), companies based in the United States with a strong union involvement (Southern Company and NYNEX), organizations in the midst of a turnaround (National Semiconductor), and firms based outside of the United States (Bank of Montreal). Companies with strong earnings and world-class brand images (Anheuser-Busch) and government agencies are also "reinventing" themselves (Department of Defense, Defense Acquisition University) using the corporate university model.

These efforts have started for many reasons: as an outgrowth of re-engineering, cultural change, new top management, the result of new legislation, even the restructuring of an entire industry, as in the case of utilities, telecommunications, and healthcare. In almost every case, the basic goal is the same: to increase work force productivity and create a competitive advantage in the marketplace.

A number of corporate universities resulted from the restructuring of the entire organization's education function. Some have outlived their CEO champion, others have not. The lessons drawn from these corporate university initiatives are relevant to any organization that asks how to launch a learning infrastructure that becomes a competitive advantage for the organization.

The general lesson is that launching a corporate university is iterative; it goes through several phases with each phase building on another and takes on average about 18 months. Skipping steps may create the illusion of speed, but will not produce an end result that allows the organization—in the words of McDonnell Douglas CEO Harry Stonecipher—"to strengthen the capacity of its people to learn."

Once an organization's management has resolved to create a more value-added role for learning, there are ten building blocks necessary to build a corporate university successfully (Figure 3-1). These building blocks include forming a governing body, crafting a vision, recommending the scope and funding strategy, creating an organization, identifying stakeholders and their needs, developing products and services, selecting learning partners, drafting a technology strategy, instituting a measurement system, and communicating the vision, products, and program throughout the organization and beyond.

Not every organization, of course, puts the same emphasis on these ten, but an organization that skips or slights one or more finds that its corporate university may not be as performance-based and business relevant as desired. It is better to take the time and spend the resources on each step than to jeopardize the entire effort.

Let's consider each of these ten building blocks carefully and follow a number of organizations—University of Chicago Hospital Academy, the Bank of Montreal's Institute for Learning, National Semiconductor University, Tennessee Valley Authority University, Van Kampen American Capital University, and others—as they launch their corporate universities using these building blocks.

**FIGURE 3–1**

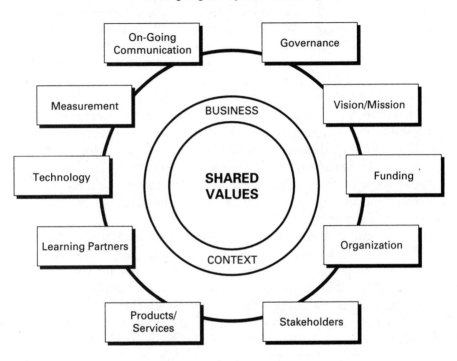

**Ten Building Blocks**
In Designing A Corporate University

© 1997 Corporate University Xchange, Inc.

## TOP MANAGEMENT IS THE DRIVING FORCE BEHIND A CORPORATE UNIVERSITY

While middle managers, human resource executives, or training directors may see a clear need for a corporate university, they usually do not launch one from the bottom up; rather, a senior leader—in many cases the CEO—is the impetus. In contrast to the past when many CEOs halfheartedly followed the training director's recommendations, the CEOs behind the best-in-class corporate universities profiled here proactively plant the idea of launching a corporate university. Why? In many cases, these CEOs' businesses—utilities, financial services, healthcare, or technology—are undergoing profound change. The goal in these "knowledge industries" is to learn faster than competitors. These CEOs recognize that only as learning spreads widely and deeply throughout the company will the organization be able to successfully compete in the global marketplace. These top executives often start by asking a series of questions: What skills do our employees need to allow us to achieve our goals in the twenty-first century? How are we training our employees? What are we spending on employee education? How are we managing this investment? What are we getting for the investment?

This first step is critical because just getting the effort underway requires top management's support and the cooperation of many individuals and departments within the company. Top management must create a sense of urgency or the effort will be stalled. To research the issue, to assemble a cross-functional task force, and to recommend how to re-engineer the education department requires top level support.

While benchmarking the current state of education and training, the company must begin to ask the difficult questions: Where is the industry going? What are the challenges the industry faces? What are the skills and competencies major job families need now and will need in the future considering new technology, new competitors, new legislation, and changing customer needs?

It is no coincidence that the industries changing the most—utilities, healthcare, and financial services—are actively interested in launching corporate universities. Executives in these industries are in the midst of evaluating their business model in light of such external forces as the 1992 Energy Policy Act, the emergence of Health Maintenance Organizations, and the restructuring of the financial services marketplace. In these industries, CEOs understand they can no longer continue to do business as usual.

The research often culminates with a frank assessment of unpleasant facts: employees do not have the skills, knowledge, and competencies to move the organization successfully into the next century; customers are not satisfied with the skill level of the organization's work force; employee morale is low; employee turnover is high; and the education function is redundant, fragmented, and not cost-effective.

The experience of the Tennessee Valley Authority (TVA) provides an interesting example of how a comprehensive inventory of all education and training contributed to the sense of urgency to launch TVA University. Catherine Hammon, general manager of TVA University, says, "Our audit of the entire function uncovered redundancies, a lack of alignment to the business, fragmentation, and, importantly, cost inefficiencies. For example, we found that TVA had 137 separate arrangements with vendors and contractors supplying us with education and training. Just by negotiating bulk vendor contracts we were able to show a significant savings and benefit to centralizing the strategic management of education and training. The audit provided top management with the hard facts to support a new infrastructure, TVA University."

Lynn Hodges, manager of External Education Programs at TVA University, goes on to say, "Some of our managers were invested in maintaining the status quo. One of the purposes in conducting the education inventory was to show that maintaining the status quo was probably the most dangerous thing we could do."

How did this audit really provide the sense of urgency to invest in TVA University? Dr. John Turner, senior vice president of Education, Training, and Diversity, elaborates, "TVA's board and executive committee examined the facts and publicly supported the launch of TVA University by participating in the learning process. In other words, top management gave our employees the time and encouragement to learn."

When is the level of urgency high enough? From our perspective, when most of the company's senior business managers are convinced that providing corporate education in the current state is totally unacceptable, cost inefficient, and will, in fact, cause the organization to lose market share to competitors, the time is ripe for recommending how to restructure the education function.

University of Chicago Hospital (UCH), which has about 4,600 employees at its Hyde Park, Illinois site and 9,000 employees in the system, was under pressure to change because of the restructuring of Medicaid and Medicare, and the emergence of managed care. While the hospital is a distinguished academic medical research center, it was also one of the most expensive in the market. Ten years ago, hospitals did not advertise on the radio or in the newspaper; today they do because they are competing for business on three levels: cost, clinical outcomes, and service. Hospitals that cannot compete fail, as some already have, or merge with other hospitals.

Management at the University of Chicago Hospital recognized

they had a serious challenge. Senior executives spent eight months talking about the changes in the healthcare industry and translating these changes to a new set of skills required of all employees. According to Judy Schueler, director of the University of Chicago Hospital's Academy, "The chief executive officer told employees, 'If you are willing to change, we are going to find a spot for you, but you are going to have to acquire new skills and knowledge. We are committed to keeping you here, if you are committed to learning these new skills.'" One of the University of Chicago Hospital's human resources policies that emerged from this is known as "shared time education and training," meaning the UCH employee is released from his/her regular work assignments for 50 percent of instructional time and contributes 50 percent of his/her own personal time for the opportunity to learn new skills.[1]

Another example from the financial services industry underscores a similar impetus to change: industry deregulation. In 1989, the Canadian banking industry was transformed overnight with the 1989 Canadian Bank Act. Any financial institution could now engage in any facet of the financial services industry—from managing trusts and/or mutual funds to stock brokering to insurance. This shift had a profound effect on the Bank of Montreal in terms of who comprises the bank's major competitors, as well as customer expectations.[2]

The Bank of Montreal, founded in 1817, underwent a much-needed but radical re-engineering in the late 1970s and early 1980s. By 1987, the bank had successfully "modernized" its internal processes, but at considerable cost. The bank had used a traditional, heavy-handed approach to bring about this radical change, but as a result there was resistance and low morale among the 35,000-employee work force. Given these internal and external pressures, the bank's chairman, Matthew Barrett (named as the youngest president in the bank's history in 1987), toured the organization from one end to the other, asking employees at all levels about their thoughts on banking, the future of banking, and their roles within the new financial services industry.

In April 1990, the Bank of Montreal announced a new strategy called Vision 2002, "to become a full-service North American bank" and to achieve and sustain a distinctive competitive advantage with its customers. James C. Rush, senior vice president and executive director of the bank's Institute for Learning points out that "the fundamental belief underlying this vision is the strategy that learning is our only sustainable competitive advantage."[3]

In fact, Barrett has said that without a commitment to learning, there will be no customers. With the sense of urgency pumped up that high, the Bank of Montreal planned and designed its Institute of Learning, a $50 million commitment to employee learning launched in January 1994. But once you have a sense of urgency, then what?

## TEN BUILDING BLOCKS IN DESIGNING A CORPORATE UNIVERSITY

### *Form a Governance System*

The vision for creating a corporate university often starts with top management providing support for restructuring the education function. This theme was cited by many corporate university directors and summarized best by Jackie Vierling, program manager of General Electric's Management Development Institute (Crotonville), when she said, "We have hundreds of companies a year coming to Crotonville. And in every talk given to these companies, we at GE stress the importance of visible support from the CEO. By this, we mean actually having the CEO come to Crotonville and facilitate learning."[4]

While strong visible support from the top is certainly a critical factor in the overall success of a corporate university, a coalition of managers is also needed to give the effort a minimum mass in its early stages. We are referring to the creation of a governance system, where not only the top champion is involved but another 15 to 50 business managers come together to develop a shared vision for the corporate university. In our experience, this group never includes all the top managers, because some people just won't get involved in the early stages of a new initiative. Some perceive it as just too risky. Many times, these "nay-sayers" believe the effort might fizzle out quickly and they don't want to be involved. Our advice is not to be discouraged by resistance because it is a normal response to change. The team leader must learn to work with those who do participate, acknowledge the rest, but not let them sap his/her energy.

Once the organization decides it needs a governance structure, the next step is to recommend the role and responsibility of this governing body. Kevin Wheeler, founding dean of National Semiconductor University (NSU) describes its board of regents as operating under a federal structure. The individual business units have responsibility for delivering skill-based training and the corporate university has the responsibility as the strategic umbrella for setting the organization's learning policy (see Figure 3–2). In this scenario, NSU has centralized the administration and measurement of employee learning, but has left the delivery of the learning programs in the hands of the individual regions—similar to the structure of the United States government where local decisions are left to the individual states. Under this federal model, the firm delivers employee learning and development as close to the individual employee as possible, be it at the work site or the desk top.

Ideally, this type of governance structure links key business strategies to the design and development of learning solutions. In essence, a governing system provides four key roles:

1. *Identifying and prioritizing current and future learning needs.* What are the company's learning needs to support business strategies? How is the business expanding globally, and what new skills do employees need to participate in this global expansion? This gives corporate education its strategic direction.

2. *Linking training to these key business strategies.* How should they be linked? What are the investment priorities? For example, if top management decided that expansion efforts should concentrate in China, then the governing board would say, "Help us expand in China." This means developing state-of-the-art training programs, language programs, cultural programs, and whatever else is needed to be successful in China.

3. *Ensuring consistent design, development, delivery, and measurement.* What are the procedures, processes, and standards to first determine if training is the best solution and then to cost effectively design, develop, and deliver the learning programs?

4. *Providing direction for the development of a philosophy for*

**FIGURE 3–2**

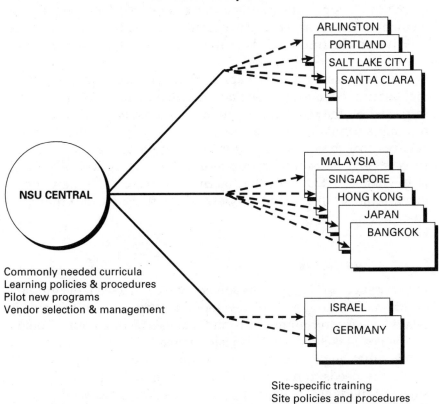

### National Semiconductor University
### Governance System

Courtesy of National Semiconductor University

*learning.* What is the organization's learning philosophy? Will all employees be required to participate in learning for a certain number of days per year? Will this occur during the work day or on the employee's own time? Will the organization develop a culture of continuous learning where employees recognize they must continually upgrade their skills? If so, how? How will this learning philosophy be communicated throughout the organization?

One of the keys to the success of the National Semiconductor University governance system has been the careful criteria used to select the members on the governing board. Sharadon Smith, the current director of National Semiconductor University, says, "We set out three important criteria to select a technical advisory board member. Each prospective participant must: 1) have a broad perspective on the future needs of the technical community, guiding us in creating a technical learning and development roadmap for key job families; 2) have the ability to meet once a quarter in formal board meetings and then ad-hoc via e-mail; and finally, 3) be respected by the technical community and assist NSU in communicating and marketing the curricula for key job families." Smith believes that the governing board is a significant factor in NSU's success. She points out the long-term value of the governing board is to connect NSU with the internal and external experts on a given topic so their point of view is incorporated into the NSU curriculum.

### Create a Vision

In every successful corporate university we have seen, the guiding coalition of board members develops a picture of the future that is relatively easy to communicate and makes a lasting impression on all the key stakeholders. This vision is really the group picture of success that helps to clarify the direction in which the corporate university needs to move. Sometimes the first draft comes from a single individual—usually the team leader charged with launching the university—but after the governing board works at it for a couple of months, something better emerges through a combination of analytical thinking and visioning. Eventually a strategy for achieving the vision also emerges.

Many training departments passionately believe they should be totally responsible for creating the vision statement and the charter and everything that goes with it; it is their baby. Yet to be successful, the governing body must have a major role in the visioning process. The head of training can certainly craft a working vision and a working charter to bring to the first board meeting, but it is the whole governing body's responsibility to decide the ultimate vision and charter. Ideally it is a collaborative effort.

A vision statement should be inspiring, memorable, credible, and concise. It should also evolve. When the Southern Company launched its corporate university in 1991, the vision statement talked specifically about creating programs and curricula for major job families aligned to the corporation's business strategies. The initial vision was, "to be the preferred partner in providing non-technical education solutions to the people within the Southern Company and be regarded as an energizing force to the business success of our managers." There was nothing wrong with that vision, but, as Southern Company College evolved over the next four years, the managers felt the vision statement should change. It now says, "To champion and accelerate learning." The new vision signals Southern Company College's commitment to not only provide world-class non-technical education, but also be actively involved in the transfer of learning throughout the Southern Company.

Before the University of Chicago Hospital Academy opened its doors, the senior executive staff realized they needed a vehicle for organizational learning, so they visited corporate universities at Motorola, Disney, Intel, Herman Miller, and others. Says Schueler, "They came back with some of the best and brightest ideas of existing corporate universities, and developed what we call an 'enabling document.' That enabling document actually provided the framework in which we operate." Schueler argues that it is impossible for a highly bureaucratic organization in a regulated industry to move directly to a learning organization, "It takes years to get there, and there are developmental steps along the way. For us, the corporate university is based upon multiple learning tracks; multiple learning offerings; learning that is targeted for all employees, as opposed to just management or just physicians or just nurses. And it provides career development ladders to move into other positions within the organization."

## Recommend the Scope and Funding Strategy

At the onset, the corporate university must define its scope of operation—the range of employees served and programs offered. The "full service" corporate universities at Motorola and Arthur Andersen have the largest scope of operations. They train the entire spectrum of the value chain from internal employees and teams to current customers and suppliers, and even potential customers in emerging markets. Motorola, which has a Motorola Customer and Supplier Institute, licenses its training programs to its suppliers. In addition, Motorola offers numerous other courses in which the firm attempts to mix employees and outsiders in the classes. The thinking behind this approach is that the company is not a self-contained entity. To be successful, the organization must train all the key elements in the value chain. It has to train—or at least embrace—customers and suppliers and let them know the strategies behind the organization.

Figure 3–3 outlines two major areas where corporate university objectives are clustered. One objective is to be an agent of change for the organization. This involves serving as the communication vehicle for disseminating the corporate vision and creating a new corporate culture. While this objective is present in varying degrees in nearly all of the corporate universities with which we have worked, it is the primary objective cited by General Electric. GE's CEO Jack Welch uses Crotonville as a model of what he calls the "two-way radio" to give and receive information about the company. As Welch says, what he hears is as important as the knowledge, culture, and war stories he imparts to Crotonville participants. In recognition of the importance of this "two-way radio" as a vehicle for creating a boundary-less organization, Welch said at the April 1991 annual shareholders meeting, "Walls are tumbling, productivity is growing, and while we have a long way to

FIGURE 3–3

---

### Initial Scope of the Corporate University

*Where Do You Fall on the Continuum?*

←――――――――――――――――――――――――――――――――――――→

Agent of                                                    Competency-Based
Cultural Change                                             Skill Development

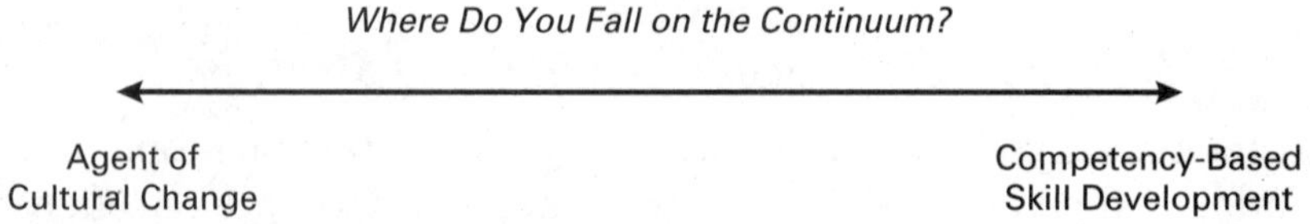

© 1997 Corporate University Xchange, Inc.

go to become a truly boundary-less company, we can see the outline of that company in the mist ahead of us."[5]

At the other end of the continuum is the objective of enhancing job-related skills, knowledge, and competencies. While some "corporate culture might also be disseminated" the goal is squarely on upskilling the work force. This is the case in The Next Step program where, with two unions—Communication Workers of America and the International Brotherhood of Electrical Workers—Bell Atlantic created a customized degree program in telecommunications technology. Participants earn an associate degree (64 credits) from one of 23 colleges in the Buffalo, Syracuse, Albany, New York City, Queens, or Nassau County areas.

After agreeing on the scope of the initiative, corporate university directors must next address how to fund the corporate university. When governing board members first address this issue, they initially consider what the competition spends on education and training as a percentage of payroll. Our *Annual Corporate University Survey of Future Directions* found that, on average, 100 corporate universities spend 2.2 percent of their payroll on education and training. This figure includes the design, development, and delivery of training programs and excludes the salaries of the participants while they were involved in the training programs.

In addition to considering the magnitude of the corporate university budget, the next issue is how should this initiative be funded—corporate allocation or chargeback to business units. As we discussed in Chapter 2, while corporate funding continues to account for the majority of surveyed corporate universities' budgets, the trend is toward funding through chargebacks to business units. In fact, by the year 2000, our *Annual Corporate University Survey of Future Directions* expects 70 percent of their funding to come from chargebacks, with only 30 percent of funding from corporate allocation. In addition, funding from licensing training to customers, suppliers, and key organizations within the value chain is expected to increase and contribute to the overall budget.

### Create an Organization

One issue that someone inevitably raises at the mention of a corporate university goes something like, "Does that mean you want

**FIGURE 3-4**

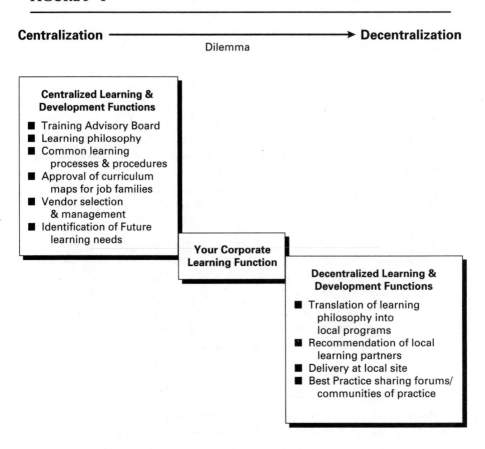

Centralization ——————————————————→ **Decentralization**

Dilemma

**Centralized Learning & Development Functions**

- Training Advisory Board
- Learning philosophy
- Common learning processes & procedures
- Approval of curriculum maps for job families
- Vendor selection & management
- Identification of Future learning needs

**Your Corporate Learning Function**

**Decentralized Learning & Development Functions**

- Translation of learning philosophy into local programs
- Recommendation of local learning partners
- Delivery at local site
- Best Practice sharing forums/ communities of practice

to put all training under one umbrella?" The answer is that some functions are centralized for cost and efficiency reasons, and others continue to be decentralized—those that make most sense to be close to customers. Figure 3-4 presents a sample of what functions are best centralized and decentralized. The litmus test for deciding what to centralize and what to decentralize is to determine where you can receive the greatest cost efficiencies while still linking employee learning to business goals. The answer often rests with centralization of the strategic functions of employee education: setting the learning philosophy, overall governance, design, development, registration, administration, measurement and marketing; and then leaving the responsibility for delivery to the local sites and/or regions.

### Identify Stakeholders

One of the many things that distinguishes a corporate university from a traditional training department is the breadth of the audience the corporate university serves; it includes the entire value chain—not only employees, but suppliers at one end of the chain and customers at the other.

As corporate universities evolve over time, they re-evaluate their stakeholders and often shift their original target audience. For example, Southern Company College was originally created to focus only on executives and managers in its role as an agent of change; however, since its 1991 inception, Southern Company College has expanded its focus to include the entire work force, a shift that has had a positive impact on employee morale. As Al Martin, dean of Southern Company College says, "Southern Company College was originally targeted to top managers. Now, the college has widened its stakeholder audience to include learning solutions for every employee."

Once you determine the target audience of your corporate university, your next mission is to identify your customer's needs and focus on the needs that give the organization its greatest leverage. As Jim Rush, senior vice president and executive director of the Bank of Montreal's Institute of Learning, says, "Essentially we ask who's in the best position to create maximum influence, and what can we do to help?"

Rush gives an example: "We're doing a learning program targeted with developing a sales culture. Largely this is going to be a business line-led program, so it's clear that the first program has to be 'Train the Trainer.' So we bring line managers together and train them on how to teach the program. Next, we decided to create a program called 'Leading the Sales Culture.'

Essentially, this is a leadership program that says, 'Your people are about to go through a learning intervention and they're going to be asked to change their behavior in the following ways,' which we enumerate. 'For this to stick, we need you to provide the appropriate direction and coaching and deep understanding of how different this is from what they've done before.' So, we think these leaders really ought to go through the training before the people whose behavior you're really trying to change go through their program."

It's important to identify your objective, target audience, and business issue, and the gap between current and future skills, knowledge, and competencies needed for the organization to be successful.

## Create Products and Services

Once it is clear what skills, knowledge, and competencies the business will require in the future, your next charge is to develop a template of learning solutions. The Bank of Montreal's $50 million investment in a building symbolizes the importance it places on employee education, but there are other less concrete factors involved in its corporate university. As Jim Rush says, "While the building itself plays an important role as a symbol of the value the organization places on continuous learning and growth, becoming a world-class learning institution means more than bricks and mortar. It really means becoming a professional service firm that is dedicated to helping clients achieve exceptional performance. To accomplish this broad mission, Bank of Montreal Institute of Learning's strategy is to offer not only traditional training courses on core banking skills but comprehensive well-integrated performance solutions."

Rush believes that what is not so straightforward is the learning that happens simply because people are thrown together. "On any given week, we're going to have 250 people in the Institute who represent a cross-section of the bank. We want to create an atmosphere that could really enhance their learning. How can you help the East know what the West is doing? The corporate bank know what the retail bank is doing? What the U.S. is doing and Canada and vice versa."

Under Rush's leadership, Bank of Montreal Institute for Learning is trying to encourage—if not actively manage—a form of interaction that spreads informal and incidental learning across an organization. Rush elaborates on this when he says, "This is knowledge transfer, although your traditional forms of needs analysis don't work here. But somebody who understands the opportunity and understands how knowledge is transferred knows there is learning taking place. The first level of learning is the course you came to take. But the next level of learning acknowledges in a subtle way that you were here with your colleagues, and you shared your best practices and knowledge and in the process created another level of learning."

The process the Institute goes through to create this template of core formal products and services involves forming ad hoc professional service teams made up of a client relationship manager, a subject matter expert, and a learning manager. The roles of each are spelled out:

| | |
|---|---|
| Client Relationship Manager | Relationship managers work directly with major client groups. |
| Subject Matter Expert | SMEs address what learning will occur; they understand the specific skill requirements needed for future success. |
| Learning Manager | Learning managers address how learning will occur; they recommend how to best leverage the methods, technologies, and environment where learning will take place.[6] |

These client teams are responsible for curriculum development in each of the schools of learning: Leadership and Change, Technology, and Core Banking Skills. This curriculum includes both formal training programs as well as a myriad of informal learning initiatives that promote on-the-job learning.

### Select Learning Partners

Once the template for learning has been created, the next step is to select learning partners. These run the gamut from training vendors, consultants, and institutions of higher education to for-profit education firms. What is striking is how much more choice corporate university deans have as they select their learning partners.

Because the job of continuously updating an employee's knowledge base is so formidable, corporate universities are joining forces with conventional universities and a vast array of partners to merge the goals of the individual employee, the corporation, and the educational institution into one mutually beneficial three-way partnership.

One of the most innovative partnerships is between AT&T School of Business and the University of Phoenix, a rapidly growing for-profit educational firm that provides AT&T employees the opportunity to continue their education by pursuing a degree at one of the 51 University of Phoenix campuses and learning centers spread across the United States. AT&T School of Business currently outsources over 50 percent of its educational programs to create unique value-added learning programs that provide college credit for internal training programs without maintaining a large permanent staff. As corporations continue to focus on core competencies, a plethora of learning partnerships similar to AT&T and University of Phoenix will grow.

Chapter 6 includes a detailed framework and model for creating these alliances, as well as a list of selection criteria to consider when entering into a learning partnership.

### Draft a Technology Strategy

How will you use technology to train more people, more often, more cost effectively, and also track results? Today, instructor-led training is becoming less and less significant. In fact, the *Annual Survey of Corporate University Future Directions* found that while 17.5 percent of all training is currently delivered using technology, 50 percent of training will be delivered using technology by the year 2000. In fact, that estimate may be low when one considers that Don Tapscott, digital economy guru, estimates that by the year 2000 there will be over one billion users of the Internet, with traffic on the network exceeding telephone traffic.[7]

Companies typically select learning technology and media at the end of the analysis phase of instructional design, but they should really consider their delivery options at the outset of the design phase.

If one looks at the range of technologies used by companies profiled in this book, the common theme that emerges is the commitment to using a combination of technologies to distribute learning throughout the organization. Examples include desktop learning using an Intranet or electronic performance system—embedding learning in the workstation; distance learning; and even centralized learning labs where people can go during a lunch hour and learn at the computer.

One company that is extensively using the self-paced learning model is Van Kampen American Capital University, the corporate university of the mutual fund firm Van Kampen American Capital, the fifth largest broker-sold mutual fund group. Van Kampen American Capital University has successfully moved beyond traditional delivery methods of audio and video to offering both product training and leadership skills training in a myriad of online, satellite, video teleconferencing, and desktop solutions. Currently the university offers 500 plus self-paced courses to employees. In fact, this emphasis on self-directed learning has led Van Kampen American Capital Dean Tamara Scott to create a Customer Fulfillment Center to keep track of the inventory associated with these technology-based products. Scott's advice to others in using technology for learning is to consider the various media options early on in the process and to ask the following three questions:

- Does the technology fit the learner's needs?
- Is it available and justifiable?
- Does it simulate real working conditions?

In the Van Kampen American Capital environment, with its heavy commitment to professional licensing delivering personalized, easily updated, and learner-controlled products, training has become essential to the organization.

### Create a Measurement System

The primary objective in launching a corporate university is institutionalizing a culture of continuous learning tied to critical business strategies. This is a significant challenge for a traditionally oriented training and development manager who has been measuring the success of his/her programs by developing a catalogue of classes, building training facilities, or measuring the number of training hours completed in a given year. Today, the new chief learning officer must create learning experiences embedded in work, that address critical business needs, and result in improved performance on the job.

How will the corporate university's governing board (or the corporation's CEO and board of directors) know whether this loftier goal is actually being accomplished? How will the corporation know whether its corporate university has "real business impact?" It may not be measurable in the way one can measure a machine's output or a salesperson's sales revenue. Jay Zimmerman, the manager of Research and Quality at the Bank of Montreal's Institute for Learning, says, "I like to talk about evidence or indicators of impact. When people talk about value and measurement of the corporate university, my concern is that they are looking for a dollar impact, or a bottom line flow-through, and I think that's extremely difficult to show."

Zimmerman cites an example of how training impact can be measured: "We've instituted a regular level three three-month follow-up assessment. We go out to participants and we say, 'Remember three months ago you took the XYZ course.' We ask them to reflect back on the course, and then ask, 'Given you've had three months to apply what you learned, have you had an opportunity to apply it?' Maybe they've changed jobs; maybe their environment hasn't let them apply learning to the job. If they had the opportunity to use what they learned, to what extent are they actually applying it? If they're applying it, what impact are they seeing, in terms of quality of their work, efficiency, customer retention and satisfaction, and timeliness?"

Zimmerman adds that in addition to the traditional training measurements, Levels 1 through 4,* measurement should be a team approach. Is the corporate university aligned to the business

---

*Kirkpatrick's Four Levels of Measurement are defined as:
Level 1: Participant assessment (do the trainees think they've learned anything?)
Level 2: Knowledge/skill acquisition (can they pass a test on the material?)
Level 3: Transfer to the job (do they apply the learning when they get back to work?)
Level 4: Return on investment (is the new skill saving or making money for the organization?)

strategies and developing targeted programs, for example, to enhance customer service by so many percentage points?

The real action, of course, is around business impact measures, and those are highly customized. There is no recipe. The dean of the corporate university has to work with the members of the governing board or the advisory council to decide what these measurements should be. "One thing I think is important to keep in mind," says Zimmerman, "is the kind of change you are trying to effect. If the change is a cultural one, then you need to be creative in how you look for culture change." He points out that anthropologists understand culture as well as anyone; they almost own the term. "We have used an economic anthropologist to come in for an ethnographic evaluation. I think that's a direction that people need to go — to focus on more than numbers. That's not to say that numbers may not be legitimate at a particular moment in time, but, you need a much more holistic approach in looking for evidence for the corporate university's impact to the organization."

University of Chicago Hospital Academy provides an example of using traditional measurements with customer and employee satisfaction surveys. For example, UCH first measures on the four Kirkpatrick evaluation levels. "Probably like everyone in the world, you have your immediate measure after formal learning," says Judy Schueler, "We use classroom assessment techniques, course evaluation forms, instructor rating forms, etc. The second level is, did learning occur in the structured environment? So, we do pre- and post-skill testing. That would be appropriate for more didactic types of information. Level three is focus groups for managers: 'As a result of this learning, what changes are you seeing in your area?' The fourth level, which is essentially why we have an entity for organizational learning asks, 'What impact does it have on our patients and internal customers?'"

In addition to using these traditional quantitative measures, the UCH Academy measures its success by external patient and physician satisfaction ratings, and its internal customer ratings, that is, the satisfaction ratings of senior business managers. This does not mean satisfaction with a course or instructor; it means satisfaction connected to resolving a particular business challenge. For example, the UCH Academy is preparing employees to work in a managed care environment, therefore it asks questions on customer satisfaction surveys about a customer's experience as a managed care patient: "Did the staff advise you to bring your referral form? Did you receive your bill in the required time period? When you were referred to another specialist, did they advise you to obtain another referral form? As a result of these types of services, would you return to the University of Chicago Hospital?" The questions all relate to the UCH's specific business goal of providing exceptional customer service.

Finally, one of the keys to measuring the success of a corporate university is for the corporate university dean to manage the expectations of key stakeholders. In other words, this means advocating a "patient capital" mindset where long-term investments are made in human capital. How long is "long enough?" We believe taking a long-term view of an investment in learning means longitudinally measuring what happens to the "graduates" of these corporate university learning programs. Do these graduates go on to be promoted and assume leadership positions within the organization? What specific accomplishments do they point to? Are they held up as role models for young aspiring managers? What is their long-term impact on the organization? The key here is to have in place an administrative system that allows this type of long-term student tracking.

Too often the results of training are measured in the number of hours of training per employee per year, the number of employees in training, and the percentage of revenue spent on training. While these indicators are important, they measure only training input and not the training outcomes. Measuring business outcomes will ultimately lead to institutionalizing a corporate university after the "champion" has long retired.

### Communicate . . . Communicate . . . Communicate

It is impossible to communicate too much about the corporate university and its role within the business. We've seen several patterns with respect to communication, all very common. First, some organizations develop an inspiring vision for the corporate university and then proceed to communicate it by holding a single meeting or sending out a single memo. Having communicated so sparsely, the corporate university management is somehow startled to learn that few people seem to understand what a corporate university is and why their company had decided to launch one. In a second approach to marketing a corporate university, much effort goes into developing "roadshows" to individual business units along with placement of articles about the corporate university in company newsletters, but most of the senior business managers still "don't get it." The net result is that cynicism increases among the employees and belief in the value of the corporate university goes down.

Now what? Successful communication programs recognize that to effectively convey the value of a corporate university requires hundreds—perhaps thousands—of employees get involved in understanding the "why, wherefore, and what" behind the decision. This effort must address the basic "man in the street" questions about a corporate university. Some of these frequently asked questions are presented in Figure 3–5 and we have found that they must be addressed early so employees understand the "big picture" associated with launching a corporate university.

One of our surprises has been how often employees ask about how much the corporate university "costs the individual employee." Many of these employees are paying big tuition bills to send their children to college and they associate the corporate university with the costs of a traditional university. Once these ques-

## FIGURE 3–5

---

### Ten Frequently Asked Questions about the Launch of a Corporate University

1. What is the corporate university?
2. Why is learning important to our company?
3. Where will learning at the corporate university take place?
4. What types of learning programs will be available through the corporate university?
5. How is the corporate university different from our company's training department?
6. Who pays for the learning programs reflected in the corporate university catalogue?
7. When will the corporate university be operational?
8. Who is in charge of the corporate university?
9. How do I enroll in the corporate university?
10. Are the learning programs in the corporate university eligible for college credit?

tions have been answered, a corporate university dean should consider the following lessons in promoting the corporate university throughout the organization:

**Target board members first in your communications.** You want senior business managers to begin advocating the corporate university in their hour-by-hour interactions with employees. For example, in a regular performance appraisal managers should address how an employee is participating in both formal and informal programs developed under the corporate university umbrella. In a review of a division's quarterly performance, managers should not only talk about the numbers, but also about how the division's executives are role-modeling learning within the organization. Finally, in a routine discussion about a business problem these managers should propose how such problems can be addressed with learning interventions. The goal here is to build enough awareness about the corporate university, including its rationale, core purpose, and benefits so that business managers become ambassadors of learning.

**Create branded communications vehicles.** Think of your corporate university as you would a consumer product. Your first challenge is to create positioning for your corporate university. This means developing in the minds of your customers a unique, motivating benefit for your corporate university. This benefit should be communicated in just a few words, such as National Semiconductor University, "Moving and Shaping the Way National Learns." This positioning then fuses with the corporate university's overall branded strategy and becomes the consistent message around which all communication about the corporate university is delivered.

This positioning often times develops into a logo. At AT&T Universal Card University (UCU) the positioning is "Facimus Ut Fiat" or "We Make It Happen." This motto is reinforced in all the communications materials and shows how AT&T UCU contributes to the business success of the organization. This UCU symbol adorns everything connected with employee training. Says Robert O'Neal, founding dean, "When people see that symbol, it's like a branded product. It's a Universal Card University offering, and it tends to pull people into our programs and special events."

**Develop bold communication vehicles.** Think beyond the traditional catalogue, newsletter, and e-mail announcement to include broad-scale marketing programs that highlight the rationale and contribution of the corporate university. For example, AT&T Universal Card University produces an annual conference targeting a theme of vital interest to the organization. The conference brings together experts, practitioners, and senior AT&T Universal Card business managers to examine an issue related to their future growth. One recent conference entitled "Virtually There," looked at electronic commerce and AT&T's role in it.

**Market the success the corporate university has with both internal customers as well as external stakeholders.** Think of the corporate university as a stand-alone business with several target audiences, namely the different lines of business. The customers are not only the people who participate in the training, but it also includes their sponsors, the supervisors that approve their participation. Moreover, the business' senior executives have certain perceptions about the corporate university and must be told over and over, and in many different ways, what the corporate university is doing and why, and how it is impacting performance on the job.

James Rush at Bank of Montreal's Institute for Learning notes, "We need to communicate the importance of learning and the kind of commitment the organization needs to make around learning. You've got to make sure that your clients understand that you're running your business efficiently and effectively. I try to continually benchmark against other corporate universities, to show how our costs are competitive or are often even better than others. All this shows that we're running our business effectively. Management has to understand that this is a business with a strategy and a plan and good operating practices."

Pat Parker, president of SBC Center for Learning, communicates the strategy and operating principles of the corporate university in the form of an annual report. Parker, a former executive vice president of a line business at Southwestern Bell, believes in the need to run the Center for Learning as a role model business unit.

The SBC Center for Learning, started in 1996, is the education and training subsidiary of SBC Communications Inc., the parent company of Southwestern Bell, Pacific Bell, and Nevada Bell. In the 1996 annual report, the Center for Learning created its own mission and listed a number of accomplishments and developments within the organization. These include the consolidation of several education departments, the establishment of a human resources group to design appraisal and reward systems, and the formation of a communications group. The latter development is significant because it illustrates how organizations are beginning to see their corporate universities as entities that add value and whose accomplishments must therefore be communicated to customers and suppliers.

Like most corporate universities, the Center for Learning conducts a number of standard measurements, such as level 1 and level 2, to quantify training inputs. The center's annual report includes other input data such as the number of student classroom days, students trained, vendor training classes, and alternative media delivery. A 31 percent increase in instructional days and a 9 percent decrease in "average intervention cost" were cited as major achievements.

The ultimate goal of the center's annual report, however, is more strategic. According to Don Highley, performance consultant for evaluation and measurement at the Center for Learning, "This is a way of helping to communicate the value that we're adding to our clients. It's a concise document that we can pass on to our clients to let them know what we are doing here at the Center for Learning.

"We still report basic input information because company officials are accustomed to looking at that kind of information. But we're moving forward and are going to report measures beyond customer satisfaction. In the future we'll be able to demonstrate the students' achievement of competency—with test scores tied to performance objectives—by discipline. Also, for targeted projects the Center will be evaluating the business impact, levels 3 and 4, for our clients."

As alignment with business needs continues to emerge as a critical issue for corporate university directors, Parker's annual report will play a key role in communicating to SBC's customers the value of the corporate university.

Finally, there is an opportunity to also develop a communications strategy targeted to investors—the ultimate stakeholder in a corporation. Institutional investors, investment analysts, and brokers live by their knowledge of which securities will increase in value faster. Investors are rarely told of an organization's investment in their intellectual capital, except for an organization like Skandia, profiled in Chapter 2, which creates a supplement to their annual report outlining their intellectual capital investment strategy. We can foresee a future where organizations will routinely communicate to their investors the costs, as well as the ongoing benefits, of a human capital investment. In fact, John Stevens, director of Professional Policy for the Institute of Personnel and Development in the United Kingdom, has been studying this issue of educating investors and says, "We believe companies in the United Kingdom should be required by law to say in their annual reports what they are trying to achieve through their people management strategies."[8]

## THE CHIEF LEARNING OFFICER AS LEADER OF THE CORPORATE UNIVERSITY

While the ten building blocks offer guidance in launching a corporate university, the key issue for a top manager supporting this function is what skills, knowledge, and competencies should the corporate university's leader have? As Steven Kerr, chief learning officer of General Electric's Crotonville facility, says, "Managing a learning function is essentially managing a central paradox: How to develop strong leaders while the organization is decentralizing and delayering."[9]

The job of launching a corporate university is chaotic, challenging, and often quite rewarding. In this atmosphere the experience a chief learning officer brings to the whole enterprise is critical to the university's ultimate success. In the *Annual Survey of Corporate University Future Directions* four roles of the chief learning officer were cited as critical to the overall success of the initiative. Figure 3–6 illustrates these four roles: Business Partner, Systems Thinker, Education Officer, and Alliance Builder. By far the majority of these deans indicated that assuming the role of a business partner was their most important contribution to the organization. What are the common characteristics of these four roles?

**FIGURE 3–6**

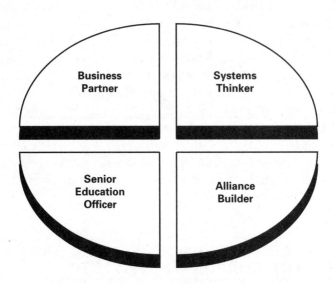

Roles of a Chief Learning Officer

© 1997 Corporate University Xchange, Inc.

Being a business partner essentially means being a student of the business. This translates into understanding the company's strategic direction, its products, services, customers, competitors, suppliers, union issues, and how the organization is positioning itself in the global marketplace. This was cited by 72 percent of our sample of 100 corporate university deans as the most important contribution of the director. Acting as a business partner also means understanding the issues facing the business and industry, attending strategy meetings, reading business unit strategic plans, developing working relationships with senior business managers, and recommending learning solutions to meet business challenges.

Next, the role of systems thinker comes into play as the chief learning officer crafts a vision for how the whole learning and development operation fits together as a system bound by interrelated actions. This vision is often tightly linked with the business objectives of the organization and carefully crafted in collaboration with an advisory council. High performance chief learning officers do not "shotgun" ideas and programs. They are able to function and deliver value because all the parts (vision, staff, development, organization, use of technology, funding strategy, measurement approach, and communications vehicles) work together as a unified whole. This ability to be a systems thinker was cited by more than half of the 100 corporate university deans in our research sample as critical to their overall success in the organization.

The chief learning officer's next role is as senior education specialist. As the functional expert for learning, the chief learning officer must shape the vision for continuous learning. To this end, it is critical to promote large, even audacious goals for the organization. For example, a chief learning officer must be willing to take risks and focus on developing the long-term effectiveness of the corporate university, such as: extending training and development beyond internal employees to all members of the value chain, eliminating business unit inefficiencies and radically improving internal stakeholder satisfaction. Dr. John Turner of TVA University says, "I am committed to creating new ways for employees to learn on the job and will strive to ensure that employees are accountable for their own learning."

Finally, the chief learning officer must be an alliance builder forming partnerships not only with internal senior business managers but also with external customers, union leaders, and deans of institutions of higher education. As an alliance builder, the chief learning officer must operate strategically, formulating a business plan and recommending how to implement the plan by developing a global web of learning partnerships.

As companies look to the twenty-first century, change will be constant. New customers, new products, services, new alliances and new opportunities merge from these changes. The corporate university's real goal is to prepare all of an organization's employees to take full advantage of these emerging changes and to institutionalize a culture of continuous learning aligned to the business' core strategies.

## Chapter Four

# Learning Programs at Best Practice Corporate Universities

*As Chancellor of Fidelity Investment Service Delivery University, I believe our most important goal is to align all training with our major business objectives: setting the industry standard in customer service; sustaining double-digit annual growth, and continuing to achieve profitability in all segments of our business. Every formal course, case study, and exercise must address this goal.*

—Ellyn A. McColgan, president,
Fidelity Investments Tax-Exempt Services Company

## THE CORPORATE UNIVERSITY CURRICULUM

As companies face rapidly changing technologies, increased customer expectations, and escalating competitive pressures, the workplace is becoming a dynamic, interdependent one, where thinking and acting must be done by all employees. The increase of knowledge workers pervades our workplace. While many jobs may still entail manual skills, they now also require theoretical knowledge that must be refreshed on a continuous basis. In fact, Peter Drucker estimates that knowledge workers will comprise two-thirds of the work force by the end of this century.[1]

Across industries and occupations, the chief concern for knowledge workers is the shortened shelf life of the knowledge they possess, hence the need to constantly retool their skills. In other words, what we know today will not add value tomorrow unless we have the ability to learn new skills and broader roles. These new skills run the gamut from enhanced technical abilities to creative problem-solving and leadership development. The key goal for an organization is to provide its workers with the ability to continually retool their skills and knowledge.

## The Three Cs of the Core Curriculum

The formal learning programs at corporate universities represent an expanded effort to train all levels of workers in the skills needed for today's changing workplace. A key goal of such programs is to build among workers the knowledge and skills necessary to support the company's overall competitiveness. While each company's training programs differ, interviews with deans of corporate universities have revealed a set of common themes found in nearly all outstanding corporate university programs. For the purposes of discussion, this set of common themes will be referred to in the remainder of the book as the university core curriculum. This core curriculum incorporates a range of formal learning programs in operation across leading corporate universities.

Figure 4–1 shows the components of a core curriculum for a financial services firm. Its overall emphasis has been expanded from simply teaching technical skills to communicating the corporate culture and values; providing employees with an understanding of the company relative to its customers, suppliers, and competitors; and building within employees a set of core workplace competencies that define the company's competitive advantage. In fact, this core curriculum is what distinguishes corporate universities from traditional corporate training departments of past decades that have historically focused only on providing employees with the technical skills needed for their immediate jobs. The corporate university approach recognizes the importance of each employee having a firm foundation in the company's values, culture, traditions, the contextual framework in which the organization operates, and the organization's core competencies, as well as job-specific capabilities introduced in each school of learning.

Taken together, the core curricula of corporate universities exam-

**FIGURE 4–1**

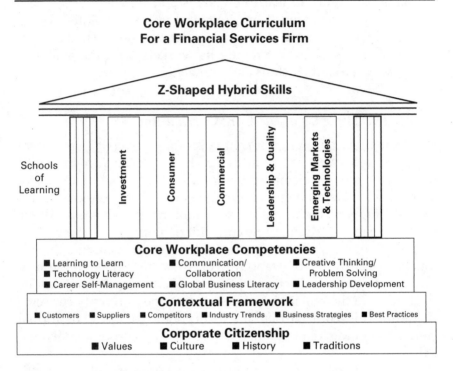

Core Workplace Curriculum
For a Financial Services Firm

Z-Shaped Hybrid Skills

Schools of Learning

Investment

Consumer

Commercial

Leadership & Quality

Emerging Markets & Technologies

**Core Workplace Competencies**

- Learning to Learn
- Technology Literacy
- Career Self-Management
- Communication/ Collaboration
- Global Business Literacy
- Creative Thinking/ Problem Solving
- Leadership Development

**Contextual Framework**

- Customers
- Suppliers
- Competitors
- Industry Trends
- Business Strategies
- Best Practices

**Corporate Citizenship**

- Values
- Culture
- History
- Traditions

© 1997 Corporate University Xchange, Inc.

ined in this book promote employee development in three broad areas, termed here the three Cs. They include:

**Corporate citizenship.** Inculcates all levels of employees to the culture, values, traditions, and vision of the company. Implicit in this concept of citizenship is a strong identification with one's company and its central values. This inculcation in the corporate cultural identity is similar to the approach taken by many Japanese companies.

**Contextual framework.** Gives all employees an appreciation of the company's business, its customers, competitors, and the best practices of others. Employees become grounded in the features and benefits of the company's products and services, how the company makes money, how its business stacks up against the competition and, most importantly, how to learn from the best practices of world-class companies that determine standards of excellence within an industry.

**Core workplace competencies.** Develops a set of specific workplace competencies that define the company's competitive advantage. The common core workplace competencies identified by companies interviewed for this book were discussed in Chapter 1. To recap briefly, they include:

*Learning to learn skills.* Knowing how to understand and manipulate new information quickly and confidently is a primary workplace competency. Showing a commitment to self-development, constantly improving one's ability to learn new skills and competencies, and being able to handle ambiguity and chaos within an organization are crucial learning skills.

*Communication and collaboration skills.* Knowing how to listen and communicate with co-workers and customers is essential, but beyond that, the knowledge worker of the twenty-first century must also know how to work effectively in groups, collaborate with team members, resolve conflicts, and share best practices across the organization.

*Creative thinking and problem-solving skills.* Knowing how to recognize and define problems, implement solutions, initiate new ideas, take action, and track and evaluate results is a fundamental part of sustaining competitive advantage. Above all, possessing the cognitive reasoning skills necessary to transcend sequential thinking and leap to creative solutions is a paramount problem-solving skill.

*Technological literacy.* Being able to use technology to connect with team members, network with new professionals, and research the best practices of an organization, as well as what other companies and competitors are doing in the global marketplace, is essential. The ability to navigate the web is becoming crucial to operating in the anywhere/anytime marketplace.

*Global business literacy.* Having an understanding of hard business skills, such as knowing how to read a profit and loss statement, understanding an internal rate of return, having a command over the capital allocation process and knowing how to evaluate a business's potential are key to workplace competency.

*Leadership development.* Being able to empower co-workers and "envision, energize, and enable" a group or team to achieve the corporation's business initiatives is also imperative. To operate in this knowledge economy leaders must know how to define a shared vision and lead an organization in achieving this vision.

*Career self-management.* Having the ability to proactively manage one's own development and career, rather than just passively following a training plan laid out by one's manager is important because companies are increasingly focusing attention on developing their workers' employability. Hence, the ability to successfully manage one's career is the first step in this process.

Finally, corporate universities are beginning to recognize the importance of hybrid skills, which I have coined Z-shaped skills. These skills combine the core workplace competencies with thorough business expertise across functional areas. In other words, world-class engineers must also understand the basics of sales and marketing as well as economics and finance in order to work effectively in a cross-functional team. Hence they must be conversant in a set of overlapping, hybrid skills. Similarly, financial customer service representatives must learn about operations, risk management, leadership, sales/marketing, and how to deliver exceptional customer service. While these customer service representatives do not necessarily need to know how to process a loan, they should understand broad concepts involved in operations management. These Z-shaped skills can be acquired through a series of formal courses, working in communities of practice, or even in developmental assignments. The goal of developing these hybrid Z-shaped skills is to have employees understand the complex demands of each other's work and how the various parts of the business create an integrated whole.

Let's examine in detail how these three Cs of the core curriculum are translated into action within the curricula of some corporate universities.

## CORPORATE CITIZENSHIP

### Training in the Values, Vision, and Culture of the Organization

Formal learning programs that train every employee in an organization's corporate values have undergone a resurgence. The fantastic pace of change in many industries has created the need for new hires to understand not only their own job, but also how all the other jobs fit into the overall corporate mission and strategic agenda of the organization. Increasingly, companies are designing two-for-one learning experiences where employees learn essential skills as well as absorb the corporate culture. Consider the healthcare industry for a moment to understand how the rapid pace of change mandates the need for a cross-trained work force. According to Judy Schueler, University of Chicago Hospital's (UCH) director, "Our vision in creating the orientation program for UCH was to develop a program where our employees could learn to be good citizens. To us, a good citizen moves beyond performing just the job tasks. Rather a good citizen acts like he/she is the owner of the business, desires to satisfy customers, understands that customer satisfaction comes from how a job is done, and takes responsibility for continually striving to do a better job." The UCH orientation program actually uses actors from the Chicago-based LaSalle Street Management Theatre to create a dramatic slice of life to act out examples of good and bad customer service.

This increased focus on acculturation training is driven by the need of an organization to develop a shared mindset. Gradually, more companies are focusing on training employees in their vision, values, and culture, especially those committed to building a world-class work force. The vehicle for delivering this is the totally redesigned company orientation program. Instead of a half-day event characterized by paper shuffling and benefits briefings that outline everything from vacation days to retirement policies, orientation is increasingly seen as a strategic process and an opportunity to immerse the employee in the company's shared mindset. This new orientation model works to lay the foundation of employee empowerment and achievement of the company's total quality vision.

Companies who are giving new priority to orientation are doing so in part for practical reasons. First, employers are concerned about the cost of turnover. According to a human resources study, 50 to 60 percent of all new hires leave their jobs within the first seven months, so companies realize they must focus on increasing employee retention.[2] Secondly, employers point to demographic trends which project that by the year 2000 there will be 27 percent fewer 16- to 19-year-olds available for work than there were available in 1975.[3] Because this traditional source of new workers is forecast to be shrinking through the year 2010, employers recognize the importance of retaining employees.

Economic considerations notwithstanding, companies who are developing a more strategic approach to orientation are motivated by a conviction that by doing so they strongly enhance the organization's customer service culture. They believe that employees who feel they have been treated well will, in turn, treat customers well. This is known as the service-profit chain concept first advanced by Heskett and Schlesinger in the *Harvard Business Review* article, "Putting the Service-Profit Chain to Work." The authors adhere to the belief that instead of beginning with profit and growth, companies should begin with employee satisfaction and loyalty. A loyal, satisfied employee population will drive customer satisfaction— which in turn will drive profit and growth.[4] What better way to leave an indelibly positive first impression on employees than through a strategically designed orientation process? It almost guarantees that new employees will start out on the right foot.

### Metaphors Teach the Corporate Values, Culture, Big Picture, and Traditions of the Organization

The concept of ordinary citizenship implies a degree of identification with one's city or country that comes in part from a close familiarity with its values, customs, and culture. Progressive companies want to cultivate in their work forces a similar sense of connectedness and pride. They are doing this by *formally* training employees in the corporation's unique values, culture, traditions, and the specific employee behaviors that go along with "living the values" on the job.

One of the ways that an organization's culture is brought to life is through the use of a metaphor. Metaphors are powerful because people can use them to represent thoughts that are implicit and unspoken.

**AT&T Universal Card University: passport to excellence journey on the UCU express.**   AT&T Universal Card University (UCU) is the corporate university of AT&T Universal Card Services, the Jacksonville, Florida-based division of AT&T. AT&T UCU's two day orientation program, known as "Passport to Excellence," is a preparatory and experiential assimilation where new AT&T UCS hires learn the culture and organization of UCS through a symbolic train journey, with the final destination culminating in the participants' new career at UCS. In this scenario, participants embark on a journey in a new career. At the end of the two day journey they are able to explain the principles, values, and culture that make UCS a unique company. They are also able to state their own personal missions with regard to how they approach their careers at UCS.

Day one of the program begins with an ice-breaking activity where participants unpack their old cultural baggage and explore where they came from and what values they carry around with them. Understanding the old baggage and discarding what they don't need creates room for the values and culture of AT&T Universal Card Services. Then everyone boards the train and the journey begins. Each stop along the way is an opportunity to explain Universal Card's values of teamwork, quality management, empowerment, delighting customers, and continuous improvement. The train metaphor gives the participants the chance to leave the train, get involved in a classroom activity, and then re-board the train. Along the way, they fill out postcards about what they've learned, and the postcards actually end up on the classroom bulletin boards.

As the journey unfolds, participants get involved in a simulation: something has killed quality and they have to work in teams to solve the mystery. It sounds like Agatha Christie's *Murder on the Orient Express*, only in this case the winning team is rewarded when the mystery is solved. At the end of the journey, participants talk about what they've learned, what souvenirs they have picked up along the way, and the various postcards they've acquired. The power of the train metaphor is that during the two day program participants return to the packing and unpacking exercise and discuss what they have discovered during their trip and how it compares with their expectations. Finally, the program ends with an actual passport symbolizing certification of the new hire program.

Bob O'Neal, founding dean of AT&T Universal Card University, describes the rationale for this two day orientation program:

"We believe when new employees join our organization we must communicate and reinforce our values, vision, and mission so these new hires will know what we believe in and importantly what will make them successful in their careers at AT&T Universal Card Services. This means we must not only train them in how to do their jobs, but also in what philosophical framework we expect it to be done: how we want them to interact with our customers and more importantly with each other."

**Orientation goes high tech: Oracle University uses CD-ROM for new hire acculturation.** Oracle also concentrates on educating employees in the vision, values, culture, and big picture of the firm but uses technology to do so. Their CD-ROM orientation for new hires, *Inside Track,* a version of which is also deployed on the company's intranet, uses the metaphor of an automobile racing car to provide a media-rich approach, combining graphics, movies, and a rock'n'roll/jazz fusion soundtrack to deliver orientation training that is also entertaining.

*Inside Track*'s interface is designed around racing themes and the content on each of its seven discs is separated into "tracks" that are broken down into "turns" and "sub-turns." Racing imagery accents the theme and is used to control screen and navigation functions. Road signs, checkered flags, and other racing paraphernalia dot the various menu screens. When a track is selected, a secondary menu displays turns and sub-turns as stops along a winding racetrack. When an item on one of these menus is selected, the presentation screen looks like the dashboard of a racing car and its speedometer, gearshift, and ignition can be clicked to move to other menus or control the information on the screen.

The movie of a racing car speeding down a track begins this orientation CD and the first turn on the first track is a film of CEO Larry Ellison discussing the genesis of Oracle, the company's guiding philosophy, and its goals for the future. "Company History," "Key Personnel," and "Internal Resources," are some other tracks on this CD. The other *Inside Track* CDs include: "Executive Messages," "Sales," "Oracle's Service Information," "Server Product Information," "Tools Product Information," and "Applications Product Information."

The *Inside Track* presentations generally comprise either movies or slideshow-like displays that combine voice-overs with charts, graphs, and bullet-points. *Inside Track* offers a high degree of navigational choice and individual topics can be skipped, repeated, or viewed in any sequence. There is also a "score" screen that gives the user a picture of which subject tracks and turns have been completed. Finally, the new hire can actually take a test and be certified on their knowledge of Oracle, its vision, mission, values, and strategic goals.

The advantages of this kind of technology-delivered orientation are obvious. New hires can access information when and where they want—and as often as necessary. Also, *Inside Track* can actually facilitate intimacy and give new employees the opportunity to familiarize themselves with senior managers. For example, seeing a film of President and Chief Operating Officer Ray Lane sitting beside his credenza and discussing Oracle's strategic intent is more memorable than having Oracle employees simply read about the company's strategies and business goals. *Inside Track* is Oracle's way of keeping the culture alive, enhanced, and spreading throughout the organization.

The companies with corporate universities make a deliberate attempt, through formal course offerings in the company's values, culture, and history, as well as technology-based tools, to develop a strong sense of corporate citizenship among all members of the work force. Rather than rely on employees to learn about the company in a haphazard fashion, the companies profiled here consider the assimilation process a critical first step in building a world-class work force. In many ways, this is similar to training and development practices used by Japanese companies, where training is broadly defined as a way to inculcate workers in the foundation of the company.

## CONTEXTUAL FRAMEWORK

### Know the Company's Big Picture: Customers, Competitors, Industry Trends, and Best Practices of Others

The companies profiled in this book believe that corporate performance is enhanced when all employees, not just management, operate from a shared vision about the organization's industry and the key players within it. Contextual training is the second component of the core curriculum. This training aims to develop in workers a very specific and practical know-how about the company, the industry, the customers, the suppliers, and how the company stacks up against competitors. But how does a company "train" employees in what an old-timer instinctively knows about the company and the industry?

**Fidelity Investment employees learn the big picture of the company.** One company that has done an innovative job of helping service people become business people is Fidelity Investments. Because many Fidelity Institutional Retirement Services Company (FIRSCo) service representatives do not have face-to-face contact with customers, the job of understanding the big picture of the company becomes more difficult. FIRSCo is responsible for managing corporate retirement 401(K) plans for more than 3,400 clients with a total of 4 million individual participants. In 1995, FIRSCo created Service Delivery University (SDU), a virtual university with five colleges, a well-developed curriculum, and a goal for every Fidelity associate to receive 80 hours of development activity per year.[5] Figure 4–2 presents an overview of these five colleges: Customer Service, Operations Management, Risk Management, Leadership and Management Development, and Sales and Marketing.

SDU began as a service initiative rather than a training initiative. The driving force behind SDU came from line management

**FIGURE 4-2**

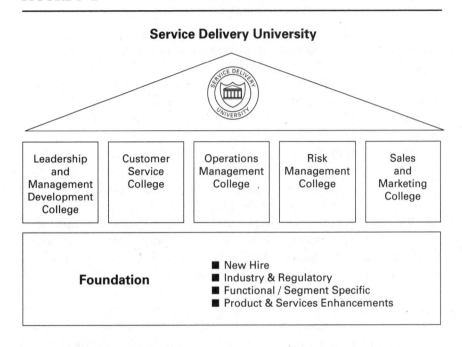

**Service Delivery University**

| Leadership and Management Development College | Customer Service College | Operations Management College | Risk Management College | Sales and Marketing College |
|---|---|---|---|---|

| Foundation | ■ New Hire<br>■ Industry & Regulatory<br>■ Functional / Segment Specific<br>■ Product & Services Enhancements |
|---|---|

Courtesy of Fidelity Investments

rather than training or human resources. In fact, when the SDU concept was first explored, FIRSCo discovered that while the organization was able to articulate a funding strategy for investments in new technology, it was not able to estimate how much it spent on training or how this spending was tied to business objectives. The lack of a business model for training was the impetus to create SDU.

Additionally, explosive growth during the early 1990s reinforced the need to inculcate all Fidelity employees with the big picture of the business. As Ellyn McColgan, the founding chancellor of Service Delivery University (SDU), says, "Our employee population in client service positions grew from 450 to 1400 in just three years, with roughly 60 percent of our employees having less than one year of service. This growth caused us to focus not only on training employees in the technical skills to do their jobs, but also in how to understand the cross-functional aspects of their jobs, such as the need for sales associates to also understand the basics of operations management and risk management."

A key contribution of the SDU experience is that concepts presented in class can be applied by the participants on the job. In a course known as "Managing Risk During Change," participants are taught to assess the regulatory, financial, operational, and reputational risks associated with the business. Here, they are put into teams and presented with a real case from FIRSCo. In these teams, participants discuss what risks they face and what they should do differently. In this way, they learn the link between SDU and what they do on their jobs every day.

What McColgan did not anticipate was the resistance to SDU from the FIRSCo Learning and Development Department (L&D). "At first the L&D group wondered why we had come into their expert domain," says McColgan. "In fact, many questioned whether the creation of SDU was an implicit acknowledgment that L&D was not meeting user needs." Over time SDU and Fidelity's Learning and Development Department worked out their corresponding roles, with line managers being responsible for determining the content of learning and development activities, while L&D concentrates on how to design and deliver the content.

As McColgan said in the opening quote for this chapter, the most important goal of SDU is to have all employees develop a common understanding about the importance of achieving FIRSCo's business goals of exceptional customer service, double-digit annual growth, and profitability. How does SDU bring these goals to life? One way is by bringing the customer into SDU training through case studies and exercises based on actual FIRSCo situations, as well as videotapes of customers describing their positive and negative service experiences.

To bring home the shared value of exceptional customer service, all FIRSCo participants are trained in how every employee has an impact on the customer, even if they have no direct contact with customers. SDU does this by educating participants in what Fidelity calls the "hierarchy of customer needs." This hierarchy shows which needs have to be met before a client is interested in continuing a relationship with the company. According to research conducted by Fidelity Investments, the first of these needs is accuracy and timeliness, that is, delivering accurate and timely financial information to its customers. Then the "hierarchy of customer needs" focuses on the importance of availability, responsiveness, credibility, and finally culminates in developing a long-term partnership between Fidelity and the customer. McColgan stresses the importance of this type of education when she says, "We believe that significant change has come directly from our employees learning about the customer hierarchy in SDU culture classes. Here's one example: in the past, withdrawal specialists at our company thought of their job as collecting all the documentation necessary for processing hardship withdrawals for expenses like college tuition and making sure it complied with government regulations. In other words, they were focused on how to get the withdrawal through the system. Our culture classes reoriented that focus toward the customer's needs: getting the right amount of money (accuracy) by a certain date (timeliness) while delivering reliable service that was responsive to the customer's needs. Obviously these customer service specialists must know the process, but they must also be alert to the need to provide solutions that are meaningful to our customers—even if someone else in the organization is the actual point of contact."[6]

The SDU Customer Service class concludes with participants making a pledge that identifies how they will change their performance to better meet customers service expectations. In this way, participants see the link between what they learn at SDU and what they do on the job.

Ellen Rentfrow, a team manager who completed a series of courses in the Operations Management College, believes the classes she took were immediately applicable to her job. Rentfrow explains, "Our area—Financial Operations Cash Management Services—receives approximately 350 to 400 wires each day in FIRSCo bank accounts. In class we learned the process mapping concept and how this concept can help us to look for more efficient ways to handle a process. When we used this tool on the job we were able to identify components in our current process and determine the areas to be strengthened. For example, we decided that we needed to develop more detailed client communication in order to specify our wiring requirements and ensure we met the client's needs."[7]

Ultimately, the goal of SDU is to help FIRSCo service people broaden their skills so they can become more effective business people. McColgan notes that before the creation of SDU, employees could take any of the 125 classes offered by the FIRSCo Learning and Development Department; all they needed to take a class was a manager's signature. But managers did not have a framework for approving or denying employee requests to take classes and sometimes there was a disparity between learning and job roles. For example, some telephone service representatives were taking classes on advanced regulatory reporting procedures that would not have had an impact on their daily work. SDU's primary contribution has been to create an environment where employees participate in learning and development programs that have a direct impact on their jobs.

**The Southern Company College trains employees in how to be a "student of the business."** The Southern Company provides another example of contextual training with their "Student of the Business Program," designed to build in-depth understanding of the profound changes in the electric utility business.

The Southern Company, an umbrella group for five utilities in the southeast United States and several affiliated companies that span eight countries, employs more than 30,000 workers and has 4.8 million retail customers. Its key leaders began to prepare for a future of deregulation nearly a decade ago, when it became evident that an increasingly deregulated environment and fierce global competition would necessitate new and better ways to finance, generate, and deliver electric power. Southern Company needed to broaden its expertise in all aspects of the business, including power generation, finance, marketing, and company culture.

The company had many technical specialists who had grown up in a particular section of the business, but not enough people with the broad experience necessary to compete on the new playing field. The "Student of the Business" course was conceived and developed to illustrate the complexities of generating power, setting rates and pricing structures, and working with market variables in different economic environments. It uses a combination of live speakers and computer simulation to immerse participants in the challenges of running a utility.

After hearing from experts about such topics as power generation, finance, marketing, customer service, and regulatory and leg-
islative affairs, students are put into 12 teams of four to run a utility. The teams, which compete against one other, are constructed
so that each member has a different background, hence, they can
learn from each other. Using the computer simulation known as
the "Electric Utility Game," each team makes a series of decisions
about its company's generation plants, transmission and distribution operations, rate levels and rate design, service reliability, employee policies, and customer satisfaction determinants. The
"Electric Utility Game" simulates typical business issues facing a
prominent utility with assets of $6.5 billion, revenue of $2.5 billion, and a territorial base of 1155 customers—a mirror of one of
Southern Company's subsidiaries.

The simulation starts with a traditional regulatory environment
that was common in the late 1980s. Students then move through
eight years in which the regulatory and competitive parameters
for operating the business change. Teams must develop a strategy
to position their company. Will they be low cost, value added,
and/or international in scope? How will they respond to different
markets and market variables? How will they compete for customers in a competitive environment?

At the end of each decision, participants enter the data onto a
diskette. Each team's input is consolidated into a massive spread-
sheet that contains detailed industry data, market share information, customer information, and financial data. Teams then review
the results of their decisions and learn which decisions work and
which do not. The simulation allows each participant to see how
all the functional pieces of the business fit together, assess market
conditions and growth opportunities, think strategically about a
company's situation and future prospects, make decisions from a
company-wide perspective, and assume responsibility for achieving acceptable corporate performance. "The ultimate goal of the
Electric Utility Game is to assist our managers in making better
and faster business decisions and then measure the merits of these
decisions by how well the 'simulated' company compares to its
peers on such performance indicators as growth in revenues,
growth in after tax profits, overall level of customer satisfaction,
and the return on equity investment," says Jim Greene, Southern

Company College Team Leader. "When we started this program five years ago, we were helping people prepare for the future. Today, we are using the program to simulate current changes in the industry." The computer simulation continues to be updated to emulate different competitive environments and regulatory structures.

Greene says that 700 employees have already gone through the "Student of the Business" course and the feedback has been very positive. One of the strongest components of the simulation is the heavy emphasis on building financial analysis skills. "While many of our engineers have advanced degrees," says Greene, "they needed a better understanding of how to read a financial report and make a series of business decisions. The 'Electric Utility Game' provides them with an opportunity to practice these skills in a safe environment."

### Know and Practice Core Workplace Competencies

As the workplace shifts to a more open paradigm, lower-level workers are required to assume more responsibility and develop broad, interchangeable skills. The flexible organizations of the future need adaptable workers who know how to work in teams and have the self-sufficiency to acquire new skills as the workplace and marketplace change. Hence, it is no longer enough to have workers simply upgrade their technical skills; now they need to develop a set of core workplace competencies that give the company its competitive advantage.

A *competency* is defined as any knowledge, skill, set of actions, or thought patterns that reliably distinguishes between superior and average performers. In other words, a competency is what superior performers do more often and with better results than average performers on the job. By practicing a core set of competencies, workers have the opportunity to raise the bar in terms of their performance.

This section provides examples of core workplace competencies identified as critical by deans of corporate universities interviewed for this book. These competencies fall into seven areas: learning to learn skills, communication and collaboration skills, creative thinking and problem-solving, technological literacy, global business literacy, leadership development, and career self-management.

## CORE WORKPLACE COMPETENCIES

### *Learning to Learn*

As John Naisbitt, author of *Megatrends* says, "In a world that is constantly changing there is no one subject or set of subjects that will serve you for the foreseeable future, let alone for the rest of your life. The most important skill to acquire is learning how to learn." Now workers must have a broader set of skills and not only understand their own jobs but also the jobs in their immediate departments, and continuously think of ways to improve their own work processes. In short, these workers must adopt a learning to learn attitude that will make them vital individual contributors to their organization.

The American Society of Training and Development defines the skill of knowing how to learn by breaking it down into four component skills:

- Asking the right questions.
- Identifying the essential components within complex ideas.
- Finding informal ways to measure one's understanding of pertinent material.
- Applying these skills to the goals of specific job tasks.[8]

It is important to remember that learning to learn is a never-ending process. The companies who have made inroads by instilling in employees a commitment to continuously learn have done so by providing them with a framework for learning new skills plus a vehicle for self-management.

Saturn Corporation, the Spring Hill, Tennessee automotive company, has created a course known as "Introduction to the Learning Organization." The course incorporates many of the ideas of learning theorists such as Peter Senge and Howard Gardner. During this course Saturn team members learn about "multiple intelligences," which are: intrapersonal, interpersonal, visual/spatial, musical/rhythmic, bodily/kinesthetic, verbal/linguistic, logical/mathematical, and emotional.

"One of the things that we're trying to do," says Gary Carter, technical training coordinator at Saturn, "is to make employees appreciate that there are many ways they can learn. The typical academic background introduces you to only two intelligences: verbal/linguistic and logical/mathematical. Our course fosters an appreciation of these other multiple intelligences."

"Most of our Saturn team members are very high bodily/kinesthetic individuals. They work with their hands and their bodies. We try to help them understand that a large part of their capacity for learning is through this bodily/kinesthetic intelligence," adds Carter.

This course is designed to inculcate the necessity for continuous, self-paced learning. "We've come to the realization," says Carter, "that if we're going to stay up with technology we can't just train people. We have a lot of people, and if a change occurs that affects everyone, we literally don't have the classroom space or methods to teach them all they need to know. And if we could accommodate them in the classroom, the technology would change before we could get them all trained. So we must teach Saturn team members various ways they can take responsibility for their own learning."

"The paradigm of school says, 'If we want you to learn something, we'll tell it to you or have you read it.' In reality, most of us are never taught how to learn. We regurgitate what we hear or read. 'An Introduction to the Learning Organization' was initially targeted to Saturn learning specialists, but now Saturn is making this course available to all team members. Ultimately, after taking this course, Saturn team members will understand their own optimal way to learn and then seek out opportunities for continuous learning. After completing the 'Introduction to the Learning Organization' course we want team members to say, 'Here's my strength, here's how I learn best, so I need to participate in learning programs which fit my learning style.'"

Another company, First Union Corporation, the Charlotte, North Carolina-based banking company with retail branches from Connecticut to Florida, has made significant headway in promoting the concept of learning to learn through a series of broadcast seminars on the First Union Employee Television Network. One example is "The Leadership Success Series." They are broadcast at a specific time across First Union Network and are also available for sale to individual First Union branches in the form of a videotape and accompanying handouts. "The goal of these broadcast series is to provide employees with a learning tool to help them take more responsibility for their own learning," says Patsy Linker, dean of First University Leadership College.

"The Leadership Success Series" provides information and guidance to employees in how to become a self-directed learner. During the 40 minute broadcast, First Union employees are presented with a definition of self-directed learning—deciding what's worth learning and how to learn it—as well as examples of why becoming a self-directed learner is so important in today's workplace. Kathryn McCurdy, a learning specialist at the First University Leadership College, is the moderator of a broadcast that resembles the *Today* show, with special appearances from First University learning specialists in Investment College, Quality College, and Consumer College. Each learning specialist introduces a particular component of the self-directed learning process—identification of one's learning goals, completion of a learning plan, review of the plan, and measurement of the results—and explains why self-directed learning is so critical for success in today's fast changing workplace.

The broadcast starts with an exercise, asking employees to list one or two things that have affected their work lives in the last two years. Employees are challenged to think about changes in their jobs, job functions, and the introduction of new technologies. In each case, employees uncover how change has caused them to learn something new. Hence the message: most of what we learn is a response to what occurs naturally in life.

During the 40 minute broadcast, employees are encouraged to answer six questions:

- What do I need to know or be able to do?
- What steps will I take to learn this?
- What obstacles will I encounter?
- What resources will I use?
- What is my time frame?
- How will I measure my success?[9]

The intent of this broadcast series is to have First Union employees understand their individual learning styles and what resources are best suited to help them. In addition to these broadcast seminars, First University has also created a resource center that includes self-study materials, CD-ROMs, audiotapes, videotapes, and books—all intended to make self-directed learning accessible and easy for First Union employees. Both Saturn Corporation and First Union provide best practice examples of *how* to be a self-directed learner. More corporations will follow this lead in developing the learning to learn competency.

### Communication and Collaboration

While learning to learn is essential, the activities of communicating, collaborating, and working within a community really keep the work force humming smoothly. These skills are growing in importance within the twenty-first century organization.

The importance of the ability to communicate as a prerequisite for nearly all jobs is being increasingly understood by employers. Linked to this is a growing emphasis on the skill of listening. Compelling statistics compiled by the American Society for Training and Development (ASTD) regarding the types of interpersonal skills workers use on the job indicate why. According to the ASTD, the average worker spends 8.4 percent of his or her communications time writing, 13.3 percent reading, 23 percent speaking, and a surprising 55 percent communicating either virtually or in person with others.[10]

Who teaches workers to communicate with others? Traditionally, it has not been the American primary and secondary schools, who currently offer little instruction in oral communications or listening. The scant instruction they do provide in oral communications is often in the context of drama or debating classes, with virtually no instruction in listening. So, companies have had to take up the slack in training workers in these interpersonal, or soft, skills.

Being able to communicate effectively is really a prerequisite for a higher order skill—collaborating with co-workers. The more one explores the world of day-to-day work, the more the power of tacit knowledge emerges. With individuals, tacit knowledge essentially means using one's intuition and judgment to get the job done without necessarily being able to explain how to do it. With teams of employees, tacit knowledge exists in the practices and relationships that emerge from working successfully over time.

With tacit knowledge, learning becomes less about "absorbing or communicating chunks of data," and more about operating within a community of knowledge workers. Essentially work and learning become social activities and what holds the community together is a common sense of purpose and a need to know what each member of the community knows. As the community evolves, members develop a shared sense of what is necessary to get a job done. The term "communities of practice" was first coined by Etienne Wenger and Jean Lave in their 1991 book *Situated Learning* where they described a community of practice as a group of people who share a common way of thinking about how work gets done and, more importantly, learn from working together.

While community practices exist by the thousands, the challenge is to uncover ways to foster the growth of what occurs naturally when people share common work issues and a desire to learn from each other. National Semiconductor has gone further than most companies in promoting what has come to be known as communities of practice. In fact, one of the best documented cases of fostering communities of practice occurred at National Semiconductor a couple of years ago. It turns out that product groups across the company were seeking advice from an informal group of design engineers who had gained a reputation for doing superior reviews of chip designs. National management essentially left the group alone, recognizing that this self-made community needed to develop grassroots support and recognition so other engineers would interact with it and thereby become members of the group.[11]

National Semiconductor does not always take such a laissez-faire view to fostering communities of practice. One of the more innovative community of practice vehicles created by National Semiconductor University (NSU) is known as Faculty Clubs, which represents an organized way for senior National Semiconductor managers to participate in a dialogue and exchange of ideas with team members. This is not a replacement for formal training programs developed by NSU, rather, Faculty Clubs provide an avenue for managers to share successes and lessons learned. The topics of recent Faculty Club seminars ranged from opportunities in emerging markets to the latest innovations in manufacturing. There's even a seminar called "Alligators and Gotchas," where chip designers share common mistakes and ways to avoid these mistakes in manufacturing a new chip. Says Sharadon Smith, NSU dean, "Faculty Clubs facilitate group inter- actions so new members of a community can, over time, migrate into the group and share a common issue." When asked whether these types of interactions can occur over the National Semicon- ductor intranet, Smith says, "The web can facilitate collaboration, but it cannot create it. We believe people need to gather together in one room to see each other, develop a sense of community, and then use the technology to sustain the community."

Smith does say that NSU is experimenting with videotaping the Faculty Clubs and then sending out the videos to new community members so they can download these videos from the web onto their desktop. The goal then becomes to use the technology to con- tinue the dialogue.

### Creative Thinking and Problem-Solving

The main venue for creative thinking and problem-solving train- ing has been the classroom, where individual managers were ex- posed to issues and perspectives on how to enter a new market or solve a problem arising with co-workers and customers. Today, the venue is most likely the workplace, and rather than learning the five or seven steps to creative thinking or problem-solving, managers are now involved in action learning exercises and com- puter simulations where they examine business strategies and rec- ommend real-time solutions. Action learning is "training" that takes the form of an actual business problem for teams of learners to solve together.

Through action learning, an organization can convert individ- ual learning into organizational know-how by addressing real-life business issues. Because most of the action learning workshops are conducted in teams, learning is shared by all members, net- working is encouraged, and new perspectives are heard.

Eastman Kodak Company, the Rochester, New York-based photography firm, uses action learning in holding its biannual learning events targeted to the senior executives responsible for driving the strategic direction of the company. These events bring top level executives from such Kodak partner organizations as Disney, IBM, Intel, and Nokia to discuss a range of critical initiatives such as emerging technologies, shifts in consumer bases, new markets, and competitive moves. Rather than teach a static course on any of these topics, Kodak has instead focused on using action learning to encourage creative thinking among the participants. As June Delano, Kodak's director of Organization Development and Executive Education says, "Our ability to learn has become the heart of our ability to compete." Hence, these learning events created for the executive audience look forward and discuss what to do next rather than looking backward at the past.[12]

Another example of action learning is a formal course known as "Business Analysis," developed by Whirlpool Performance Centre for middle to senior Whirlpool managers who play a role in the analysis of business issues. Rather than bringing in an outside expert and engaging in passive listening, these Whirlpool managers bring a business issue to the program and analyze this issue in order to recommend a creative strategy and generate alternative business solutions. After working in small groups on their particular business issue, the Whirlpool managers address a "real Whirlpool case"—The KitchenAid Business, which details Whirlpool's unsolicited offer to acquire KitchenAid from its parent, Dart & Kraft. Whirlpool managers in the "Business Analysis" course use the KitchenAid case to evaluate the strategic rationale of Whirlpool's purchase of KitchenAid and then work in teams to use the KitchenAid case as a springboard for strategically thinking about their own business issue.

Andersen Consulting provides an innovative example of using a highly interactive learning by doing approach to develop problem-solving skills among its new hire consultants. For years, Andersen had new hires go through 80 hours of classroom lectures and workbook exercises known as the Business Practices School (BPS). Essentially, this was a Business 101 course that emphasized memorization of data and de-emphasized experience.

Now, this course has been redesigned into a self-paced computer simulation known as BPC-Business Practices Course, with

15 modules simulating various business challenges an Andersen consultant might encounter in a consulting engagement at the hypothetical Perrin Printing and Publishing Company (PP&P). The simulation "lasts" for a period of 48 months, during which time the consultant uses audio and video clips stored on a CD-ROM to interview PP&P personnel, receive phone calls, get advice from senior Andersen consultants, review internal Andersen memos, and attend meetings with representatives from the client. Finally, at the end of the BPC, the Andersen consultant delivers a presentation outlining client recommendations.[13]

What makes BPC particularly innovative is that the simulation keeps throwing situations at the trainees, asking them to make decisions each month and then the consequences of these decisions are played out on the computer screen with the real-life consequences attached to them—users get reprimanded, promoted, or even fired. As each scenario unfolds, experts appear on the screen to tell users stories related to the decisions they've made. This approach to learning, coined "goal-based scenarios," by Roger Schank, director of Northwestern University's Institute for the Learning Sciences, helps users achieve a certain goal during the learning experience while also having some fun.[14]

The economics of the Business Practice Course are quite compelling. At least half of the 30,000 member Andersen organization requires business practices training. Moving these consultants to the Andersen St. Charles facility is very costly, but by creating educational tools that consultants can use on the road, learning moves from the classroom to virtually anywhere in the world. Andersen estimates a savings of 40 percent reduction in training time, translating to a payroll savings of $2 million.

Equally as important as the cost savings is the opportunity to incorporate the experiences of some of Andersen's most senior consultants into the self-paced learning tool. Creating a corporate memory accessed through a computer is the real innovation delivered through the Business Practice Course.

### Technological Literacy

The integration of technology into learning is creating opportunities for corporations to think in entirely new ways about how employees access information and distribute knowledge. First, let's think about how much new information is being added to the Internet daily, if not hourly. Microsoft, for example, adds 500 MB of information to its web site every day—that's an entire CD-ROM full of information. In this dynamic new environment, Bill Gates, chairman and CEO of Microsoft, believes students will be the explorers and faculty will be the expert guides, helping students navigate new, uncharted territories.[15]

Learning in this environment requires the worker to know how to access Internet list servers, news groups, and web pages in order to research new products, services, and competitive offerings. Workers will need a new skill set—technological literacy—in order to use the latest software tools to access information and explore new data at an even deeper level.

As the corporate world moves more of its operations on-line, technological literacy becomes more crucial. In companies that are moving on-line, knowing how to access and move around the company's intranet is one of the first things new hires need to learn. At Dell, Internet business currently generates a million dollars a day in customer orders, so technological literacy has become a necessity for employees at all levels and in all functions of the company. Dell University has developed a course for new managers and employees with limited or no PC and web-browser experience using Microsoft's Internet Explorer, the web browser used to access the company intranet and the Internet.

Dell has been growing so fast that new managers often are charged with hiring a staff within a week of being hired themselves. They need to go on-line to find the appropriate policies for hiring, instructions for how to use their voice and e-mail, instructions on obtaining purchase order forms, and other information that once was contained in the company's printed policy manuals.

While many managers have the technological skills to find the information they need over the intranet, others do not. Managers, as a whole, are the last group to have hands-on computer skills because they often did not need to develop these skills in school. As things move faster in corporate America, on-line materials prove to be more efficient than printed materials or classroom sessions. They can be updated faster and can be distributed at a reasonable price to various locations throughout the world.

Dell University starts with classroom-delivered courses on the web browser. This allows employees with no PC experience to get their questions answered immediately. Equipment can be demonstrated and students practice what they learn in the classroom. Then Dell employees move on-line to self-study courses. A manager's orientation course delivered on-line, for example, is accessed with a browser window in a framed environment, which means there is always a point of reference to which the employee can return. Dell University's on-line orientation program also has links to information the manager will need to set up operations, such as a directory of employees, information on how the company is organized, and a page that explains all of Dell's products. Dell University has found that assessments of on-line education tools indicate most "learning events" are very brief; people use these tools to get what they want and then leave. They don't, as a rule, move sequentially through an entire course or body of material, yet they are still able to extrapolate and eventually ascertain the whole from the sum of its parts. To address this tendency, Dell University decided that the best learning tools should be intuitive and rely on employee self-reliance rather than traditional, classroom-based learning modes. This assumption has led to the development of many practical on-line learning tools that can be used on the job and on an "as needed" basis.

## Global Business Literacy

Too often participants attend executive education programs but do not implement new learning because the programs do not match company strategic objectives, run too long, lack flexibility, or simply lack action learning. Southern Company College's new focus on training the top 500 managers in deep business and leadership skills provides an interesting example of the growing emphasis on building what I have called "global business literacy" within the top management of an organization. When Southern Company College was launched in 1991, the emphasis was on the top 1,200 executives—from the CEO down to the plant manager level. Focusing on such a broad target audience resulted in many courses that provided an overview or awareness of a particular topic, but did not go into depth in any particular area.

Then in 1995, Allen Franklin, president of Georgia Power Company, took over as chairman of the Southern Company College Board of Advisors and focused the college on the need to develop deep business literacy skills for the top 500 managers. Allen Franklin describes the driving force for this transformation as the uncertainty and new competitive nature of the electric utility industry, "With the future of the electric utility industry, including more competition and greater demands from customers, the challenges faced by electric utility managers will be substantially more complex. Hence, we need to integrate Southern Company College into the company strategic goals and use the college to train our top 500 managers in how to be successful in operating in this uncertain and highly competitive environment."

The result of this top management involvement in Southern Company College was a new curriculum for the top 500 senior leaders of the company that focused not only on building leadership skills, but also building a core set of deep global business skills deemed necessary to operate in a highly competitive and uncertain business environment. This curriculum of business courses and leadership experiences is an example of global business literacy, shown in Figure 4–3, and is referred to by Allen Franklin as the "initial required courses" for the top 500 Southern Company managers. Franklin continues describing the focus of

**FIGURE 4–3**

---

### Southern Company Corporate Strategic Education Focus

| **Business Curriculum** | **Leadership Curriculum** |
|---|---|

- Competitive Energy Markets:
  A Strategic View
- Emerging Competitive Markets
- Electric Utility Cost Structure
- Financial Analysis
- Student of the Business

- Performance Management
  Workshops
- External University Programs
- Leading Empowered Leaders

Courtesy of Southern Company College

this curriculum when he says, "Our goal is to actively involve our senior managers in the courses so a new Southern Company style could permeate the organization. Our objective in focusing on the top 500 managers is to provide these individuals with an intense educational experience with measurable results." The goal of this curriculum is to focus on training top leaders in a required set of formal learning programs in finance, strategic analysis, and leadership skills.

Three of the changes coming from Franklin's involvement in Southern Company College stand out as representative of best practice corporate university processes: 1) Incorporating a clear linkage to Southern Company issues to clarify the firm's strategy, values, and priorities. This means building company-specific case studies, simulations, and action learning exercises into the business literacy coursework; 2) Developing expectations and accountability for participants to learn and apply their new skill sets back on the job. This includes a clear message from leaders like Allen Franklin on the necessity of participating in Southern Company College Leadership offerings; and 3) Linking participation in these courses to the individual development and compensation processes of the organization. Involvement of senior managers in Southern Company College becomes necessary for advancement in their careers.

**CIED builds leadership and business skills.** While the Southern Company College defines global business literacy in terms of developing deep leadership and business skill sets, Petroleos de Venezuela, S. A. (PDVSA) emphasizes an integrated program to train PDVSA managers in business management and leadership skills. PDVSA maintains a training infrastructure of 14 learning centers across Venezuela, befitting the second largest oil company in the world. Their corporate university, Centro Internacional de Educación y Desarrollo (CIED), is divided into three institutes: Industrial Training, Professional and Technical Development, and Management Development. Each institute of CIED, like most major corporate universities, is geared toward training employees in accordance with the strategic goals of the company and fostering skills that will produce employees capable of steering PDVSA toward its business objectives.

The expansion of CIED and the assurance of its success is particularly important for PDVSA because it has ambitious plans for the future. Their goal, by the year 2004, is to double oil production, and increase the petrochemical output, while maintaining the same employee population. They also plan to increase their oil reserves by more than five times through increased exploration. As part of these plans, PDVSA, which is a state-owned company, is inviting private oil companies to participate in partnerships in some selected areas of the business. This initiative is known as "The Apertura" or opening. The Apertura aims at specific sectors of the company that senior management believe would benefit (become better able to help increase productivity) by the entrepreneurial mindset associated with private sector enterprises.

CIED provides training that fills gaps left by traditional education and instills corporate values in PDVSA employees. The training is fully aligned with the overall business plan and relies on a combination of customized and standardized programs. CIED's integrated training follows a tightly focused curriculum model that is most apparent in the Management Development Institute (MDI).

MDI provides learning and development needed by PDVSA's executives for today's volatile and complicated economic climate. The MDI training model, illustrated in Figure 4–4, is divided into three focus areas or dimensions: corporate, business, and managerial.

The corporate dimension of MDI training is chiefly concerned with instilling corporate culture and values within the PDVSA work force. PDVSA employees are trained in the vision, history, and strategies of the organization and its subsidiaries. This is especially important in a large company with more than 20 subsidiaries, many of which have developed their own identities and have a tendency to compete among themselves.

Next, the business dimension focuses on developing leadership and negotiating skills to foster a competitive mindset among PDVSA managers. The leadership aspect of the business dimension is designed to strengthen leadership and negotiation skills that correlate with business plan requirements. Finally, the managerial dimension of MDI includes courses that might be found in a traditional MBA program; including finance, marketing, accounting, strategic planning, and supervisory skills.

**FIGURE 4-4**

---

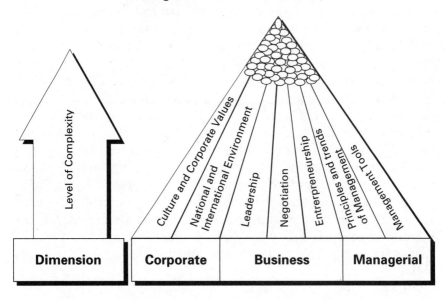

**Centro Internacional de Educacion y Desarrollo (CIED)
Management Education Model**

Courtesy of Centro Internacional de Educacion y Desarrollo

Together, three dimensions of the Management Development Institute represent an integrated business literacy curriculum promoting cross-functional skills PDVSA managers need for success on the job. As illustrated in Figure 4–4, the training programs at the bottom of the pyramid are very specific to each dimension—corporate, business, or managerial, but as the training increases in complexity, the focus is more on developing cross-functional skills. For example, PDVSA managers must develop both strong leadership skills, as well as hard business skills of finance and marketing, and an appreciation of the PDVSA core vision. This progression toward an integrated training curriculum reflects CIED's core belief that managers cannot be specialists in one area but must be conversant in a diverse set of overlapping, hybrid skills, noted earlier in this chapter as Z-shaped skills.

In addition to the curriculum of the Management Development Institute, CIED also has developed alliances with local and international institutions of higher education, such as Wharton, Harvard, Cornell, MIT, Babson College, and the Center for Creative Leadership. These alliances supplement the integrated training curriculum with customized executive education programs that meet the specific business needs of PDVSA managers.

### Leadership Development

Perhaps one of the most important distinctions of the past decade has been the emphasis in the corporate university curricula on leadership development. Participating in a leadership development program at a corporate university today is a very different experience than it was in the 1960s and 1970s when participants arrived with little understanding of the curriculum that lay before them. At check-in they were given books and a detailed outline of how each hour of the program was to be spent. Also included in the registration package was a lot of blank paper, signaling to the participants that their primary job was to listen.[16]

That model has evolved tremendously over the past few decades and now participants expect to not just listen, but to work in teams, engage in case discussions, debate recommendations, and make presentations based upon their conclusions during the program. What's more, these participants devote a significant amount of time to demonstrating their ability to apply concepts to real challenges through some form of action learning. In fact, what really sets apart today's leadership development programs from those of the past decades is what is included in the registration packages—airline tickets to go on-site to study a business issue, laptops, software to access the Internet, instructions on how to participate in a chat room, and the e-mail addresses of one's team members.

Motorola's innovative leadership development program— China Accelerated Management Program (CAMP)—is an example of a cutting edge leadership development program where learning is always tied to a real business issue and includes case discussions and action-based exercises. CAMP is an integrated management development system, designed to train local Chinese managers in Western management and leadership development practices. P. Y. Lai, president of Motorola China Electronics Limited (MCEL), puts the goal of CAMP into perspective when he says, "We want to be known as the education company in China. We are the only company who comes here with our own university—Motorola University. We want to share our good fortune with China by providing education not only to our own employees, but also to our customers, suppliers, and friends as well."[17]

Despite the enormous potential of the People's Republic of China (PRC), one of the world's largest emerging markets with 1.2 billion potential consumers, Motorola soon found that doing business there is unlike doing business elsewhere. The transition from state socialism to a market economy is both a crisis and an opportunity for the Chinese people. Once taken care of by their government, the Chinese are now expected to be entrepreneurial and work effectively in a competitive, market-driven environment.[18]

Here is Motorola's dilemma: by the year 2000, MCEL expects to triple its Chinese work force from 3,500 to 10,000. These new hires will be mostly middle managers and technical people, not laborers, but as an internal Motorola University document recognizes, China has "a shortage of management talent in the labor supply." MCEL has been plugging the hole with more than 100 U.S. expatriates, stationing them in Beijing. This reliance on expatriates has slowed down the company's strategy of "localization,"—relying on Chinese managers who are closer to and more imaginative about local market opportunities.[19]

While Chinese recruits are typically strong in the areas of functional and technical knowledge, most lack exposure to a global business environment and Western-style management skills. In the long term, Motorola realizes that not only are expatriates expensive, but the real issue that has emerged is the linguistic and cultural barriers of doing business in China. These issues are best understood by native-born Chinese managers.

The China Accelerated Management Program (CAMP) was designed to address this crucial problem and systematically transform Chinese nationals into Motorola business leaders. The need is certainly acute. Leo Burke, director of the Center for Management and Organizational Learning at Motorola University, puts this into perspective when he says, "Essentially we have to teach business to 10,000 Chinese workers." CAMP was designed to address this work force explosion by developing talented native-born employees who can replace expatriates. The goal is to use CAMP to develop the future leadership at the general manager level.

At the core of CAMP is an innovative five phase leadership development program that incorporates six weeks of classroom work, spliced into ten months of on-the-job training, including action learning, project management, job rotation, and coaching/mentoring. During this time, Chinese new hires learn the basics of a market economy, value creation, business process design, benchmarking, and systems thinking. CAMP also teaches presentation style, situational leadership, and team facilitation skills—all subjects that are particularly challenging in China, where improvisation is generally frowned upon. For Burke, breaking through this inhibition is the most compelling dimension of CAMP. Figure 4–5 shows how all these phases are brought together into a holistic leadership development approach.

The percentage of Motorola managers who are expatriates now stands at 90 percent, but in five years the number of MCEL managers is expected to grow substantially, with expatriate managers representing a much smaller percentage of the total manager population. The remainder will be Chinese managers who are graduates of CAMP. "Korea, China, Indonesia, and India represent half of the world's population. We want to bring the best to these markets and leave a legacy of good community leadership. Leadership is a big concern of ours. It is important that we are good corporate citizens and develop the kind of communities of learning that CAMP represents," says Burke. "China is the great success story of the next century," Burke continues, "and Motorola has the opportunity to contribute a part of the DNA to a future business culture. CAMP curriculum teaches as much general management education as it does Motorola's culture, and its commitment to individual dignity that engenders "total quality." Hence, CAMP is really about the skills and values of what people in the West mean by citizenship."[20] As of early 1997, 55 managers had graduated from CAMP and another 45 were taking part in it.

FIGURE 4-5

---

## MOTOROLA UNIVERSITY CAMP

### Phase I: Training and Site Visits (Four Weeks)
■ Demonstrate understanding of Motorola culture & ethics, business practices
  & basic management principles
■ Examine best practices at Motorola facilities in Asia

### Phase II: Action Learning (Four Weeks)
■ Integrate skills and knowledge learned in Phase I into current job function
■ Apply action learning tools to the job

### Phase III: Training and Rotation (Eight Weeks)
■ Acquire advanced leadership and project management skills
■ Participants rotate for six weeks on jobs outside their country

### Phase IV: On-the-Job Action Learning (Six Months)
■ Integrate skills and knowledge learned in Phases I-III into current job
■ Teach particular skills to Motorola employees or suppliers to Motorola

### Phase V: Capstone Event (Two Weeks)
■ Integrate experiences of Phases I-IV
■ Develop career plan for furthering individual development
■ Model effective change agent behaviors

Courtesy of Motorola University CAMP

## *Career Self-Management*

The final core workplace competency is career self-management, corresponding to the responsibility all employees have to manage their own careers. You can think of this competency as the skill possessed by individuals who are self-starters. Perhaps the need for this competency is best described by Peter DiToro, a 45-year-old middle manager who has survived a half-dozen rounds of lay-offs at Computervision, a Bedford, Massachusetts-based computer company. In a *New York Times* interview DiToro discussed the importance of self-management:

Job security is gone forever. I expect a revolution in my career every five to seven years. So, I now believe I am the corporation and it's my responsibility to manage my career.[21]

This focus on career self-management comes at a time when corporate America is just recovering from severe job losses. In early 1996 the *New York Times* did a seven-part series on corporate downsizing that took more than nine months to produce and was the longest piece of journalism published by the paper since its publication of the Pentagon Papers in 1971. According to the series, lifetime employability is replacing lifetime employment as the new social contract in American business. Michael Weiss, vice chairman of The Limited, put the employer's side of this social contract in the simplest of terms: "We show you that we value you by helping you develop your career."[22]

Hence, career self-management is becoming an important competency emphasized at a number of corporate universities. Career self-management is the ability to keep pace with the speed at which change occurs within the organization and the industry and to prepare for the future. It signifies a recognition on the part of the individual employee to keep learning because jobs that are held today may evolve into something else tomorrow, or simply disappear entirely. Career self-management also involves learning to identify and obtain new skills and competencies that allow the employee to move to a new position, either inside or outside of the organization.

A company that supports and encourages career self-management may ultimately have more highly-skilled and flexible employees, because employees understand the need to continuously refresh and update their skills. One effective way to nurture and support career self-management is to create a career center within the corporate university. This career center becomes a visible sign of the company's commitment to employee development, allows employees to assess their skills and benchmark them against company and industry standards, and cultivate skills that will help them succeed better in both their current and future jobs.

In the *Annual Survey of Corporate University Future Directions* we found that of the 100 corporate university deans surveyed, 43 percent currently have a career development center and another 15 percent are contemplating creating one. By far the most important function of the career development center is to be the resource center for assisting employees in self-assessment of their skills and advising them on the range of new skills, knowledge, and competencies needed to successfully compete in the global marketplace.

The emphasis today is on promoting career self-management. Often there is no longer a clearly marked career path for employees because the nature of the business changes so fast. An individual who wants to move within a company where the traditional career path no longer exists must know how to manage his/her career. Hence, making career information accessible, providing assessment instruments and benchmarking tools, as well as opportunities to talk with experts is the first step in creating a work force that is aware, motivated, and career-resilient. However, creating a culture that encourages and sustains career self-management while maintaining employee loyalty is a challenge. It requires commitment to the idea of employee self-development on the part of managers, a workplace culture where employees recognize the need for continuous learning, and an organization that develops self-development programs for both the employee and the manager.

Raychem in Menlo Park, California has developed an innovative approach to institutionalizing a culture of career self-management. Raychem, with 1996 sales of $1.67 billion and a 1996 net income of $148 million, launched a career development center in 1994. The former CEO, Bob Saldich, made learning and self-development a visible part of the culture; employees were taught to think of themselves as self-employed and encouraged to explore many career options.

Raychem, under new CEO Richard Kashnow, is building upon this culture of employee self-development by making people development a key competency for Raychem managers, along with such performance targets as 15 percent annual growth in earnings per share. The Raychem human resources department recently launched a program called HR Review where an annual strategic plan for people development is created and Raychem managers are rated on their ability to develop their employees. This People Development Strategic Plan covers how employees should be coached and cultivated, the specific competencies needed for their success, and the employee development initiatives that will be undertaken by employees. "The HR Review process, along with management accountability for employee development, and the emphasis on feedback, will drive the movement toward supporting employee development," says HR Manager Suzanne Edises, who is responsible for people development at Raychem.

A critical component of this people development initiative at Raychem Career Development Center is currently housed in Raychem's corporate library. The Career Development Center is outsourced to Career Action Center, a local non-profit agency with expertise in the development and delivery of career management services. The Raychem Career Development Center provides employees with self-assessments, career workshops, and referrals to career resources. Raychem is now exploring the idea of putting some self-assessment materials on-line and making them accessible to employees throughout the world.

An important function of the Raychem Career Development Center is to guide employees in developing a list of competencies they need for their current job or will need in the future. By providing resources on industry skill standards, and sometimes suggesting companies to benchmark, Raychem Career Development Center helps employees see where their skill level is in relationship to what the market demands or will demand in the future. Employees can then chart their own development plan, which may include taking advantage of Raychem's tuition reimbursement program, participating in formal training programs at Raychem University, requesting developmental assignments, or seeking masters/mentors to role model on the job.

"We are looking at a variety of options in employee development," says Edises. "We want to provide development opportunities for our employees and we are seeking out the most efficient and effective ways to accomplish this. In the future, much of what we currently do may be done on-line so that we can serve our growing global population of employees."

The types of career self-management tools developed by the Raychem Career Development Center ultimately create what Robert Waterman calls a career-resilient work force, defined in the *Harvard Business Review* as:

A group of employees who not only are dedicated to the idea of continuous learning but also stand ready to reinforce themselves to keep pace with change, take responsibility for their own career management, and last but not least, are committed to the company's success. The result is a group of self-resilient workers and a company that can thrive in an era where the skills needed to remain competitive are changing at a dizzying pace.[23]

Many companies profiled here have taken a firm stand on the importance of having employees understand that it is their responsibility to manage their own development. The assumption made by these companies is that once the company sets the direction and defines the core workplace competencies, each and every employee must assess if he or she has these competencies and, if not, how they can be developed.

## EMPLOYEE SELF-DEVELOPMENT LINKED TO COMPENSATION

As more companies focus on creating a culture of career self-management and employee self-development, many are going one step further by tying completion of learning plans to compensation. Together the employee and the employer develop learning goals for the year. Saturn comes to the forefront as a leader in developing an innovative approach to link learning to compensation. Gary High, director of Human Resources Development, defines the Saturn learning culture as:

- Every team member has his/her training and development plan.
- Training has a demonstrated impact on job performance.
- Training is an investment, not a cost.
- Training is driven by the needs of the organization.
- A high percentage of Saturn team members are involved in providing training.[24]

Central to Saturn's learning culture is the partnership Saturn builds with each individual team member. Training requirements lead to higher and higher levels of professional competence. This partnership is formalized in an agreement known as the individual training plan (ITPs) where Saturn team members and their leaders outline the specific training and development activities that each team member will undertake in a given year. These activities, outlined in ITPs, range from taking Saturn-specific formal training programs, teaching a class, cross-training a team member, reading a book, completing a computer-based training program, or taking a university course. Once a team member successfully completes this combination of learning activities on the plan, he/she will have achieved the 5 percent or 92 hours learning goal. Importantly, this partnership stresses team member professional development so that each Saturn team member learns new skills to improve his or her performance on the job, not merely to complete a required number of training hours. In this way, learning becomes the goal rather than simply using training to fulfill a human resources policy.

This partnership agreement does something else—it links Saturn's commitment to training to the team member compensation system. According to the partnership agreement developed between Saturn management and the representatives of the United Auto Workers union, 12 percent of each Saturn employee's base compensation is at risk, pending meeting specific goals. Interestingly, as this "risk percentage" has increased from 5 percent in 1995 to the current level of 12 percent, the reward has also increased to its maximum of $12,500 per person, but what is critical here is how Saturn defines this risk/reward formula. Five percent of base compensation at risk is directly tied to completion of one's training plan objectives, 5 percent at risk relates to meeting product quality goals and 2 percent relates to how well Saturn self-managed teams are able to demonstrate their effectiveness in working together in teams. The reward portion of the compensation gives additional compensation up to $12,500 over the base salary. It is tied to quality and productivity results that exceed the industry standard and to the achievement of financial goals for the year. Tim Epps, vice president of People Systems at Saturn, comments on the benefits of this compensation system when he says, "Doing the right training, in the right way, at the right time really can leverage the company's ability to build better, and more cars and, in the end, increase every team member's salary level."

Linking attainment of training goals to compensation has become an increasingly important factor in ensuring that training is linked to a performance management system. According to Gary High, "As the risk percentage has increased over time at Saturn, so have our team member's salary levels. In essence, this has motivated us to achieve higher levels of performance by taking the ambiguity out of one's job and putting a spotlight on the important deliverables needed for the team to be successful. We believe one of our critical success factors in creating this culture of continuous learning is to clearly define the risk and reward formula to our work force and to provide them with the opportunity for achieving their learning goals as well as other performance goals." Saturn's use of an incentive-based professional development plan reflects the company's belief that success at Saturn is dependent upon everyone making a commitment to life-long learning.

## THEMES OF FORMAL AND INFORMAL LEARNING PROGRAMS

More and more companies realize that workers at the turn of the century will be much more involved in coaching, teaching, and motivating teammates than just executing the technical aspects of their jobs. The companies profiled here have understood the growing complexity of jobs at every level of the organization. They have observed that work is becoming less task-oriented and more people-oriented, requiring workers who can think critically, make decisions, solve problems, effectively communicate with co-workers and customers and see the business as an integrated whole. The university model for training has become their means of "upskilling" their work forces to meet these new demands. They provide an important example for other companies to follow. The common theme emanating from the core curricula of numerous corporate universities is the need to develop workers who understand the big picture of the organization, have broad yet deep business skills, and are closely attuned to the identity and strategic mission of the firm.

The core curriculum outlined here reflects the challenge of transforming a diverse working population into a powerful and cohesive *work force* worthy of the name. It is also important to remember that learning and development programs under the corporate university umbrella also include customized learning solutions where corporate university managers operate as performance consultants. This approach, combining formal learning with customized consulting, seeks to achieve improvements in performance on the job. Chapter 5 examines a myriad of ways corporate universities seek to improve on-the-job performance.

*Chapter Five*

# Corporate Universities Become Learning Laboratories

> *Advances in information technology will allow for the creation of a learning environment that is continuous, less costly, made available to the entire force and characterized by personal networking.*

—Lieutenant General Jay Kelly, commander, Air University

## TECHNOLOGY TRANSFORMS LEARNING

A rule of thumb in education is that we learn 20 percent of what we see, 40 percent of what we see and hear, and 70 percent of what we see, hear, and do.[1] If that is true, the combination of computers, satellite television, and multimedia capabilities represents a formidable educational tool.

Corporate universities are making a major contribution to this "new learning environment" by experimenting with a variety of educational tools in the workplace. Over time, classroom-based corporate training as we know it today will become only one part—and in some cases a small part—of an organization's approach to educating its employees. As jobs become more complex and the skills they require become more extensive, executives are calling into question the traditional assumptions underlying corporate training and development programs.

Until recently, the instructional format has been one trainer standing before a class of 15 to 20 trainees teaching a static curriculum. Because training has usually taken place away from employees' jobs, the training department has owned the process.

Now, the imperative is to
ganization's strategic g
movement's greatest co
managers—in partnersh
the learning process and

As Chapter 1 pointed out, the emergence of the knowledge economy has created an urgent need for companies to continually update employee skills in response to new opportunities, new competition, and new technology. The organization will call on employees at all levels to develop broader, deeper, and more specialized skills to meet the changing needs of global customers. Meanwhile, companies will continually assess their workers' current skills, measure these against evolving business needs, and provide training and learning opportunities to close the gap between skills and needs.

Today the ability to disseminate new material within a company overnight is phenomenal. With technology-based learning, employees can move through new programs a week after the organization adopts them. As a result of these technological advances, companies with corporate universities are challenging traditional training assumptions. They are the vehicles to develop life-long learning by experimenting with new ways for employees to learn in the classroom, at the work-site, at home, and on the road. Sophisticated companies no longer view training simply as a way to help employees develop cognitive understanding and acquire a smorgasbord of new skills, rather they view learning as a means to achieve strategic goals and performance improvements on the job.

Figure 5–1 looks at some of the ways companies are experimenting with developing a life-long learning mindset among its employees. These organizations believe that when they put the pieces of the learning puzzle together employees will make improvements in their jobs. Some of the ways companies are experimenting with learning include: satellite-based learning, multimedia-based learning, collaborative learning technologies, web-based learning, and virtual campuses.

As corporate universities challenge old assumptions about training and tinker with new ideas and solutions, they take on a new role in the organization: that of a learning laboratory. Just as a scientific laboratory experiments with new methods and theories,

**FIGURE 5-1**

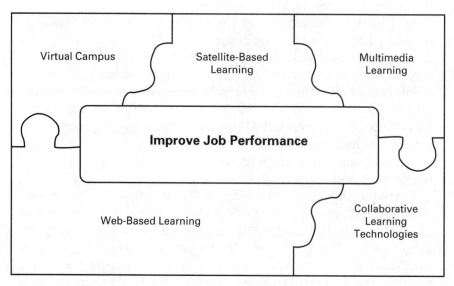

The Corporate University
A Learning Laboratory

Virtual Campus

Satellite-Based
Learning

Multimedia
Learning

**Improve Job Performance**

Web-Based Learning

Collaborative
Learning
Technologies

© 1997 Corporate University, Inc.

corporate universities explore different ways to disseminate knowledge to improve job performance. The corporate university thus fosters a spirit of experimentation in exploring new instructional design methods, learning technologies, self-development tools, and knowledge transfer.

Our *Annual Survey of Corporate University Future Directions* found that while only 18 percent of training is currently delivered using technology, by the year 2000 fifty percent of training will be delivered using technology. Figure 5-2 illustrates this dramatic shift. The cost of technology is a factor now, as shown by the differences in use of technology by a corporate university's size of budget, but this gap will shrink over the next five years (see Figure 5-3). While there is currently a slight distinction by industry between who is delivering how much training via technology, with manufacturing, transportation, communication, and utilities

FIGURE 5-2

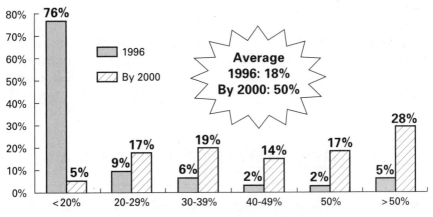

**Percent of Training
Delivered through Technology**

Source: Annual Survey of Corporate University Future Directions
© 1997 Corporate University Xchange, Inc.

FIGURE 5-3

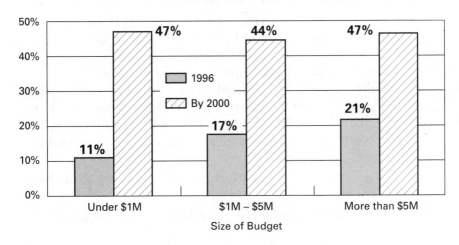

**Percent of Training Delivered through
Technology, by Size of Budget**

Source: Annual Survey of Corporate University Future Directions
© 1997 Corporate University Xchange, Inc.

firms reporting a greater interest in using technology for learning, the expected increase in the use of technology affects all
industries.

Management must guide these experiments in using technology
to accelerate learning by realistically appraising the types of learning
the organization wants to facilitate and then focus on which (if any)
technologies will work most effectively to accomplish the objectives.


## THE FIRST STEP: ESTABLISH CRITERIA FOR MEDIA SELECTION

Before an organization can employ learning technology effectively,
it must develop a plan outlining the various technologies the organization will utilize to accelerate employee learning. In pulling
this plan together it is important to focus on what sorts of learning
the corporate university wants to foster and what combination of
technologies will provide the optimal solution. We believe one
must consider the following mix of criteria:[2]

1. *Subject matter*—How complex is it? What type of flow is
   necessary for the material? Is there a need for remedial
   learning? How often will the material change?
2. *Funding*—What is your budget to fund development?
3. *Course design*—If the course exists, how will it translate to a
   new medium? If it doesn't exist, is the medium appropriate
   for the type of learning envisioned? How will
   communication between student and instructor and
   between student and student be tracked? How will students
   navigate through the information resources provided? How
   will discussions be structured? How will learners be kept
   involved? Is there room within the course design to make
   improvements easily?
4. *Design cycle time*—How much time do you have to develop
   the learning solution?
5. *Audience size*—How large is the audience for this learning
   solution?
6. *Audience location*—How disbursed is your audience in

terms of number of locations and size of employee population in each location?

7. *Learning environment*—How important is it for employees to share best practices?

8. *Access to technology*—Will employees have access to technology? Do they know how to use the technology? What sorts of hardware and software do employees need and how does it get disseminated? What technology platform has the organization committed to? Has the Chief Information Officer (CIO) been consulted?

9. *Technical support*—Who will be responsible for keeping the system running and who will maintain communications during the course?

10. *Outcome*—How proficient do you want your audience to be?

These are all important issues when evaluating technology-based solutions to learning. It is important to address the questions posed and select a combination of media that fit the learner, the subject matter, audience, and technology platform of the organization and desired outcomes.

For example, in experimenting with distance learning technologies, Air University, the educational arm of the U.S. Air Force responsible for providing professional military education, learned that high tech distance learning doesn't have to be an all or nothing proposition. In fact, Air University Chief of Instructional Design Dr. Adeline Cherry, says, "The proper mix of media is usually a combination of paper and higher tech options." In other words, it doesn't always make sense to put things on CD-ROM; if text-based lessons aren't interactive or hyperlinked, the learner doesn't need a disk. The Air Force found that learners were printing much of the CD-ROM's text, which meant that printing costs were merely being shifted to the student.

With an appropriate mix of high- and low-tech tools, Air University is experimenting successfully with providing an electronic campus format. Learners can receive the Air Command and Staff course on CD-ROM and communicate with instructors and other learners via e-mail, electronic bulletin boards, and chat areas where they can communicate in real time. These "cyberseminars" are restricted to groups of no more than eight to ten. So far more than 9,000 Air University learners have enrolled in this type of non-resident course.

Air University's Dr. Cherry believes it is important to allow for delivery of a single course in several different formats. While not all students may have access to the equipment needed for the more technologically sophisticated applications, providing a choice to learners has become a critical success factor in using technology for learning.

The technology puzzle illustrated in Figure 5–1 represents a visual way different technologies can serve a learner's needs. Ideally, an organization would use a mix of these technologies to address various needs, but only after rigorously assessing learning goals and the environment in which learning takes place. Let's look at how various companies are using elements of the technology puzzle, and in some cases elaborate combinations of technologies, to deliver learning anywhere and anytime.

### Satellite-Based Learning

Satellite-based learning can be either a synchronous (at the same time) or asynchronous (at a different time) form of learning. Satellite-based learning is able to train a large group of employees in a shorter time than traditional methods. It can deliver consistent instruction using qualified instructors and subject matter experts. It reduces employee travel costs and time away from the job by taking training to the employees, simultaneously reaching students scattered over a broad geographic area, and allowing for real-time interaction.

Satellite-based learning can also provide a record of which students received the training and how well they mastered the course. It allows subject matter experts, located at the various sites (indeed, virtually anywhere in the world), to interact with the instructor, and it gives students an interactive, participative experience, that increases their retention of the material. All of these advantages also present several challenges when an organization decides to implement satellite-based learning.

The Ford Motor Company and Southern Company experiences

with satellite-based learning illustrate the importance of several critical success factors in using satellite technology for learning.

**Fordstar trains vendors in the new technology.**   Ford has about 6,000 dealers throughout North America. Most of them have subscribed to FORDSTAR, a satellite network that allows Ford Motor Company to deliver training, provide access to experts and product information, and offer networking opportunities straight into the dealership. FORDSTAR uses one-way video and two-way audio via the One Touch System. It is the largest interactive digital satellite network in the world. In 1996, FORDSTAR delivered programming to 125,000 interactive dealer participants in parts, service, sales, technical, credit, and other dealership departments. The system can interactively "log on" participants in 1064 sites simultaneously, with typical class sizes ranging from 60 to 300 people.

According to Larry Conley, Ford's FORDSTAR networking manager, Ford's dealer training strategy is composed of three elements: self-study, distance learning over the satellite, and classroom based hands-on training. Knowledge that lends itself to self-study and has a long shelf-life is delivered through CD-ROM. Changing knowledge or information for which rapid distribution is essential is delivered over the satellite network. Skill-building training is delivered in one of Ford's 50 classrooms, equipped with engines, transmissions, and other training aids. Ford's training menu of technical, sales, marketing, and customer service training, as well as management and leadership programs, is systemically linked to the business strategies and goals of Ford Motor Company. To assure that Ford training fulfills its mission and continues to add value to the company, a FORDSTAR board of governors, equally representing dealers and Ford Motor Company, guides FORDSTAR communications and training programs.

At one time Ford delivered most of its dealer training through classrooms and hotel rooms. That meant dealers had to pull their people out of the dealership for extended periods of time in order to take advantage of Ford's training programs. Thirty-four percent of Ford's dealers are over 100 miles from the nearest classes, and they had a hard time sending employees to programs. Some curriculums required dealership employees to be out of the dealership for as many as 30 days. The use of the satellite network has meant that dealers can cut back significantly on the time their employees are away from the dealership.

Ford has found that satellite delivery means flexibility for dealers and their employees so the right student can get the right information at the right time. There is also a tremendous advantage in being able to spot comprehension problems early and do remedial teaching immediately. The system allows Ford to measure how well a student understands and then to better explain concepts, or examples, if a student is having difficulty with them. Because so much of the technical training is based on being able to grasp certain basic concepts before a student can progress to the next level, the ability to discern where remedial learning is needed and to address the need immediately provides a tremendous training advantage and impressively reduces the drop-out rate. There is also the advantage of consistency in the instruction. Ford can utilize the best instructors from around the world and is assured all students receive the same quality of instruction. Finally, satellite delivery offers the possibility for refresher courses after classroom training. For example, Ford runs a management course for dealers in Dearborn, Michigan. The participant's dealership is assessed the first day, on the second day dealers set their goals for the future, the third day consists of how to achieve their vision, and the fourth day focuses on how to maintain commitment for the vision. A classroom refresher course would have been prohibitively expensive, but using FORDSTAR to share best practices via the satellite provides course participants with the opportunity to benchmark their progress with other dealers and share solutions.

Currently, almost all Ford dealers in North America have subscribed to FORDSTAR. The training programs are packaged with communications services, some of which, previously, dealers had to pay for. The network also has the capacity to send giant data files, and to link to Ford's intranet, so that the cost of sending materials to the student can be reduced. Eventually updates to service manuals, price lists, and other vehicle information will be delivered over the network. So far, the network spans Canada, the entire United States, including Hawaii and Alaska, and Mexico. A plan for a similar system in Australia and New Zealand has recently been approved, and business plans for networks in other areas of the world are under development.

Notwithstanding all the advantages of satellite-based learning, Ford discovered that one of the critical elements in the rapid adoption of FORDSTAR is the requirement for all instructors who deliver over the network to have eight hours of practice and coaching for every hour of on-site delivery. Ford believes excellence in both instructional design for television and interactive delivery are critical to the success of a satellite-based learning program.

FORDSTAR adheres to a learner-centered approach in both the design and delivery stage. In other words, both designers and deliverers must be focused on how the learner fits into the process. FORDSTAR's goal is 30 percent interactivity in FORDSTAR-delivered content. "We're asking the instructor to do less and the student to do more," Conley says. "This means designing the learner's role in greater detail."

FORDSTAR developed a manual called "Welcome to FORD-STAR," which is written for the various vendors that contract with FORDSTAR to produce content. It includes sections on how to design a course, the goals in dealership instruction, the type of support FORDSTAR provides to the dealers, how to select a producer, the cost of a broadcast, and a list of vendors who have experience producing content for FORDSTAR.

In addition, FORDSTAR also provides orientation courses for instructional designers and deliverers that emphasize understanding the learner's mindset and focusing less on the role of the instructor and more on the learner's role and responsibility. The orientation program reinforces the need to deliver material in "bumper sticker" sized-bites of information easily absorbed by the learner. Both designers and instructors are challenged to find creative ways to involve learners in a FORDSTAR satellite broadcast.

The importance of vendor training is underscored by what lies in the future—vendor certification for the design and delivery of FORDSTAR programs. This includes not only how to best design and deliver a training program over satellite, but also courses on how adults learn and how to reinforce life-long learning. The goal is clearly to take a customer-focused view in the creation of all FORDSTAR programs.

**Southern Company College: The electronic classroom communications challenge.** While Ford focused on vendor training as a way to deliver world-class satellite-based learning, Southern Company College's Interactive Distance Learning (IDL) illustrates another best practice: the power of communicating the value of IDL to the employee population—particularly traditional trainers. In the case of Southern Company College (SCC), the experience with satellite-based learning dates back to 1992 when Southern Company Television Network was expanded to include the capability of interactive distance learning. This investment resulted in the creation of 50 downlinks equipped with keypads that relay feedback from students at the sites.[3] Participants respond to yes/no and multiple choice questions and also have the ability to hit a call button that signals the instructor they want to ask a question. Also, built-in microphones allow the participants to ask questions and talk with classmates at other locations. For example, when a student hits the call button, the instructor will see the student's name and a raised hand icon will appear on the screen. The instructor can then recognize the student either individually or collectively so all participants hear the question or comment.

The challenge in using this technology is to focus on material that can be delivered frequently to large numbers of students. "One of the first things we did," says Ron Youncker, manager of Southern Company College Learning Solutions and Interactive Distance Learning, "was to do a complete assessment of how to use interactive satellite for broadcasting for learning."

In our experience, we have found that there are three important steps to take before leaping into the "technology build mode": 1) Quantify the number and type of common and consistent training messages delivered by instructors to a large dispersed employee population. For example, if your company comes out with a new product every six months that thousands of salespeople need to know about, then the economics of a cost/benefit analysis will be quite favorable toward using IDL; 2) Understand the cultural basis within your corporation for classroom-based training. Your corporate university dean may have fallen in love with IDL, but if your business manager still says, "I think my people will really only learn in a face-to-face environment," then recognize the tremendous hurdles associated with "pulling" the technology

## FIGURE 5-4

---

### Does Southern Company IDL Answer Your Training Needs?

The following questionnaire can help determine if IDL is the solution to your training needs. If you check more "Yes" than "No" responses, IDL may be the right answer for you.

Yes   No

❑   ❑   There are a large number of students/participants in need of this training scattered over a broad geographic area of The Southern Company.

If "Yes", estimate how many: _____

❑   ❑   The target group for this training is within 90 minutes of IDL remote learning sites.

❑   ❑   The cycle time needed to train the target group is short.

❑   ❑   There is a need for students to ask questions and/or carry on conversations with the instructor and/or other students.

❑   ❑   There are few instructions qualified to provide this training.

❑   ❑   The participants' job responsibilities make it difficult for them to take a fullday or multiple-day traditional training course.

❑   ❑   A consistent and precise message is critical.

Courtesy of Southern Company College

through the organization; and 3) Appreciate the need for value-based Interactive Distance Learning communications. As Figure 5-4 illustrates, Southern Company College developed a communication tool detailing key questions in assessing whether IDL is the optimal form of delivery for a training program. Youncker adds, "We believe one of the critical success factors is to communicate the strategic vision of Interactive Distance Learning and thereby create a 'demand pull' from the business units. In the final analysis, we want the business managers to understand the value of satellite-based learning and be able to articulate the value in achieving their business goals."

So what are the results so far? Southern Company College has put 2,300 students through such courses as Performance Management, Diversity, and Regulatory Compliance using Interactive Distance Learning. When you compare the cost of having an outside

expert teach the same course in 20 locations over a six-week period versus having that individual deliver the entire course in
three days via Interactive Distance Learning, the economics are
compelling.

Economics aside, Youncker found that one of the biggest challenges is building a consensus throughout the Southern Company
training community on the benefit of a successful IDL introduction. "We did not anticipate the fact that our trainers would present communication challenges," says Youncker.

For Southern Company College the solution has been to develop communications initiatives for senior business managers
and trainers that articulate the value of using IDL. Here the goal is
to have these business managers pull the technology through the
corporation. Finally, Youncker is also investigating the feasibility
of creating a local consortium where SCC can open up its facility
to the community of Atlanta-based corporations and universities.

### Multimedia-Based Learning

The desktop is being transformed into a workstation that employs
graphics, animation, video, and audio to facilitate learning. The
goal is to create learning solutions that learners access on demand
and that engage their interests and imaginations, accelerating
learning and reducing training time and costs.

**First Union Bank delivers 30 percent of training in alter-
native delivery.**  First Union National Bank of North Carolina,
with 2,000 branches, has implemented an aggressive multimedia
learning strategy aimed at two large job families: tellers and commercial lending officers. Its first major effort was converting classroom-based teller training targeted to 10,000 tellers across the retail bank to CD-ROM. First University, headed by First Union
Senior Vice President Kathryn Heath, rolled out teller training in
12 bank regions that stretch from Florida to Connecticut. Teller
training via CD-ROM has enabled the bank to reduce the average
cost of training a new teller from $1,581 to $859, as well as decreas-
ing training time from ten days to three to five days.

"In the past, new tellers were hired and then they had to wait
for a training program to open, and this program usually took ten
days in class and five days of mentoring," Heath says. "But with

CD-ROM teller training we are able to train tellers in just two and one-half days, supplemented by three days of mentoring. What's more, we're able to send a more consistent message with the goal of ultimately increasing teller productivity and retention."

The real lesson here is that this type of alternative training delivery is consistent with the sales culture of First Union, which has over 150 different incentive systems. "Everyone from the teller to the mutual fund sales person is working on a sales incentive program, and this strong sales culture reinforces learning on one's own time. Our people tell us, 'I lose money when I'm in training, but I need to keep up my skills.' So the requests have been pouring in for CD-ROMs and even home study programs," adds Heath. The goal was to deliver 24 percent of all training alternatively in 1996; First Union surpassed this to reach 30 percent. The current CD-ROM teller training program is 25 hours in length, but because the learner controls the learning, one can "test out" of various sections.

Doug Steele, dean of First Union's College for Commercial Bankers, also realized CD-ROM could speed learning among commercial bankers. Steele decided the most practical and economical way to implement First Union's multimedia vision for learning was to enter into a consortium with Robert Morris Associates (RMA), a Philadelphia, Pennsylvania-based trade association for commercial lenders and credit risk professionals. As outlined by RMA, the goal of the consortium is to bring together a number of financial institutions who have common training needs for commercial lending professionals. The impetus for this consortium came out of a "needs assessment" completed by Robert Morris Associates Professional Development Department who found that an increasing number of their 1,800 member banks, including Royal Bank of Canada, NorWest, Mellon Bank, Bank of America, and First Union, all expressed a similar need: to have commercial lending training programs delivered on a CD-ROM rather than in the traditional ten week classroom-based training program. The RMA consortium put together a group of ten financial institutions each paying $25,000 for the license to have 250 commercial lending training programs delivered on a CD-ROM. RMA acts as the umbrella designer and retains the copyright so the trade association can in turn sell these CD-ROMs to the remainder of their 1,800 membership base.

The first series includes such areas as: Industry Business Management, Analysis of Balance Sheets and Income Statements, Ratio Trend Analysis, Cash Flow Analysis, and Loan Structuring. The goal of the consortium is to drive down the economies of scale in program design and development so an entire curriculum in commercial lending can be available on CD-ROM. Then the goal is to have this CD-ROM based commercial lending training program be eligible for college credit.

"This is more economical and convenient for commercial bankers," says Steele. "We have come together with commercial bankers across North America and have agreed on a common set of competencies needed to be a commercial lending officer. As technology advances, we will be able to convert the CD-ROM programs to be delivered in a client-server environment, so we see it as one stage in a transitional process," adds Steele.

What did First University learn in adapting traditional classroom training for CD-ROM? "Not all machines that have CD-ROM are alike," says Heath. "You can't assume just because an employee has a computer with a CD-ROM drive it will run our programs. Plus, we realized that we needed to be in the customer support business, so we installed a help desk to assist any employee who has problems, although the technology makes it easy for just about anybody to access the program," adds Heath. "We also learned that changing the way we deliver training has ramifications throughout the company. When we speed up the delivery time, eliminate the wait time, and reduce the cycle time, we have impacted many lines of business. In addition, we realized that changing the way we deliver training also changes the way we interact with our customers. To accommodate this change, we have put a Customer Fulfillment Center in place to handle requests for courseware, laptops, and other learning tools."

## Collaborative Learning Technologies

While multimedia learning requires an individual to learn at his/her desktop, collaborative learning technologies recognize the power of learning in groups. These collaborative learning technologies can be either "soft technologies," such as Learning Map™ illustrations, or "technologically advanced" knowledge databases. In both cases, the goal is the same: to become the campfire around which knowledge workers congregate, learn the business, and share successes.

Alan Webber, a founding editor of *Fast Company* magazine, observes that the best management tool to initiate learning is a conversation. "Time was, if your boss caught you talking on the phone or hanging around the water cooler, he would have said, 'Stop talking and get to work!' Today, if you're *not* on the phone or talking with colleagues and customers, chances are you'll hear, 'Start talking and get to work.'"[4]

Why has conversation been identified as a "management tool"? Because as employees converse with each other they are sharing knowledge, uncovering best practices, and, in the process, creating new knowledge. While technology can help spread knowledge, it still depends on the quality of the conversation these technologies support. Hence, the growing interest in developing collaborative learning technologies that illustrate an organization's business strategies and direction and provide an opportunity to engage in a dialogue that focuses on the organization's future. One of the companies that has developed an interesting and innovative set of collaborative learning tools is Sears Roebuck.

When Arthur Martinez took over as CEO of Sears in the early 1990s, the company was in a cost-cutting mode. Sears had severely cut back on education and training in 1988. The company included many businesses peripheral to its retail core. Both executives and employees were trapped in an entitlement mentality that did not encourage, or even allow them, to see that customer satisfaction was critical to Sears' survival.

Martinez immediately replaced half the executive committee and began hiring outside executives and closing, spinning off, or selling peripheral businesses (the Sears catalog division, Dean Witter, Allstate Insurance, the Discover Card, Sears Tower, Prodigy Services, and more). He closed 113 stores and laid off 50,000 workers. Sears then focused on five key goals for the remaining 275,000 employees:

1. Make Sears a compelling place to shop.
2. Develop local market focus in order to understand customers and competition at the local level.
3. Create a winning culture where employees on the Sears floor, their managers, and higher level executives express pride in their association with the company.
4. Focus on the core businesses, which means expansion into

related businesses, such as Sears Home Life and Sears Hardware.

5. Drive a culture of continuous improvement throughout the organization.

Sears University was formed in October of 1994 to train managers and executives in a set of leadership skills that would contribute to making Sears a "compelling place to work, a compelling place to shop, and a compelling place to invest."

In its first two years, Sears University trained more than 28,000 managers at seven United States development centers. In order to educate all 275,000 Sears employees about the critical issues facing the company, Sears University created a collaborative learning tool known as Learning Map™[5] graphic illustrations that provides Sears employees with an understanding of the contextual framework in which they operate. Sears Total Performance Indicators (Figure 5–5), an example of a Learning Map™ illustration, is de-

**FIGURE 5–5**
*The Learning Map™ illustration produced for the licensed use of Sears is the solely owned property of Root Learning, Inc., Perrysburg, Ohio.*

signed to stimulate conversation within a group of employees so they can learn the key indicators that contribute to making Sears a compelling place to work, shop, and invest.

Using the metaphor of the waterfall, the pictorial illustration of Sears Total Performance Indicators includes drainpipes of competition that illustrate what happens when key measures such as customer satisfaction are weak. In addition, water wheels are shown to depict how different indicators such as employee satisfaction drive performance. The illustration helps managers see the relationship between different measures and understand how they affect each other and impact revenue growth. It asks managers to discuss questions like: "How would you characterize a compelling place to work? As a manager, how much influence do you believe you have in creating a compelling place to work? How would you characterize a compelling place to shop?"

Steven Kirn, vice president of Education and Development at Sears, notes that, "The visual representation and the questions that accompany each illustration of our business have helped Sears employees better understand their impact on individual store performance." For example, in one store, repeated use of the illustration of Sears Total Performance Indicator was customized with actual data on employee turnover and customer satisfaction. Using this map as a tool for employees to converse with one another, managers begin to understand the relationship between employee turnover, inadequate hiring and training practices. This has helped store managers direct their energies into training and teamwork building, and refine their interviewing practices to recruit associates who have a predisposition to working well in a retail environment.

"You can't use these maps once and expect results," says John Greene, a former Sears store general manager who is now the district human resources manager for the Charlotte, North Carolina area. "The maps should be used in conjunction with other collaborative learning tools, such as workshops, meetings and facilitated discussion groups. They should be revisited so the concepts can be refreshed after employees have had time to work with them. Our maps are always hanging in the lunchroom, so both associates and managers can refer back to them as needed. We've also conducted follow-up sessions with the maps, to explore new concepts employees and managers have learned during the first use of the maps."

Greene believes that using various collaborative learning technologies such as Learning Map™ illustrations; workshops and follow-up meetings with employees has helped to address common myths about selling in a retail environment. For example, many sales associates believe that customers do not want to be hovered over, instead they want a knowledgeable sales representative who can immediately answer specific questions about the products. Hence, sales associates must learn to acquire in-depth knowledge about Sears products and services and present these to the customer to close the sale.

### Knowledge Databases on the Intranet

While the development of collaborative learning technologies such as Learning Map™ illustrations encourages "on-site dialogue" between co-workers, knowledge databases allow workers to communicate and share information and advice virtually—on the web. As defined by Carole Anne Ogahn, founder of Deep Woods Technology, "These knowledge databases go beyond e-mail to include strategic initiatives changing how companies operate."[6] The goal of knowledge databases is to integrate scattered information and knowledge into an organization's collective wisdom.

The large consulting firms such as Arthur Andersen; Booz, Allen & Hamilton; Coopers & Lybrand; and KPMG are leading the way in experimenting with knowledge databases as a vehicle to store and disseminate knowledge. To understand how these knowledge databases work, it is worth taking a look at Coopers & Lybrand's Knowledge-Curve[SM]. "Essentially, KnowledgeCurve[SM] was designed to reduce the amount of time a Coopers & Lybrand consultant spends searching for answers," says Mik Chwalek, director of Knowledge Strategies for the worldwide consulting firm.

In the past, if a Coopers & Lybrand consultant needed help on a client assignment, he or she would have to call fellow consultants and wait for days for packages to arrive via courier. Now, the consultant need only check Coopers & Lybrand's KnowledgeCurve[SM] and best practices are posted on-line. The result: Coopers & Lybrand's collective know-how is spread to individual consultants worldwide.

In developing their intranet, Coopers & Lybrand conducted a survey of 500 knowledge workers to find answers to such questions as: What do you need (content wise) and what is the frequency: daily, weekly, monthly, or once in a while? Then, Coopers & Lybrand conducted a similar survey with their librarians and information management professionals. The result validated the design of the KnowledgeCurve$^{SM}$ home page, which includes: People (experts and best practices), Clients, Firm Facts, CyberLyb$^{SM}$ (repository of research reports), Newsbytes, Yellow Pages, Hot Web-sites (hand picked for each division), and a What's New section.

Coopers & Lybrand's research has shown that the primary need among consultants (over 70,000 worldwide) is knowledge about other C&L consultants and their specific areas of expertise. For example, if you are a C&L consultant working on a client engagement and need to find a colleague who has Java expertise, you might click on "People" and navigate through the KnowledgeCurve$^{SM}$ to locate a resume that meets your criteria. What's even more compelling about using KnowledgeCurve$^{SM}$ as an information management tool is the ability to customize it for individual client needs. Suppose you have an engagement that requires you to consult external research from Gartner Group or Goldman Sachs. You can simply click on "CyberLyb," the electronic knowledge repository, and get immediate access to these external research reports.

In designing KnowledgeCurve$^{SM}$, Chwalek believes one of the critical success factors is the need to conduct knowledge profiles of key jobs in order to understand what knowledge exists, what the best practices are as conducted by top performers, and what it takes from a skills, knowledge, and training perspective to perform them. It is then possible to develop methods for knowledge acquisition and sharing to capture and disseminate content-rich information in an accessible and user-friendly manner.[7]

Knowledge databases like Coopers & Lybrand's KnowledgeCurve$^{SM}$ are really electronic support tools that enable consultants to find and retrieve "critical knowledge," organize this knowledge, and store and access it with vastly greater speed and lower cost than traditional information sharing. A survey by Forrester Research of 50 corporations finds that 16 percent have an intranet and another 50 percent have plans for or are considering one. Lehman Brothers predicts that the overall intranet market will reach $7.4 billion by the year 2000.[8] Perhaps the reason behind the creation of knowledge databases is best explained by Thomas Stewart, author of *Intellectual Capital,* when he says, "The faster newcomers can learn what the institution knows, the faster they can contribute to it. A company with a 10 percent annual turnover rate, which is better than the average, will lose half of its experienced workers in just five years, even if its total head count stays the same."[9] Hence, the need to develop electronic support tools to capture and disburse knowledge to the community of workers is becoming a critical need within organizations.

### *Web-Based Learning*

The Internet is clearly changing the way we store, move, find, and manage knowledge. As Don Tapscott points out, *The Urbino Bible* (one of the books of antiquity that predated Guttenberg) was, until recently, available to only a handful of people. Kept in the Vatican and restricted to 200 people who could view it at the rate of four pages per day, the *Bible* is now on the Internet and one hundred times as many people saw it during its first few days on the Internet than had seen it in the previous millennium."[10]

Corporate universities profiled in our *Annual Survey of Corporate University Future Directions* are already delivering one-quarter of total training (24.2 percent) on-line through the Internet or their own intranet. When asked about future learning plans, 89 percent of participating corporate universities said they had plans to use on-line learning in the future, with manufacturing and finance firms leading the pack by a small margin (see Figure 5–6).

The appeal of the web for educating a work force is its ability to customize learning experiences for each individual's learning needs and preferences. Additionally, Internet-delivered training offers automated tracking of each learning interaction. Systems can be customized to generate daily reports, including student names, e-mail addresses, time spent on-line, and screens visited.

The web also provides a central location for colleagues to share successes, ask questions about problems they are trying to solve, and download tools and tips. It is also possible to offer a wealth of collateral resources for learners without taking up space on a hard drive or producing, delivering, and continuously updating a CD-ROM.

The technology makes it easy to conduct surveys on-line and to design tests to measure performance. Employees can access not only learning programs, but also documentation 24 hours a day, from anywhere in the world. They can log on, participate in learning pro-

**FIGURE 5-6**

_____

### 89 Percent of All Corporate Universities
### Plan to Use the Internet By the Year 2000

| By age of university | % Responding Yes |
|---|---|
| 2 years or less | 85% |
| 3 – 10 years | 90% |
| More than 10 years | 94% |

| By industry | % Responding Yes |
|---|---|
| Manufacturing | 100% |
| Finance/Insurance/Real Estate | 85% |
| Services | 84% |
| Transportation/Communication/Utilities | 82% |

Source: Annual Survey of Corporate University Future Directions
© 1997 Corporate University Xchange, Inc.

grams, log off, go back to work, and log on again as time permits. The ultimate appeal of on-line technology is that it is easier to incorporate learning as a routine part of the day, whether the employee is in the office or on the road.

**SunU: An electronic learning storefront.**   The pioneer in using the intranet for learning is the company that created the intranet: Sun Microsystems. Sun's belief that "the network is the computer" has transformed the employee's desktop into a learning storefront. With more than 19,000 employees in 33 countries and with 51 percent of its revenue coming from outside the United States, Sun Microsystems has developed a "virtual" university at the desktop. Four years ago, SunU was under the gun to prove its value to the corporation. While the need for training was more important than ever, managers were finding they simply did not have time to attend classroom-based courses. "Time has become the new four-letter word in training," says Jim Moore, director of SunU. "People were asking: If I take three days off the job, will the gain be greater than the pain? And when you miss three days of work in a world this fast-paced, believe me, there is pain."

The solution: put training and information on the existing intranet so employees can search, access, and retrieve the specific knowledge they need to perform their jobs. In order to provide learning opportunities that match employee needs, SunU redesigned its approach to on-line learning. In 1993, after an unsuccessful attempt to roll out custom-made courseware for the engineering population using computer-based training (CBT), Sun began experimenting with web-based delivery.

Today, SunU believes the web is the foundation for learning and information offered at the desktop. While classroom training will always be necessary for certain types of collaborative learning experiences, Sun's intranet is a readily available supplement to the traditional classroom.

"Using the web as the vehicle of choice was a relatively easy decision," says SunU Director Moore. Within Sun Microsystems, the architecture for web-based training is in place. Most internal business is already conducted on-line; all employees have access to the technology; and it has the support of senior management as a vehicle for corporate communications.

SunU uses the intranet in two ways: as an electronic storefront for SunU learning programs and as the administrative backbone for the SunU virtual university. Many educational programs are delivered over the intranet, saving employees time away from their jobs. The intranet has many advantages over CBT as a distance learning option, principally in that it is platform independent and can be readily updated. This "real time" feature is critical since more than 75 percent of Sun Microsystems' $8 billion in revenue comes from products less than two years old. Hence, a fast and flexible development cycle time becomes critical for success. In addition, the SunU's intranet offers real-time feedback about how people use the course, how and what they learn, how much time they spend on various parts of the program, and what's working and what's not working in instructional design. Because this information can be captured instantly, instructional designers can put the first module in a series on the web and modify additional modules as they receive feedback from employees.

In addition to using their intranet for delivery of learning programs, SunU has created an educational management system on-line. Employees access Sun curricula, register for classes, receive pre- and post-class communication, are billed for learning, have student records updated, and get announcements of new classes all through the intranet. In addition, the same registration software notifies managers that their employees are registered for training, and employees can even get an individualized plan for their professional development on-line.

Because SunU is funded largely by chargebacks to business units when an employee registers for a course, the amount of money being charged is automatically credited to the SunU account. Working through the intranet eliminates much of the need for the exchange of paper between SunU and its customers.

One of the criticisms of intranet-delivered learning is that it tends to be static—just electronic page turning. Sun's Java, a programming language with "applets" of software that are downloaded along with content, is helping to change this. Java can be delivered over any network and instructional designers can use it to build some interactivity into course exercises. Moreover, Java does not take up space on the hard disk because the program is maintained on the network server and not on the individual computer. Usage of Java makes content more interactive and engaging to the learner, building in audio, video, and graphics.

"For SunU, designing education for explicit learning is always going to be a combination of electronic storefront web-based training, and the classroom," Moore says. "These are tied together; one doesn't replace the other. We need both group learning and individual learning with intranet-based learning primarily focusing on such explicit knowledge as product characteristics, industry facts, and procedures."

Sun's Eric Peterson, former manager of Research and Development for Learning Technology at SunU and now manager of Sun's Network Security Group, says, "Sun must apply the same rigor to educational offerings as it does to the development of other types of software. The best educational materials are simple and are enterprise-wide solutions to common technical problems. The intranet offers quick access to information, the ability to share knowledge among colleagues through list serves and chat rooms, and a rich bank of collateral materials that can be easily accessed."

While web-based learning provides Sun employees with the ability to customize learning to the specific needs of employees, the challenge becomes how to charge for this in SunU's current financial model where most of the budget comes from internal business units and many perceive the web as a vehicle dispensing free information. Interestingly, SunU's Moore predicts the smart card may be the ultimate solution. This scenario involves giving each employee a smart card worth $3,000 of prepaid learning. The employee can swipe his/her card each time learning is accessed on the web. While paying for training with smartcards may sound futuristic, it's the direction several corporate universities are moving as they enter the twenty-first century.

**Dell University: Using embedded learning to train a work force.**  The intranet not only offers just-in-time learning but can also design learning-centered work so learning is built right into how employees work on the job. John Coné, vice president of Dell University, talks about a link between new learning paradigms and the culture at large, "When I think of the possibilities of using the intranet for learning, I can't help of thinking of one of the most remarkable artistic compositions of this century," says Coné. "I'm referring of course to 'Woolly Bully' by Sam the Sham and the Pharaohs. The first 11 words of 'Woolly Bully' are very prophetic: 'Watch it now, watch it now/here it comes, here it comes.' I think we all know what Sam was trying to say: Change is upon us and we better be prepared for it." Coné takes Sam the Sham and the Pharaohs' message to heart. He understands the necessity of change and has embraced it wholeheartedly. To that effect, he is a vocal proponent of what he calls embedded learning—designing easily accessible learning that is synchronous with work. "With embedded learning," says Coné, "people learn naturally as part of how they work and often don't even know they're learning."

Dell University has addressed the need of employees to learn as they work by moving toward just-in-time learner-centered education. "The employees in our organization are completely capable of knowing what they need to learn, going and finding it, and learning it. We just have to make it available and tell them where to find it," says Coné. Dell University delivers 35 to 45 percent of its curriculum through web-based tools, some of which are used in conjunction with more traditional settings like classrooms and workshops. Each tool has an introduction that describes the tool, and a tutorial that provides step-by-step instructions.

The Managers On-line Success Tool (The MOST) is an example of a Dell University on-line tool. This tool is located on Dell University's intranet and provides information on how to order business cards, phone or requisition forms, as well as how to hire a new employee, and anything else a manager needs to know quickly. Another Dell on-line tool, an Electronic Performance Support System (EPSS), is the Sales Performance Support tool. This allows members of the sales force to go on-line and find specifications on product components, price, competitor information, and practically anything a salesperson needs to know to be successful on the job. But the on-line tools are just one aspect of embedded learning; Dell University has also developed follow-up classes with interactive games to involve the employees as they learn new knowledge and skills. Take for example the orientation class for new hires that combines a three-hour seminar where Dell employees are introduced to the policies and procedures at Dell with exercises back on the job. For example, when they return to the job they can participate in the Intranet Treasurehunt where they are asked to locate such information as the price of Dell stock or when the last payday was. It's this combination of on-line learning tools on the job with interactive and engaging exercises that embeds learning into work. Dell University's course catalog is also on the intranet and is updated every two weeks. Curriculum is listed alphabetically as well as by topic and includes such information as course descriptions, cost, prerequisites, what students can be expected to learn, whether the course fits the student profile, and, importantly, how the course or learning tool fits into the Dell business plan.

Using embedded learning is revolutionary because it enables Dell employees to learn in ways that are natural to them. "These same technologies provide insight into how people learn. Every page on the intranet has its own designation," says Coné. "What that means is, for the first time, rather easily, we can actually watch where people go to learn: what page they're on, what page they go to next, when do they go to the glossary, do they skip a chapter. What we saw was people going to the table of contents, finding the piece that they really wanted to know about, and going directly to that piece, and spending five minutes on it. We could watch them go and just get the part that they needed. When you put something on the intranet, it doesn't matter how you've written it, everybody uses it like a reference book; people try to figure out the most efficient way to learn."

Embedded learning is, at its root, a response to increased employee responsibility and the new emphasis on knowledge capital as a measure of a company's value. "There aren't any jobs anymore that don't require people to make smart choices," says Coné, "And, if you've got to make smart choices, the more you know about what drives the business, the more successful you're going to be."

In essence, businesses rely on employees who bring tremendous expertise, but the knowledge that is so fundamental to the success of the business must be widely shared within and across the business rather than dependent on any one individual employee. Perhaps this is the power of embedded learning as it's used at Dell University: Learning must be built into the way employees interact with each other and with the organization.

**Verifone University: A virtual university.**  It is not just large companies like Sun Microsystems and Dell Computer that use the intranet for learning. Verifone, a 15-year-old company in the electronic transaction automation business with 2,500 employees, decided that a virtual university would be the only type of training organization to meet the organization's geographically dispersed regional and manufacturing sites located in North and South America, Asia, Africa, and Australia. Verifone's clients include banks and credit card companies, retail merchants and consumers, government agencies, and healthcare providers. To date, Verifone has more than five million transaction automation systems installed in 100 countries.

How did Verifone establish their virtual university? First, the Learning and Development Group charged with the task recognized that things were moving too fast for the university to act as curriculum developer *and* deliverer. For the most part, they ceded this responsibility to subject experts within the company or outsourced it. Instead, they concentrated on creating their role as a clearinghouse of "best-in-class learning resources," and used the umbrella of Verifone University to deliver this to each employee's desktop.

Second, Verifone University recognized that 80 percent of what employees need to know to do their job is learned on the job. Hence, learning resources should be available at learning centers or at the desktops of employees. When this isn't possible, Verifone University acts as a broker—obtaining learning resources from a myriad of vendors. "It isn't complex, but it's an elaborate communications system," says Nolan

Pike, senior trainer for the Learning and Development Group, which built and now maintains the virtual university.

The university is moving employees along the path to self-directed learning by making a wide variety of relevant courses, white papers, speeches, training toolkits, books, and videotapes/audiotapes available to them. (see Figure 5–7.) Moreover, Verifone University encourages on-line learning by subsidizing employee computer equipment purchases. They are also putting course catalogue and learning resources on-line, and linking these resources to job descriptions within the company so that employees who aspire to a new position can see what qualifications are needed and how on-line learning plays a part in their development. "Everything changes so quickly that it's up to the individuals to educate themselves," says Pike. "It's up to us to provide access to world-class learning tools."

The core of Verifone University consists of about 300 pages of material on the company's intranet and is still growing, as one time

**FIGURE 5–7**

---

### Verifone University: Just-In-Time Learning

Verifone's University combines serveral familiar components with some new resources to create one-stop shopping for learning and development. It puts employees in charge of their own future. Resources available to employees include:

● **Learning and Development Group:** Can help assess learning needs, design tools and training, and help implement programs. Offer instructional design, publication development, video products, and team development.

● **On-Line Course Catalog:** A menu of courses and self-paced learning materials.

● **Virtual Library:** Access information from Verifone's own knowledge databases.

● **Financial Aid:** Reimburses employees for the cost of tuition and textbooks.

● **Computer Subsidy Program:** Reimburses employees for the purchase of home-based, job-related hardware or software as well as upgrades, maintenance, or repair of existing systems.

● **On-Line Job Posting System:** Summary of openings, location, and job responsibilities.

● **Learning Centers:** A combination of lending library and learning lab. Some centers contain audio-visual and multimedia equipment, books, and courseware.

Courtesy of Verifone University

classroom courses are being converted to virtual courses. Three such courses—two that are product-specific and the required "Bankcard 101," an overview of how bankcards work—are now on-line.

Finally, Verifone University encourages self-directed learning by linking learning with performance reviews. All managers have a comprehensive description of Verifone University's learning resources that they use in conjunction with comments about areas in which an employee needs improvement. A manager probably would not suggest that an employee take a certain course at a specific time, but will suggest that the employee consider upgrading skills in certain areas by taking advantage of Verifone University's rich collection of learning resources.

"We didn't just take our training courses and put them on-line," adds Pike. It's a whole new approach to learning and development. In order to convert classroom courses to the intranet, Pike advises developing expertise in:

- Locating a wide array of learning products and services.
- Understanding different delivery methods and which ones work best for a particular application.
- Translating educational solutions to your intranet. This is really a design question about what material to make available, how extensive, and what hyperlinks to related materials should be included in your intranet.

What makes Verifone University so innovative is its ability to be the central clearinghouse for world-class learning resources. Verifone University has become the tangible tool to put Verifone employees in charge of their own learning.


**Xerox Management Institute combines web-based learning with on-site classes.**  Web-based learning is entering a new arena: leadership development. As corporations stress learning tied to real business needs, web-based education has been identified as a powerful tool to move the classroom to the global workplace. Xerox Management Institute presents an innovative example of combining on-site, leader-led executive development programs with web-based communication and follow-up. The Xerox leadership development program responsible for this is known as Leading the Enterprise (LTE). The target audience for LTE are Xerox senior-level managers.

LTE's objectives are to give participants a broader perspective of this fast changing environment and the industries in which Xerox operates; to give them the ability to apply strategic thinking and planning to opportunities and problems locally and across the organization; and to give them the tools to stay current with and apply technology-based solutions to sustain Xerox as a leading-edge company.

LTE uses a distance-learning on-line education network to allow participants worldwide to receive and send assignments, ask questions, obtain feedback, and communicate with other participants and facilitators. "There are distance teams from all over the world," says Lida Henderson, program manager, Xerox Management Institute. "They work on real-life issues of importance to the company and learn how to build and present a strategic business case around those issues to upper management. The key factor here is that we have integrated learning with work so that the cases are real," says Henderson. "It's very applications and hands-on oriented."

The six-month program incorporates both classrooms and computers through a series of face-to-face meetings—two to five-day meetings three times during the six-month course—and on-line communication. Within this format, each Xerox manager learns about strategic thinking, broad business issues, leadership dimensions needed for success at Xerox, and develops insight into one's own leadership ability. LTE is divided into three modules, each of which lasts approximately 4 to 10 weeks, as outlined in Figure 5–8.

The participants' ultimate goal is to present and define a strategic business case. Hence, the program's real measurement of success is the quality and novelty of the solutions offered by the participants as they think outside of their regular assignments. "Interestingly, on-line classrooms remove the hierarchy problem," says Henderson. While managers introduce themselves on-line before they begin the course, the titles don't seem to matter. In a virtual world, lower-level managers and shy students are as likely to contribute as senior managers and confident types.

## FIGURE 5–8

---

### Xerox Management Institute
### Leading The Enterprise: Three Learning Models

| Module 1 (Four Weeks): |
| --- |
| **Preparing For Self-Directed Learning And An Introduction To LTE Strategy Process** |

- Orientation to on-line education
- Meets (in person) other participants
- Develops an understanding of key steps in strategy development and business analysis tools

Introductory Participant Meeting (Five Days)

| Module 2 (Ten Weeks): Strategic Situation Analysis/Opportunity Framing |
| --- |

- Introduces a systematic approach to crafting competitive strategy
- Uses business analysis tools to understand industry structure, competitive positioning and core competencies of Xerox
- Identifies and frames key Xerox strategic issues
- Introduces how to translate strategic analysis into issues and opportunities; Goal for the participant is to integrate his/her strategy with Xerox "big picture" and future strategic directions
- Evaluates synergy between each solution and Xerox core competency

Second Participant Meeting (Five Days)

| Module 3 (Eight Weeks): Preparing The Financial Case And Presenting The Strategic Plan |
| --- |

- Uses a series of financial tools to measure the financial implications of the strategic issues including market and competitive outcomes
- Identifies critical execution factors that will affect implementation of strategy
- Develops an action plan for implementation
- Works with team to present business case

Final Participant Meeting (Two Days)

Courtesy of Xerox Corporation

---

Henderson believes there are four critical success factors in designing an on-line senior management development program. First, the program must address real business challenges within the Xerox Corporation. Participants should work on problems that can be solved within their spheres of influence. They are encouraged to find the right stakeholders, market their ideas, and push forward with implementation. This makes learning immediate and generates energy and commitment around real business issues. It encourages employees to take responsibility for their own learning and helps to promote a learning organization environment.

Second, learning must take place largely within the participant's specific business environment. Groups are brought together for face-to-face meetings periodically, but these meetings are limited to occasions where face-to-face contact is the most appropriate form of interaction, such as hearing a guest speaker or making a final presentation of a strategic plan. For the most part, learning is accomplished at the same place where day-to-day business transactions are completed.

Third, learning needs to be shared across different parts of the organization. Participants are paired with managers who have different strengths and often work in a different part of the business. This makes for a richer learning experience, where strategies that have worked in one business unit can be shared in another, and new synergies can be discovered. In addition, the on-line program encourages full participation from each team member, whether a new manager, or a 20-year veteran. This creates a leveling effect and an environment where contributions at all levels are valued.

The ultimate test of relevance for programs like Leading the Enterprise is whether it is possible to observe and measure significant behavioral change. Henderson relays that of the 125 Xerox managers who have completed Leading the Enterprise, she frequently hears anecdotal comments like, "I now have a much broader view of how my position fits into the top ten business issues facing Xerox," or "I never knew the scope of resources and research easily accessible through the Internet until I participated in the LTE program."

The payback for Xerox is now being measured at the third and fourth level of evaluation needed for a return on investment (ROI). While payback is easier to calculate in programs like LTE because participants work on real business issues, Xerox is looking for direct measures of revenue growth attributable to business solutions created during the program by participants. This evaluation process has begun and results will be shared with Xerox management during 1998. As Xerox continues to have favorable feedback from the LTE program, they are sharing their experiences with other corporations who want to incorporate an on-line and on-site learning format. Xerox's Henderson believes the key success factor for scores of corporations to emulate is the ability to involve participants in a process where they actively diagnose, discuss, and resolve actual business challenges as part of their leadership development program.

## Virtual Campus

While web-based learning is gaining momentum, the virtual campus is the next opportunity to bring a community of learners to the desktop. Let's think for a moment of how a virtual campus differs from what you and I probably experienced at our traditional college campus. The traditional campus is physical in nature, features large classes organized by semester schedules, mid-term and final examinations, and research programs that occupy a lot of faculty time and energy but are accessible only to a graduate student population.

Fast forward to the twenty-first century where corporate universities emerge as dominant educators of the workplace. In their role as educators, corporations recognize the need to develop strategies and tools for life-long learning. Hence, corporate universities are experimenting with offering a range of continuous learning opportunities that are customer-oriented, technologically advanced, content-rich, and flexible for the learner. In fact, some companies have embraced web-based learning wholeheartedly, to the point where it functions not just as a component of their corporate university, but as a company-wide learning strategy. As a result, the virtual campus has emerged as an on-line learning environment using Internet/intranet technology to provide education and information tailored to the needs of the learner. The goal is to deliver learning on demand—anywhere, anytime, and with the most appropriate delivery platform for the learner.

Oracle University, the corporate university for Oracle Corporation, has created just such a virtual campus by developing an integrated performance support center for Oracle employees and their partner organizations. The reasons for the launch of Oracle University include the tremendous growth of new products as well as a growing employee population. With a product release life cycle being relatively short, Oracle's global population of 32,000 plus employees and partner organizations must have a system so they can keep current on the range of Oracle solutions. Hence, Oracle University has become a strategic initiative to equip these teams of employees and partners to compete in the marketplace. Karen Neely Jones, founding dean of Oracle University, describes the rationale of launching Oracle University: "We realized that the skills and knowledge of Oracle's employees and partners are as strategic an asset as the products and services we offer. Thus, our decision is to create Oracle University as the single point of entry for all learning."

To accomplish the goal of a single point of entry for all learning and development, Oracle University was created to provide a wide range of product knowledge, industry knowledge, technical skills, sales methodologies, and Oracle-specific processes. This combination of skills and knowledge (training) is deployed through Oracle University's virtual campus and network of regional classrooms.

Kelly Herrick, senior director of Internal Training at Oracle University, describes how this electronic storefront works for Oracle employees, "Let's take the example of a new Oracle sales representative. This employee would have the choice of talking to a field education advisor or going to the Oracle University virtual campus to search for relevant courses by topic or going to the skills assessment function to find out about the prescribed intervention for his/her job. The employee can then take a web-based class in the virtual campus or register to attend classroom training. In the virtual campus they can also access courses, plus a wealth of reference information and computer-based instruction on Oracle history, technology, solutions, competitive environment, and industry trends. This information is captured from many sources to give the employee the necessary background data. Next, more advanced courses and workshops focus on developing sales skills, and learning Oracle processes, and methods on how to sell and support Oracle's customers. Pre- and post-test results are tracked and both employee and manager receive a 'report card.'" Oracle University's Raj Prasad, senior director at Oracle Corporation, describes the overwhelming benefit of the Oracle virtual campus as offering both practical and just-in-time learning. Prasad continues, "Oracle salespeople typically do not want to participate in training unless they can use the knowledge immediately to increase sales. Oracle University's virtual campus provides learning in various formats, but we realize that it still is not going to stick until employees identify a need for it. So what we're trying to create is a compelling toolkit that makes it easy for Oracle employees to learn at the moment they need to."

The key to the learning solutions offered by Oracle University is that they are prescriptive, meaning users identify their job role and then go through a skills assessment specific to that job. The result of this assessment helps them determine which learning interventions are recommended for the user. Figure 5–9 illustrates the Oracle University learning environment designed to deploy the optimal media for employees to meet their learning needs. For example, the virtual campus is ideally configured to handle self-study reference type information on industry needs and trends and Oracle solutions, as

**FIGURE 5–9**

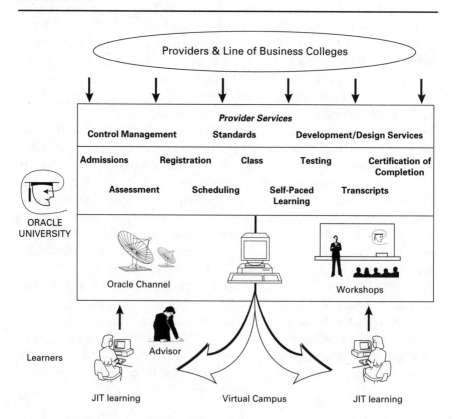

well as specific technical skill development. Additionally, regional classrooms are spread across the United States, Europe, the Middle East, and Asia to provide employees with the opportunity to practice hands-on skill building and motivational exercises. Oracle Interactive Business TV-Oracle Channel, a component of this regionally-based training, brings experts into the classroom on a mass global scale to share expertise and success stories.

The challenge of developing the virtual campus is to create an integrated learning and performance support environment so employees around the world can utilize the power of the desktop along with regional learning centers and advisors. Hence, the success of Oracle University's virtual campus is not just making instructional materials available on-line, but capturing the content of these materials electronically, at the source, so there is a seamless end-to-end process for product training. Because the shelf life of Oracle products is estimated to be between 8 to 18 months, it becomes critical that Oracle University design a system to reduce the cycle time of course development from the current time to market of six months to less than two months.

The ability to deliver on this shortened cycle time is to work with a range of content providers capturing data at the source, so Oracle University gradually reduces its dependency on traditional developers and facilitators. With the virtual campus and the range of delivery options, including the desktop, business television, and regional learning centers, subject matter expertise can be leveraged in a highly effective manner. In the past, Oracle Education had to fly someone around to various cities to give the same presentation over and over again. Now, the goal is to use the virtual campus with its variety of delivery formats—video, intranet, interactive television, and regional learning centers to provide just-in-time leaning. The result Oracle University hopes for is an accessible, customizable, and highly interactive learning solution.

## TECHNOLOGY-ASSISTED LEARNING: EXPLODING INTO THE TWENTY-FIRST CENTURY

While the surge of interest in using technology for learning has gathered momentum, an important fact remains unspoken: as more learning occurs at the desktop, at home and on the airplane, working adults are spending their own time, on weekends and in the evening, learning new skills. In fact, in the Air University and Xerox best practice examples presented in this chapter, laptops are provided as part of the registration package for the course. Rather than mandate how, when, and where participants should engage in learning, the state-of-the-art learning programs provide participants with a laptop computer/modem connection so they can make their own decisions regarding how learning fits into their already busy personal and professional lives.

We see this as a leading trend that other corporate universities will follow; both hardware and software tools will increasingly be included in the corporate university enrollment package and budget. With employers placing a premium on education and training as a way to ensure that professionals maintain their skill level, "life-long learning" needs to be as flexible, accessible, and as hassle-free as possible.

In their role as learning laboratories, corporate universities are getting an important message across to employees: that they are committed to experimenting with new ways for employees to learn, thus rendering the traditional model of once-a-week, classroom-led training ineffective in meeting the needs of corporate America. We believe distance learning is here to stay rather than a niche delivery mechanism for the busy technical professional. Why? The first and most important reason is increased Internet access. Lehman Brothers Technology Group estimates the number of end users with Internet access is expected to reach 190 million by the year 2000, up from only 25 million in 1995. With well-equipped personal computers now priced under $2,000, the Internet is rapidly changing the way busy professionals research, work, communicate, and learn.

Secondly, as we saw in Chapter 1, the shelf-life of knowledge is growing shorter across all professions, not just the technical ones, and this creates demand for life-long learning. The traditional concept of completing one's education by the age of 22 or 24 is over. According to the National Center for Education Statistics, there are over 50 million working adults pursuing continuing education, which represents a larger student body than those in grades K–12.

Finally, the Bureau of Labor Statistics projects that the growth rate in jobs between 1994 and the year 2005 will be greatest for those categories that require at least an associate degree. Jobs requiring a master's degree will grow fastest (at the rate of 28 percent), followed closely by those requiring a bachelor's degree (27 percent) and an associate's degree (24 percent). This provides us with statistical evidence for what we already know—we are operating in a knowledge-based economy where a highly skilled work force is required to assume broader roles and demonstrate deeper business skills. The goal of all these learning experiments is nothing short of institutionalizing a spirit of continuous learning throughout the entire value chain.

These forces are driving corporations to increasingly experiment with technology to educate their workforces. With the introduction of the Internet and corporate intranets, learning can be done at a time and place of one's own choosing. The Internet and intranet allow employees the opportunity to review courses, enroll in them, take a test and give feedback on the entire experience, all with the click of their mouse. This "real-time" experience enables education and training to go where the customer is and offer on-demand learning, but that's not all. Web-based learning also presents the opportunity to embed learning into work so employees learn as they interact with their team members, customers, suppliers and the organization as a whole. The goal is to make learning part of everyone's ordinary workday. These corporate university learning laboratories are allowing learning to become much more of a self-service operation, available to everyone, not just the heroic few who will learn at any cost.

The next two chapters examine continuous learning on another level—the collective learning of the entire organization. Chapter 6 looks at how various companies collectively learn by forgoing partnerships with suppliers, wholesalers, dealers and distributors, and institutions of higher education. Finally, Chapter 7 presents the emerging question of the moment: are corporate universities an opportunity or a threat to higher education?

*Chapter Six*

# Outreach: Forging Partnerships with Suppliers, Customers, and Institutions of Higher Education

*"Motorola no longer wants to hire engineers with a four-year degree. Instead, we want our employees to have a 40-year degree."*

—Christopher Galvin, president
and CEO, Motorola

## WHY PARTNER WITH VALUE CHAIN PARTICIPANTS?

Intense global competition is causing a profound reconfiguration of the marketplace. As more products are perceived to be at parity by customers, a phenomenon known in the automotive industry as *product convergence*, there is increasingly less room for companies to compete on tangible grounds. The only remaining and viable way for a firm to differentiate itself from its rivals is by focusing on intangibles, that is, the quality of the human systems and processes behind its products and services.

This new goal of carving out competitive advantage through a focus on human systems, rather than through relatively easier to achieve product or service enhancements, requires a fundamental change in a company's way of thinking. Companies can no longer think of themselves as self-contained entities, but rather as parts of systems whose links consist of the organization's relationships with suppliers, customers, and even the educational institutions that supply them with new hires. A company's efforts to improve the quality of its service and the quality of its people must take into consideration the entire system, not just the individual, isolated components. This may mean taking the initiative to develop training for the employees of customers; it may mean looking at the company's suppliers as partners rather than adversaries; it may mean proactively designing, developing, and marketing training to dealers and wholesalers; and finally, this thinking extends to building proactive alliances with institutions of higher education.

In other words, the ability to enter into and sustain partnerships is coming to the fore as a key aspect of competitiveness. The ingredients that make for successful partnerships mirror those present in a good marriage: a willingness to participate whole-heartedly, mutual trust, understanding, open communication, respect, and a commitment to continuously improve the relationship.

The idea of a company building partnerships with those parties with whom it deals in order to seek improvements in quality and productivity is really not new at all. Japanese companies routinely develop interlocking partnerships with suppliers, a process known in Japan as *kiretsu*. United States companies often work together informally with preferred suppliers, dealers, and customers. What is new is that the companies interviewed for this book have, in effect, formalized what naturally happens when a company and its value chain participants work together successfully on an informal basis. A number of corporate universities are proving a natural and effective locus for building just the sort of array of partnerships with suppliers, customers, dealers, and wholesalers necessary to improve overall competitiveness. They find that joining with members of their systems in a quest for improvement within the corporate university framework can give their relationships the kind of emphasis, energy, and purpose that distinguishes an authentic partnership. The corporate university provides an effective vehicle for encouraging such relationships because it gives companies a way to involve targeted outsiders in a sustained joint pursuit of quality improvement and continuous learning.

There is another reason companies are entering into these partnerships, namely to have the entire employee/customer/supply chain collectively learn the company's quality vision and the types of skills, knowledge, and competencies that all the links in the chain must have to successfully perform their jobs. The companies profiled in this book are increasingly engaging in a dialogue with their product suppliers, customers, and educational suppliers to ensure these value chain participants have the necessary skills and knowledge for success in the global marketplace. Companies believe this type of collective learning is vitally important to sustain their competitive advantage in this decade and the next. The *Annual Survey of Corporate University Future Directions* found a definite trend towards leading corporate universities providing special training programs for suppliers and key members of a company's value chain to learn specific skills in the areas of quality, reliability, cycle time reduction, and customer service. Companies that will be successful in creating learning organizations realize that everyone involved in bringing a product or service to market must understand the company's shared vision and, most importantly, how to realize this vision in the marketplace.

The impetus behind partnering with members of a company's value chain is the need to ensure that each link in the customer/supplier/dealer/wholesaler chain can successfully perform their job. This is especially important given the broadening of the scope and responsibilities of many businesses. As Bill Bailey, manager of Harley-Davidson University, points out, "We now have to train our dealers in how to manage and sell a myriad of new lines of business such as MotorClothes®, parts, and accessories, all businesses that Harley-Davidson has entered during the last five years." Figure 6–1 shows the various links between a company and its customers, suppliers, dealers, wholesalers, and traditional institutions of higher education. We saw in Chapter 5 how Ford Motor Company is using technology to educate its dealers. Increasingly, companies like Harley-Davidson, Anheuser-Busch, and United Healthcare are also recognizing that they have to impact their entire system to prepare their value chain to deliver exceptional customer service.

Firms are also experimenting with training the value chain for another reason: to provide a new source of revenue for their corporate university. As corporate universities face the mandate to

FIGURE 6–1

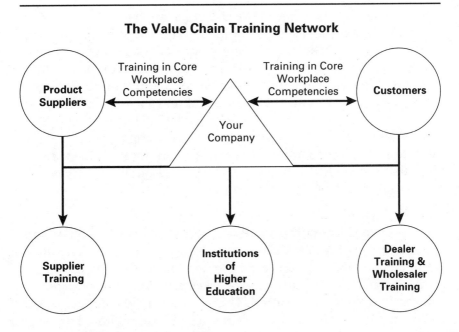

**The Value Chain Training Network**

© 1997 Corporate University Xchange, Inc.

become self-funded, they are exploring licensing their state-of-the-art training programs to their value chain and they are using these funds to supplement their corporate education budget. Licensing programs to suppliers and customers have become a key source of revenue for corporate universities intent on being self-funded organizations. For example, Motorola University in 1996 received a full 16 percent of its funding from direct charges to outsiders. Although the majority (74 percent) of corporate universities still do *not* receive funding from customer or supplier tuition, our survey showed that the number that do is up significantly from a year ago (25 percent versus 16 percent in a similar survey conducted in 1996). Also, 38 percent of corporate universities we studied expect their income from customer/supplier training to increase by the year 2000, indicating that some corporate universities not currently offering customer/supplier training plan on doing so.

## Partnering with Suppliers

The partnership-building mindset can also enhance the way that an organization manages its suppliers. The old style relationship between companies and suppliers was characterized by arm's length dealings and little involvement. American companies have watched Japanese companies create a competitive edge through a series of alliances with their suppliers and customers and have come to realize that their adversarial relationship with suppliers has hindered them. Now, more and more companies are forging long-term alliances with suppliers and working with them to ensure that both sides embrace the same set of quality practices. Often, this requires supplier training.

**Lord Corporation's partnering goal: Accreditation of supplier and distributor training.** Lord Corporation is a diversified, technology-based company employing more than 1,800 people who design, manufacture, and market a wide range of products for mechanical motion control. This privately held company, headquartered in North Carolina, with sales of $336 million, has seven sites within the United States, as well as international offices. In 1994, it created the Lord Institute for Technical and Management Training to give employees and suppliers the opportunity to learn in a manufacturing setting. The Lord Institute is based in Erie, Pennsylvania, where Lord's Mechanical Products Division is located.

Through a partnership with the Erie County Technical Institute and Pennsylvania Department of Education private school licensure, the Lord Institute has extended its in-house training into certifications and degrees for its suppliers and distributors. This is a good example of a corporate university forming a learning alliance with an outside learning institution to train external segments of the company's value chain. With the encouragement and support of the Northwest Pennsylvania Technical Institute (NPTI), chartered as a community college in 1991 by the state of Pennsylvania, the Lord Institute applied for and received state licensure as an educational institution. This enables Lord to train suppliers and distributors cost effectively and to use the revenue from this training to offer Lord employees a richer employee development program.

In 1994, Lord Institute was granted its private school license by the state of Pennsylvania after an 18-month application process. This process involved writing a curriculum so it conformed to state guidelines, making sure classrooms were designed to conform to the accessibility requirements of the state, and providing the resumes of instructors to the licensing board. The initial licensing fee was $2,500 and it must be renewed every two years. With state licensure, the Lord Institute was able to create certificate programs with educational credits in manufacturing, management, and sales technologies that encompassed many of Lord's existing training programs.

"We were an anomaly and didn't fit the world of the state education licensing board, so we had to convince them that we could provide training that would contribute to the economic development of the region," says Debra Douglass, director of the Lord Institute. "We wanted this licensure as a seal of approval and a measure of our credibility. Once we had it, NPTI could refer people who needed the types of programs we provide, which include many of our distributors and suppliers. At the same time, we want access to additional funding to supplement our training budget."

NPTI, a virtual education institution chartered in 1991 as a Pennsylvania Community College, gets state and county funding and support from the businesses in the area. It contracts with area colleges, universities, and licensed trade schools to offer a curriculum that is shaped and driven by its 700 customers—a variety of companies in a seven-county area of Northwest Pennsylvania. NPTI approved some Lord Institute courses as fitting the needs of the community. When Lord Institute has slots open in classes being offered to Lord employees, it publicizes these courses to the community through NPTI, area newspapers, its web page, and to those distributors and suppliers that Lord thinks will benefit from the training. NPTI pays Lord Institute a fixed price as a provider for each student enrolled in the course, NPTI then bills the employer of the student. For those students who come from outside Lord, Lord recovers the full cost of tuition from NPTI, thus supplementing its internal training budget. A little over a third of Lord Institute's budget is received from funding channeled through NPTI.

Distributors, for example, have asked Lord Institute to provide training in customer service, telephone skills, and goal-setting. Suppliers have asked for and are receiving training in meeting Lord's rigorous quality standards. Lord is continuing to develop curricula to meet new needs identified by suppliers and distributors.

"This is a way for us to upgrade our employee training programs and to be good corporate citizens at the same time," Douglass says. "We can bring in experts in those areas where only a few of our employees need training. This saves us having to send our people away for the course and at the same time offer it to other companies in the area that need it. Students who take the course get college credit from NPTI and can work toward certificates or degrees. While our main focus is still Lord employees, this arrangement also benefits us by having people in our classes who have other perspectives. We expand our employees' thinking by exposing them to other points of view."

"NPTI is unique in its design and its philosophy," says Institute President John Nesbit. "We are not a traditional education institution. We have no faculty, no buildings, no residence halls, or library. We believe our model for educational delivery is more efficient and effective. Many companies have the knowledge and expertise that higher education doesn't have. By buying educational courses as a cooperative for our customers, NPTI is able to give local industry the courses it really needs."

Lord Institute is exploring partnership arrangements with community colleges in some of its other seven sites throughout the United States. Lord Institute's partnership with NPTI illustrates one creative way to train suppliers and distributors, enrich the employee development program for Lord's own employees, be a good corporate citizen of the community—and, importantly, supplement funding for internal training.

### Extending Customer Training to Dealers and Wholesalers

The progressive companies profiled here have also developed training under the university umbrella for their customers, the client companies who sell their products. Initially, many customer training programs started as a way to train a customer in how to use the company's products, but over time the concept of customer training has broadened to include training customers in how to run more successful and profitable businesses. What better way to increase brand loyalty than by helping customers build more profitable business operations?

**Harley-Davidson: Continuous learning for the dealer network.** The phenomenal growth of Harley-Davidson has been a double-edged sword for Bill Bailey, manager of Harley-Davidson Worldwide Training. Harley-Davidson University is part of Harley-Davidson Worldwide Training, which is responsible for developing training programs for 600 domestic dealers, corporate-owned subsidiaries in the United Kingdom, Japan, Germany, France, and the Netherlands, plus a network of more than 300 dealers and distributors throughout the rest of the world. What's more, products carrying the venerable name now go beyond motorcycles to include MotorClothes®, accessories, and collectibles. "Strategically, we're doing things we've never done before as a company," says Daniel Snell, director of Customer Service, Harley-Davidson Motor Company. "That means training plays a much more important role in developing a shared understanding among our dealers of what it takes to build a successful global organization. Essentially, we focus on improving the performance of the dealer operation—which means finding the business problem and facilitating change."

The broad scope of training needs for dealer principals, managers, and employees has led to a multi-pronged approach to continuous learning that combines formal course offerings, a library of self-study learning opportunities, an intranet training site called HDNet, and an annual conference, known as Dealer Operation Training Conference and Expo, to share best practices with Harley-Davidson dealers from around the world. The conference has grown from 475 attendees in 1991 to over 1,400 attendees in 1997. The conference combines formal learning programs in ten areas ranging from facility management to marketing and people management (see Figure 6–2).

"The idea behind the conference is to provide our dealers with a fun, relaxed learning environment where they can learn from top business gurus as well as share valuable lessons among themselves in how to build a successful dealership," says Bailey.

**FIGURE 6-2**

---

### Generations of Commitment

### Dealer Operations Training
### Conference & Expo

| | |
|---|---|
| Facility Management | People Management |
| Financial Management | Personal Enrichment |
| Inventory Systems | Sales |
| Marketing | Service Operations |
| MotorClothes & Collectibles | Parts & Accessories |

Courtesy of Harley Davidson University

Over the past six years, the Dealer Operations segment of Harley-Davidson University (HDU) has evolved from offering four courses in the areas of general business management for dealer principals to developing an integrated curriculum offering hard business literacy skills such as: dealer operation, financial analysis, inventory control, and smart buying practices, as well as "softer" skills in customer service, negotiation, and team building.

This combination of formal and informal learning targets every level of the dealer network from the dealer principal to the sales, service, and middle manager. Additionally, all these new offerings have been "Harleyized" to reflect the real life business challenges that Harley dealers face everyday. Bailey says Harley-Davidson

University's structure has three main tracks. The service track is for the technician and centers around the motorcycle itself; the sales track covers marketing, merchandising, departmental management and staffing issues; the third track, dealer operations, "is where we really feel the pain today," says Bailey. "As our business changes so fast, some of our dealers now manage restaurants and Harley cafes and clothing stores in addition to selling and servicing motorcycles. As one dealer said to me, 'Yes we're in the motorcycle business but once someone visits a few dealerships, they are reminded of mini-malls—complete with parts, accessories, clothing, shoes, boots, children's toys, and even juke boxes.' So these dealers need to understand not only how to manage the hard parts inventory but also the clothing, merchandise, and collectibles side of their business."

When Harley-Davidson University begins its developmental efforts each year, four key questions are addressed:

- What's in it for the dealers?
- How will this learning add value to the dealers' business today and in the future?
- Does the learning improve business operations?
- Can a dealer get something useful from the university to improve the business?

These four questions guide Harley-Davidson University in deciding what types of formal training programs to develop, as well as what experts to involve in the annual conference. It has also led to offering a broader range of learning tools. For example, Bailey estimates that a growing number of Harley dealers have a web page, but many more are trying to develop one and get involved in the Internet. Consequently, Harley-Davidson University developed a toolkit for dealers in how to launch, maintain, and use a web site as a market research tool. In addition, the Harley-Davidson University intranet, HDNet, is being expanded to become a communications link between Harley-Davidson and its dealers, providing information on warranties and financial reporting guidelines.

The four questions have also focused Harley-Davidson University on providing learning that solves a business need. Bailey continues, "It's our job to find the business problems and help facili-

tate change and improvement." One of the ways Harley-Davidson
Motor Company does this is through the dealer advisory council,
a group of ten dealers that are elected by dealer representatives
within the territories to act as the link between the dealer network
and Harley-Davidson. Harley-Davidson Worldwide Training
Group works with these dealers to keep tuned into their critical
business issues as a way to enhance and revise Harley-Davidson
University. "We're constantly asking our dealers, 'What's working? What do we need to add and at what level?'" says Bailey.

For example, the Dealer Operations Training has an entire program on "Best Practices in Managing MotorClothes® Inventory,"
which showcases several Harley-Davidson dealers as best practice
case studies in inventory management and is facilitated by an out-
sider charged with drawing out the best practices from the dealer
as well as conference participants.

Harley-Davidson's strong training program for its dealers holds
two important lessons for other manufacturers with a dealer network. First, manufacturers should recognize that the dealer network is the frontline to a manufacturer business. Dealers, like all
managers, must be trained in both analytical as well as customer
service skills to successfully run their operations. Just as manufacturers invest training dollars to enhance the skill sets of all their
internal employees, they must also extend this continuous learning mindset to the entire dealer operation and go beyond training
just the dealer principal to training the vast numbers of middle
managers in the sales, service, and parts departments. Secondly,
manufacturers should build into dealer training an array of continuous learning tools that go beyond classroom-based programs
to web site training, self-study courses, and conference-type
events to encourage global sharing of best practices. Finally, Bailey
adds, "Dealers want training programs which will help them immediately improve their businesses. We never lose sight of our
goal: to be the business partner for every Harley-Davidson dealer
worldwide."

**The Busch Learning Center: Performance enablers for
Anheuser-Busch.** While Harley-Davidson has focused its resources on training the dealer network, Anheuser-Busch has
developed Busch Learning Center, a comprehensive learning

resource center supporting its sales network of 34,000 wholesale employees and a field sales force of 500. The evolution of Busch Learning Center started with one strong need: to broaden the skills, knowledge base, and competencies of this sales network in order to increase market share. The process of selling beer has become much more sophisticated with a growing share sold "off-premises" to retailers rather than on-premises to taverns and restaurants. Hence, the emergence and importance of the retail category manager in the selling process. This category manager is demanding more quantitative and analytical skills from the Anheuser-Busch sales team, as well as suggestions for increasing sales and reducing costs.

During 1996, the Anheuser-Busch Business Development Group (the group responsible for the design and launch of the Busch Learning Center) decided to gather research data from their "customers"—the wholesalers and field sales force—on the types of knowledge, skills, and competencies required to meet the increased demands of retailers. The survey uncovered employee training as the second key business challenge facing the sales network, after increased competition from conventional competitors and the grass-roots efforts of microbreweries. The survey also tapped into another wholesaler need: to share best practices among wholesalers. David Vaughn, Director of Busch Learning Center, says, "It turns out one of our biggest challenges was not simply to provide more training to the wholesalers, but rather to access information and best practices from the wholesalers and share this with the entire sales network in order to improve job performance."

Vaughn has addressed this communications need by creating an elaborate toolkit of marketing vehicles to share best practices via 30 minute drive-time audiotapes, e-mail updates, video tapes, 15-minute segments on Busch Satellite Network, and an intranet site. Essentially, Vaughn is using the power of Anheuser-Busch consumer marketing to communicate the vision of continuous learning and improvement.

This emphasis on performance improvement has moved the Busch Learning Center training from its previous "cafeteria-style approach" to a customer-driven curriculum. As Vaughn explains, the mission of Busch Learning Center "is to provide the necessary training, consultation, and tools to dramatically improve the knowledge, skills, and performance of our business partners—the network of 34,000 wholesaler employees and field sales staff."

Vaughn firmly believes that mass training activity-based solutions simply will not deliver improvements in job performance; simply providing "more of the same" in terms of training and manuals will likely decrease performance. Vaughn launched Busch Learning Center with much the same vision as Harley-Davidson University: to provide an integrated curriculum for every position in the sales network from principal and general manager, to department manager and route sales representative. Each curriculum spells out a set of core and elective courses necessary to achieve performance goals.

According to Vaughn, the survey results demonstrated just how dramatically the beer business has changed over the last five years. Bill Lazzerini, president of Advanced Beverage, a Bakersfield, California beer wholesaling company, is hopeful about Anheuser-Busch's learning initiatives: "We need to understand how we can work with the retailer in partnership to create increased market share. Busch Learning Center is our vehicle to train the wholesaler operation in relationship-based selling." In order to accomplish this goal, Busch Learning Center has created a virtual university offering a wide range of learning solutions to major job families in a wholesaler operation.

The challenge of developing the curriculum for Busch Learning Center was significant: how to leverage a rather small training department—composed of 30 professionals—to service a potential audience of 34,000 wholesalers and 500 Anheuser-Busch field sales employees. The virtual university (Figure 6–3) has become the solution offering a range of leader-led classroom seminars, computer-based training programs, web-based training solutions, home study materials, as well as access to Busch Satellite Network, a satellite network broadcasting approximately three hours a week of short training segments on such topics as merchandising, coaching, and inventory control. Eventually Busch Learning Center wants to offer college-level courses as well as home study courses via Busch Satellite Network to the entire wholesaler employee population, from the wholesaler principal to his children and grandchildren. The goal is clearly to use Busch Learning Center as a competitive advantage and vehicle for building brand preference in the marketplace.

## FIGURE 6–3

| | Place | |
|---|---|---|
| **Busch Learning Center**<br><br>**Virtual University** <br><br>Time | *Same Place Same Time*<br><br>**Classroom Session<br>Seminars<br>Professional Conferences<br>Business Unit Meetings** | *Same Time Different Place*<br><br>**Busch Satellite Network<br>Help Desk** |
| | *Different Time Same Place*<br><br>**Computer Based Training<br>Laboratory<br>Resource Library** | *Different Time Different Place*<br><br>**Busch Satellite Network<br>Video Library<br>BLC Bulletin Board<br>Computer Based Training..<br>Web Based Training<br>Audio Tapes<br>Publications** |

Courtesy of Busch Learning Center

For the future, the Busch Learning Center is also planning a new retailer training curriculum to teach the different business literacy skills needed by retailers. "Retailers are dealing with aspects of influencing consumer decisions that are different from wholesalers influencing retailer decisions, or employees influencing wholesaler decisions," Vaughn notes.

### Building Alliances with Institutions of Higher Education

The advent of the corporate university has redefined the relationship between business and education. As Christopher Galvin, president and CEO of Motorola, said to a recent gathering of The American Society of Engineering Education, "Motorola no longer wants to hire engineers with a four year degree. Instead, we want our employees to have a 40 year degree." An employee now must expect to continually reinvent his/her knowledge base. Increasingly, learning and work are becoming the same thing and they are happening in the workplace rather than in the classroom.

As the pace of change increases with the introduction of deregulation, competitive pressures and technological advances, corporations will increasingly become the "chief educators" of the workforce.

Because the job of continuously updating an employee's knowledge base is so large, corporate universities are joining forces with conventional universities and merging the goals of the individual employee, the corporation, and the educational institution into one mutually beneficial three-way partnership. While the business community has traditionally invested significant sums of money in the local schools and universities, much of this investment has been piecemeal. Companies have recruited college graduates, depended on higher education to carry out basic research, reimbursed employees for college tuition, and sent managers to university-run executive education open enrollment programs. While these piecemeal efforts have endured, business has become frustrated by its inability to increase on-the-job performance in the workplace.

The new partnership between business and higher education is, by contrast, proactively involved in making sure the skill needs of tomorrow's workforce are met. For example, rather than simply giving a list of requirements to higher education, businesses are now spelling out the specific skills, knowledge, and competencies needed for success in an industry and in the process creating joint, accredited degree programs.

We have developed a model for how corporations can build these state-of-the-art learning partnerships, with lessons in how various companies have entered into and sustained these alliances.

## A FRAMEWORK FOR BUILDING A CORPORATE/COLLEGE PARTNERSHIP

The basic process for building an alliance with an institution of higher education is shown in Figure 6–4.

The key starting point is for both the corporate university and

## FIGURE 6–4

### A Framework for Building Corporate/College Partnerships

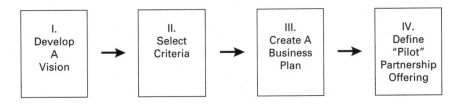

© 1997 Corporate University Xchange, Inc.

the institution of higher education to openly discuss and develop a shared vision for the alliance. In successful collaborative partnerships no one organization dominates the effort or defines the goals and outcomes unilaterally. Instead, both sides take the time to develop a shared vision of how a successful partnership operates in terms of expectations, processes, outcomes, and support systems. Creating this type of shared vision usually starts with a review of the strategic rationale for creating the alliance and an articulation of the various selection criteria in choosing the learning partner. While specific selection criteria differ by institution, the following list of criteria is relatively comprehensive, compiled by interviews with scores of corporate university deans, and can be used as a guide to help articulate specific criteria for selecting a learning partner. These criteria include:

1. Shared mindset where customer service, innovation, and continuous improvement are paramount to success.
2. Clear expectations for setting learning objectives and developing courses.
3. Flexibility and responsiveness in building a corporate/ college alliance. (This may include "teaching on-site," sharing libraries, laboratories or equipment.)
4. Complementary needs and goals. This may range from funding joint research to developing customized executive education programs.

5. Reputation and prestige of the educational institution.
6. Ability to collaboratively develop a clear path of study leading to a "new" accredited degree program.
7. Openness to experimenting with technologies to accelerate learning.
8. Ownership rights in intellectual property clearly delineated at the onset of the partnership.
9. Financial and non-financial measures carefully spelled out in advance and agreed to by the key players.
10. An infrastructure that is open to experimentation (for example, having the corporation assign a full-time equivalent to the academic institution to work on partnership matters).
11. Global education capabilities and network.
12. Commitment to building an open dialogue and continually renewing the partnership with fresh thinking.

Interestingly, when our *Annual Survey of Corporate University Future Directions* asked 100 corporate university deans to rank these criteria from most important to least important in their selection process, 68 percent of our sample cited flexibility as the most important criterion in building a corporate/college partnership (see Figure 6–5). Amazingly, the prestige of the academic partner or the "Ivy League Factor," ranked last on this list of criteria. Our survey reinforces the interest among corporate university deans to look outside traditional academic circles to locate flexible and responsive learning partners. The United Healthcare case study that follows later in this chapter even compares the process of selecting an academic partner to one used in choosing an advertising agency.

Once the vision is developed and the academic partner chosen, the next step is to develop a business plan that outlines the goals, strategies, and implementation methods needed to achieve the shared vision. If the business/education partnership is to be successful it must directly affect critical business issues important to each partner. Developing a successful partnership also requires developing a shared vocabulary and sense of trust among stakeholders who have not worked together in the past. The language, approaches to problems, and ways of solving problems differ be-

**FIGURE 6-5**

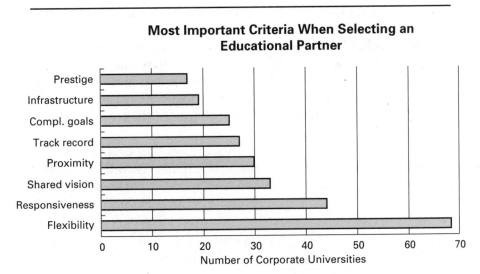

## Most Important Criteria When Selecting an Educational Partner

Source: Annual Survey of Corporate University Future Directions
© 1997 Corporate University Xchange, Inc.

tween business people and educators. If business people are to communicate with educators, each needs to learn the other's language and understand the other's perspectives.

While we have stressed a model in which the company is the customer and the educational community the supplier, there should be—as in any good customer-supplier association—a collaborative effort to achieve common goals. A clearly articulated business plan functions as the strategic document detailing the key goals, cost, timing, selection of team players, and lead champion for the project.

Finally, once the planning has been completed, the corporate university dean and academic partner are ready to define the pilot offering or offerings of the partnership. This can range from offering a degree program on-site at the corporate university to designing an entirely new educational degree program targeted for an industry. In designing this new offering, what's important here is to rethink the basics—including curriculum content, the frequency of changing this content, teaching methods, and the criteria for awarding credit. The emphasis should be on creating a dynamic curriculum, one tied to the strategic issues the organization grapples with each day.

The familiar excuse—"It's the way we've always done things"—must be changed to recognize that the educational process must focus less on the adult lecturer and more on the student learner. This shift in mindset will foster increased responsibility on the part of learners to take charge of their own learning and hence, their careers.

Based upon our interviews with scores of corporate university deans and deans of graduate business schools, as well as continuing education, we have identified four types of corporate/college partnerships as best practice examples. These include: the development of customized executive educational programs, the creation of customized degree programs, the formation of a learning partner consortium and finally, in some cases, actual accreditation of the corporate university.

## *Customize Executive Educational Programs*

Customized executive education programs serve the needs of both business and education. For companies, they meet the need to infuse the curriculum with their own corporate culture, use company-specific case studies, and emphasize a common language for jobs across the organization.

For universities, they bring in large amounts of revenue. The growth of MBA programs in general has been phenomenal. Charles Hickman, director of Special Projects at the AACSB—The International Association For Management Education—estimates that there are now 94,000 MBA programs in the United States, a growth rate of 33 percent since 1975. The range of executive education programs—from short seminars to full-fledged executive MBA offerings—bring universities approximately $3 billion a year.[1] In fact, it is the customized executive education programs that are growing far faster than the open enrollment segment. Albert Vicere, associate dean for Executive Education at Pennsylvania State University's Smeal College of Business Administration, estimates that of the $3 billion American companies spend each year on university-delivered executive education programs, customized offerings now account for about 40 percent and are growing much faster than the open-enrollment segment.[2]

**Whirlpool Brandywine Creek Performance Centre.** Whirlpool Corporation is one company that has proved the value of developing a relationship with several leading business schools in order to meet their unique needs. In 1986, when David Whitwam was appointed chairman of Whirlpool Corporation, the firm was mainly a North America-based appliance manufacturer. In 1988 Whirlpool shut down its corporate training center, moving sales and leadership training into the organization. Then in 1989 Whirlpool purchased the appliance division of Phillips, N.V., which did business in Europe, Asia, and parts of Latin America. Following that acquisition, Whirlpool held a global conference in Montreux, Switzerland to review the implications of the recent purchase. Coming out of that conference, says Kent Price, director of Training and Education Development, "were a number of what we now call 'One Company Initiatives,' major initiatives we felt would drive Whirlpool forward as a global company. One of those talked about was the development and strategic management of our corporation's talent pool." From the One Company Challenge eventually came the training and education strategy, which mandated the launch of the Brandywine Creek Performance Centre, the strategic umbrella for all corporate education and development of Whirlpool employees. The mission from David Whitwam was clear: build a global training and education strategy as a vehicle to communicate the company's strategic vision, cultivate current and future leaders, develop core business competencies to win in a global marketplace, and encourage continuous improvement of all company-wide processes.

Price took this mandate and decided that what was needed to carry it out was to forge learning alliances with three world-class university partners: Indiana University, University of Michigan, and INSEAD in France. Price considered many options in meeting this challenge from the chairman, and ultimately decided that the strategic umbrella of global training and education was indeed a core competency of Whirlpool, while the design and delivery were not and could be outsourced. The solution for Whirlpool was to create a consortium of leading business schools. As Price says,

"Rather than going to a host of independent training vendors, we decided to forge an alliance with a network of universities offering us a global expertise and a research capability to strategically think through the changes affecting our industry and assist us in developing customized programs to meet our unique business needs."

Price set out to develop a set of selection criteria for choosing the university partners. First, he thought about what he wanted to accomplish with the partnership. For Whirlpool, the major consideration was the ability to design, develop, and deliver world-class training programs without creating a large internal staff. There were also other important considerations, such as the creation of a breadth of resources to address a wide variety of organizational developmental challenges, the need for flexibility and responsiveness on the part of the universities to rapidly address changing organizational learning requirements, and, importantly, the ability to offer global learning solutions. Price adds, "We could not work with a university that has a long drawn-out process for working with corporations. Rather, universities must listen to the needs of corporate customers and then quickly marshall the resources to solve the learning requirement."

While Whirlpool did consider other business schools, over time it had developed a good relationship with Michigan and Indiana, primarily through on-campus recruiting and Whirlpool Foundation grants. The Phillips acquisition ushered INSEAD into the equation, and this gave Whirlpool a strong Euro-Asian educational center. Ultimately, Indiana University, University of Michigan, and INSEAD were selected as the learning partners and they have helped with all aspects of Whirlpool executive development, from consulting, research, and custom design of courses, to creating student internships and on-campus recruiting.

One issue that came up in the process of developing this network of learning alliances was the control of intellectual properties as an outgrowth of the learning alliance. While all three universities signed confidentiality agreements, this proved to be only the first step. The second important step was the creation of a creative assets agreement, which allows the universities and Whirlpool rights and protection to utilize certain models that the universities create for Whirlpool, or if they created them for another purpose, Whirlpool reserves the right to use the model with the university's permission. "Over time, we want to use these models for a profit," says Price. For example, certain customers might someday want to take management courses. At present, Whirlpool Brandywine Creek Performance Centre does not offer its executive education programs to outsiders, but it is something Whirlpool is considering over the next two to three years. The output of these university alliances has resulted in the development of customized management development programs in the areas of economic value added and project management.

What advice does Price have for entering into these learning alliances with university business schools? "From Whirlpool's perspective there was no real problem in creating the alliances, but where the problem arises is between the universities," adds Price. For example, while Whirlpool works with one university at a time in the design and development of a management training program, the true vision is to take the best of what each university has to offer at different points in the design, development, and delivery process.

While University of Michigan and INSEAD professors worked with Brandywine to develop a "World Class Manufacturing Program," that has unfortunately been the exception rather than the norm for the partnership. Price believes the reason for this hesitancy lies with various faculty members from different schools who often find it difficult to work together. Of the 30 programs Whirlpool has developed with these three universities, only four have used more than one university partner. This is the direction that Whirlpool wants to go: create a network of university partners and use the creative resources and energy from the entire network to design and develop new training programs.

One of the biggest benefits universities can offer corporations is the ability to help in the early stages of developing a new strategy. As Price says, "When we started working with INSEAD, we had little expertise and experience in dealing with Asia. We had a small internal group called the Whirlpool Overseas Corporation, but we just sold the products through independent reps in Asia. INSEAD helped us in developing a new learning strategy which focused our efforts on educating senior Whirlpool managers on how to deal effectively with joint venture agreements in Asia."

Another example is that Whirlpool is currently working with Indiana University to create a new training program on economic value-added (EVA). The new training program will be targeted to mid-level and senior managers so they can apply EVA principles to business decisions.

Price forecasts a dramatic increase in the number of customized executive education programs managed by a carefully selected network of university partners. The reason is that executive and leadership development are increasingly being viewed as key levers for strategic change rather than a series of disconnected programs and initiatives. As such, generic programs are becoming less appropriate as corporations demand executive development programs that support their strategic objectives and reflect their vision.

Price offers guidance for those thinking of forming a corporate/college partnership: first consider where your business is evolving over time and select the best learning partner to help you achieve your business results. "We know over time, that we wanted the Whirlpool/university partnerships to help us educate more people more cost effectively than we could do on our own, provide us with specialized global expertise we clearly did not have as a training organization (that is, training on product introductions in the Asian marketplace), and finally, customize the executive development program with Whirlpool-specific case studies."

## *Launch a New Accredited Degree Program*

Many of the companies profiled in this book realize they need to take radical steps in preparing their work force. Sometimes this radical step actually leads to creating a new degree program. David Sprague, director of the Center for Professional Excellence in Central Michigan University's College of Extended Learning (one of the colleges that has built a strong alliance with local business) believes the concept of "customized education" will gradually replace straight tuition reimbursement among quality-driven companies.

This concept of customized education refers to the alliances corporations make with colleges and universities to build a customized training curriculum for specific job categories. These customized training programs are eligible for college accreditation while also meeting the requirements for workplace competencies outlined by the corporation.

Customized degree programs are growing in interest as organizations reach a startling conclusion: many universities are not preparing employees with the skills, competencies, and knowledge to work successfully in a growing number of career paths. Companies have found that the ability to offer training that is eligible for college credits offers benefits for both the employee and the company. For many employees, such training is often their first encounter with college-level work. Furthermore, the companies who offer training eligible for college credit are often viewed by prospective employees as more desirable places to work, and hence these companies become premier employers within an industry. The real motivation, according to John Craig Eaton, CEO of T. Eaton Company, a large retailer in Canada, is to produce the best employees possible: "Retailing represents 30 percent of Canada's gross national product, 1.4 million jobs, and an annual Canadian payroll of $22.2 billion dollars. But with all this there is no formal set of courses focused on the unique set of skills needed to be successful in retail selling and management. We changed this by forming the Eaton/Ryerson Polytechnic University partnership, leading to an associate degree in retail management."

**T. Eaton Company and Ryerson Polytechnic University.** The partnership between T. Eaton Company and Ryerson Polytechnic University is one example of customized education in the form of a degree program. T. Eaton Company believes that delivering exceptional customer service involves a discrete set of skills in retail marketing, communications, information systems management, and retail management. A partnership in building a degree program to meet these needs seemed to be the perfect solution. "We actively sought an educational partner who understood our vision, was flexible in wanting to work with industry, and also had a strong desire to create a professional program in retail management," says Jim Chestnutt, general manager of the Eaton School of Retailing.

Before 1995, there was no business degree with a retail and services major in Canada, although the University of Alberta has recently approved one. In recent years, though, there has been a growing academic interest in serving the needs of the retail and services sector. The Center for Retailing at the University of Florida, the European Institute of Retail and Services Studies at Einhoven University of Technology in the Netherlands, and Ryerson's own Center of the Study of Commercial Activity are examples of the academic world's attempts to focus on the needs of the retail industry.

While Eaton School of Retailing started with the vision of offering an accredited degree in retail management, Chestnutt says that it was important to start first with retail management certificates. These could be offered within a relatively short time to sustain the momentum and enthusiasm for the entire project. The types of courses that make up this retail management certificate and ultimately the degree program are shown in Figure 6–6. The purpose of the program is to train students in a set of skills deemed by the T. Eaton Company and Ryerson Polytechnic University as critical to success in a retail environment. This partnership between T. Eaton Company and Ryerson Polytechnic University has redefined retailing as a knowledge-based, professional career choice. The creation of a professional certificate and degree program in retailing management has changed the way a university carries out its mission and the way a corporation invests in individual and corporate learning. The Retail Management Certificate is open first to Eaton employees and then to Eaton suppliers such as Levi Strauss. Soon, any retailer will be able to take advantage of the program via a distance learning partnership with Bell Canada.

One of the keys to the success of the Eaton/Ryerson partnership was finding the right champion within Ryerson Polytechnic University. Philip Schlam, director for Business Continuing Education, was the ideal candidate. An enthusiastic advocate of moving education closer to the needs of business, Schlam was delighted with Eaton's offer to work closely to develop the program. In fact, Schlam felt Eaton's desire to create retail management certificates and ultimately a new degree program was the catalyst needed to mobilize the university's internal resources to support the retail industry. Schlam moved forward in developing the curriculum for the retail management certificate by inviting representatives from

## FIGURE 6-6

---

### Retail Management Certificates

The Eaton School of Retaining and Ryerson have developed two introductory certification programs that are designed to provide the core knowledge and competencies needed by retailers. They form the base for an advanced certificate that will enable students to develop specialized knowledge in store operations, buying and merchandising, entrepreneurship and planning, and logistics and supply chain management. All of the courses in these certificates earn advanced standing in the Bachelor of Commerce (Retail Management) that is in the final stages of academic approval at Ryerson.

**Certificate in Retail and Services Management I**

Issues and Innovations in Retailing I

Service and Professionalism

Introduction to Retail and Service Management

Human Resources Management (for non-H.R. Professionals)

Principles of Marketing

Organizational Behavior I

Introduction to Retail Management Communication

Entrepreneurship & Enterprise Development

Information Systems Applications (non-credit)

**Electives*** (choose 2)

Retail Operations I: Human Resources Challenges and Strategies

Retail Operations II: Planning for Profitability and Productivity Franchising

Buying Process II

Strategic Logistics Management I: The Demand Side Approach

Strategic Logistics Management II: The Supply Side Approach

**Certificate in Retail and Services Management II**

Retail Information Management

Retail Technology

Buying Process I

Geodemographics

Visual Merchandising & Display

Principles of Accounting

Consumer Behavior

Financial Management

Buying Statistics I

Store Design and Planning

Retail Advertising

Design, Commerce and Culture

Retail Location I

International Retailing

Relationship Marketing

Issues and Innovations in Retailing II

Courtesy of Eaton School of Retailing

Eaton, other retailers, and Ryerson colleagues to provide input on course content. In hindsight, Schlam says it took some courage. Through negotiations and discussion, the group was able to reach consensus on the direction and content of courses and ultimately approve them. Consensus had to be developed within various parts of the university that would have a stake in the curriculum, which ultimately included courses in business management, information management, and technical communications.

Marilyn Booth, dean of Continuing Education at Ryerson Polytechnic University, sees the Eaton/Ryerson partnership as an effort to create a learning culture that values both individual and corporate needs. "In Canada, corporate education has traditionally been one-of-a-kind workshops, seminars, and courses. But we know we must move beyond the events to develop a comprehensive, integrated program where threads run through all the courses and link together to form a whole that's much more powerful than any individual learning event."

Booth admits that part of the struggle in putting the program together has been challenging the sacred cows of Ryerson Polytechnic University. These challenges center on who owns the curriculum and what role the corporate world should play in curriculum development. The resulting partnership between Eaton and Ryerson Polytechnic University was successful because both the corporate as well as academic players were flexible in listening to the needs of the other and creating a curriculum that is truly responsive to the business community.

The Eaton funding for the Center for Research in Lifelong Learning at Ryerson Polytechnic University has advanced the partnership by promoting greater experimentation with both new learning models and research data to measure the effectiveness of the Eaton School of Retailing. One of the interesting research findings uncovered by the Center for Research in Lifelong Learning was the desire among graduates of the retail management program to remain in contact with Ryerson Polytechnic University after returning to work. These graduates told Ryerson and Eaton School of Retailing how important it was to obtain support in transferring new knowledge and skills back to the job. In response to this need for more ongoing support and follow-up, Ryerson Polytechnic University in cooperation with Eaton School of Retailing has developed ESR: The Next Steps, a facilitated series of change management workshops designed to accelerate and transfer learning on the job.

One of the outputs of these workshops was a detailed set of guidelines managers and employees can use before, during and after a course. These guidelines (shown in Figure 6–7) offer specific actions a manager can do to create an environment that is supportive of learning. These guidelines begin to show managers how to walk the talk and support learning on the job. Research efforts such as the one described here are strong evidence of the need to focus not only on providing an outstanding learning experience, but also on developing strategies to transfer learning back to the worksite.

## FIGURE 6–7

### What Managers Can Do To Support Learning

**Before**
- Learn about courses
- Take courses
- Meet with employees
-    to identify objectives
- Provide an outline
- Put the student at ease

**During**
- Send more than one person at a time
- Drop in on courses
- Keep interruptions to a minimum
- Make the classroom a safety zone
- Clarify that marks are confidential

**After**
- Use the language and strategies of the course
- Be open to new approaches
- Ask for input
- Establish networks
- Follow through on commitments
- Meet to debrief the course
- Make learning a part of the workplace culture
- Structure opportunities for students to use their learning

Courtesy of Eaton School of Retailing

**Megatech Engineering and Central Michigan University.**
Megatech Engineering, a $50 million Warren, Michigan-based design company, and Central Michigan University (CMU) have created a unique bachelor of science degree with a major in vehicle design. It is the only such program in Michigan and was created to alleviate a shortage of qualified designers in the automotive industry. In fact, this partnership is so unique that it was recently bestowed with the Innovation Award by the National University Continuing Education Association.

The Megatech/CMU partnership got its start because of the shortage of vehicle designers. In an effort to deal with this shortage, several vehicle design firms, led by Megatech Engineering, initiated a series of meetings with Michigan colleges and universities during March and April 1995. The objective was to create a program to produce world-class designers for the automotive industry. Automotive designers are a major resource to the industry. They take car concepts created by artistic stylists and make working designs out of them with input from engineers. "The designer is the link between the stylist and the engineer, who both have bachelor degree programs available to them, so this degree is a natural evolution," says Patrick Kirby, president of Megatech and initiator of the degree program.

Megatech approached several schools about partnering to create the design degree, but only Central Michigan University was willing to address the needs of the marketplace. Megatech wanted state-of-the-art education in a framework that was convenient to working adults. The resulting partnership required that technical courses specific to vehicle design would be taught at facilities in Megatech Engineering's Megatech Academy (their version of a corporate university).

Recently, Megatech Academy received Michigan state licensure as an educational institution and is located within Megatech Engineering's vehicle design building complex—giving students and instructors access to the most current technology. Courses taught at Megatech Academy are structured to provide a mentored, practical learning experience. Besides counting toward the degree, they can also be used by Megatech employees to complete the Academy's technical design certificate. Building this type of innovative partnership ensures that the program stays current with technological advances.

"The vehicle design program was innovative in another aspect as well," says David Sprague, director of the Centre for Professional Excellence in CMU's College of Extended Learning. "We listened to input from the vehicle design industry who told us they needed well-rounded employees who not only have technical expertise but also possess a breadth of education." CMU created the vehicle design program to consist of 133 credits versus the traditional 124 and included appropriate courses in both technical areas as well as liberal arts.

The degree went from concept, through development, approval, and implementation in a little more than one year. That is an amazing accomplishment and attests to the benefits of using a "champion" model rather than the traditional academic "committee" model. After a period of languishing under the committee model, the program finally was launched because of the role that David Sprague played as facilitator/cheerleader/liaison for both partners, Megatech and CMU. Sprague looks back on his role and says, "Business and universities each have distinct cultures and the cultural differences get in the way of doing the job at hand. My recommendation for others attempting to create a corporate/college partnership is to appoint a project director who can bridge the cultural gap and mend the glitches that get in the way of accomplishing the desired goal. My advice to the project manager: Push the program through the bureaucracy, knowing there will be many sacred academic cows standing in the way."

### Create a Corporate University Consortium

Rapidly gaining in recognition and respect is the consortium model of executive education. This model is really a unique combination of open enrollment and a custom program where a group of companies come together with a university to share resources in achieving innovation, quality, reliability, and value. The consortium model is really just like any other type of strategic alliance that a company enters into with a supplier, but in this case the supplier is higher education. This distinction is key—both the corporation and the university must recognize that they are in a customer/supplier relationship where risks and rewards are shared by both partners.

**Southern Company and the Emory University Consortium.** The Emory Consortium is a good model to understand how a company might use such an education vehicle to train senior managers and those ready to move into these positions. The consortium got its start in 1992 when Ed Addison, president and CEO of Southern Company, believed his need for cost-effective, high value executive education must also be one that was shared by scores of other Atlanta-based corporations. To test the water, Addison wrote a letter to the local CEOs of Atlanta-based corporations and personally advocated the consortium model as a way to save money, time, and developmental efforts in training high potential managers.

As soon as Addison brought together a group of 12 local companies, Southern Company College took on the task of interviewing several local universities in the Southeast area to recommend an optimal university partner to provide the educational experience for these consortium members. According to Al Martin, dean of Southern Company College, they had three important criteria for selecting a university partner:

> "First, we wanted to work with a university that had faculty with a predominant "real-world," experience base. In other words, we were searching for faculty that had experience consulting with corporations and were interested in spending time learning our business, our industry, and our competitive challenges. Second, we wanted to work with a university that was flexible and responsive and willing to experiment not only in terms of program design and delivery but also in terms of selection of faculty. This is a very sensitive issue. For example, we were interested in having the best of the best as faculty and that does not mean from one single university. So, a university's willingness to involve faculty from other universities was critical to our selection process. Finally, we recognized the importance of reaching a common agreement on the financial and non-financial terms of a partnership. This primarily means the ownership rights surrounding courses. Courses from the consortium are owned by the consortium rather than any one university or company."

The Emory University Consortium that emerged from this development process delivers a three-week educational experience spread over a four-month period. Week one focuses on corporate strategy with an emphasis on creating and managing shareholder value; week two concentrates on leading a corporate transformation in a global business environment; and week three emphasizes building leadership skills. The nature of the educational experience provided by the consortium is different from open enrollment programs—it is more strategic and less tactical and functional. Also, there are more application-oriented projects that involve best practice teams from consortium member companies. The consortium membership requires member companies to send at least two participants annually to the programs, each paying a tuition ranging from $9,000 to $11,000 per participant.

In analyzing the launch and design of the consortium model, what is apparent is the similarity to launching an internal corporate university: the necessity of the top management commitment, the importance of a clear vision, and the need to develop strategic goals for the initiative.

**United Healthcare/Rensselaer Learning Institute Consortium.** While the Southern Company College/Emory University consortium focuses on developing executive development and leadership skills, United Healthcare, a Minnitonka, Minnesota-based healthcare provider with 30,000 employees worldwide, entered into a consortium as a way to ensure consistent and cost-effective management and technical training to information systems managers.

The consortium approach grew out of a need for United Healthcare to find an effective way to provide training to its remote staff. While United Healthcare's training budget had more than doubled to $2.3 million, Allen Stein, director of United Healthcare Learning Institute, believed much of that budget was spent without any strategic consideration.

Stein set out to find an alternative solution—one that would systematize the training operation and provide high quality, cost-effective learning solutions. Stein quickly set up a task force to assess the current United Healthcare training offerings and evaluate potential learning partners who had a national presence and could deliver management and technical training at a distance. Here the consortium selection process differed quite significantly from Southern Company, where CEO Addison created a list of companies with similar needs and then went to find the learning partner. In the case of United Healthcare, the selection process was very similar to that of an advertising agency search—a task force drew up key criteria and invited a list of seven firms to make a presentation. The list was eventually narrowed to three finalists, then a panel representing human resources, business line managers, and the purchasing department came together to make the final selection. Rensselaer Learning Institute (RLI), an engineering college based in Troy, New York, was selected mainly because they were able to deliver both technical and management training at a distance (RLI is now licensed to deliver Center for Creative Leadership courses over Interactive Compressed Video). RLI was ultimately selected because of its experience as a learning partner and broker of training programs for Hartford-based United Technologies. (Hartford is one of the many locations where United Healthcare has a concentrated employee population.)

RLI serves as a broker offering programs from Boston University, Carnegie Mellon University, Stanford University, and Massachusetts Institute of Technology, all delivered through Interactive Compressed Video (ICV) at specified work sites without employees ever having to visit these campuses. The employees participate in accredited degree programs from one of these universities. In its role as a broker, RLI arranges non-degree seminars, technical related courses, as well as desktop training in management education, all at the best possible rate.

The RLI partnership is akin to finding the best faculty in the world and then negotiating a bulk rate discount on behalf of the total 200,000 employee population—the number of employees in both United Healthcare and United Technologies. The goal of this consortium is to share resources and leverage the volume of students so that the consortium receives the lowest possible rate.

While this will not replace the consortium model used by Southern Company, United Healthcare's innovative learning partnership with RLI illustrates the extent to which new methodologies and synergies are being experimented with in the consortium. As the cost of designing and delivering technology-based training increases, we will see many more consortia forming as a way to achieve efficiencies in the training process.

## Consider Accreditation of Your Corporate University

Our *Annual Survey of Corporate University Future Directions* has found that four in ten corporate universities now expects to start creating accredited degree programs jointly with an institution of higher education. These new degree programs range from certificates to associate level and graduate level programs, as shown in Figure 6–8.

Granting college credit for job training puts a value on the training that extends well beyond a narrow job description for one company. One of the reasons these best practice organizations are pushing towards accrediting their curricula is the need to offer employees "portable credentials," in an era where lifetime job se-

FIGURE 6–8

### A Sample of Degree Programs Offered by Corporate University/Higher Education Partnerships

| Organization | Corporate University | University | Degree Program |
|---|---|---|---|
| T. Eaton Company | Eaton School of Retailing | Ryerson Polytechnic University | Retail Management/ Associate Level |
| Bell Atlantic | The NEXT STEP | Consortium of 23 Colleges in New England | Telecommunications Tech./Associate Level |
| American Express | American Express Quality University | Rio Salado Community College | Customer Service/ Associate Level |
| Megatech Engineering | Megatech Academy | Central Michigan University | Vehicle Design/Bachelor of Science |
| University of Chicago Hospital | University of Chicago Hospital Academy | Network of Learning Partners | Healthcare Management/ Associate Level |
| Arthur D. Little | Arthur D. Little School of Management | Fully Accredited | Management/ Masters Level |

© 1997 Corporate University Xchange, Inc.

curity is a thing of the past. In some cases corporate universities will be competing directly with traditional higher education institutions in granting such degrees. More frequently, however, once a corporate university decides to grant a degree, it looks at all the components involved in the process and recognizes the advantages of partnering with traditional institutions of higher education. The movement toward accreditation is really a statement of the commitment organizations are making to be proactive customers of education.

The Arthur D. Little (ADL) School of Management recently became the first non-traditional school to be accepted into precandidacy for accreditation by the AACSB—The International Association for Management Education. The ADL story illustrates the risks and benefits of gaining accreditation.

**Accreditation of Arthur D. Little School of Management.** As corporate universities go, the Arthur D. Little School of Management is unusual. It was never set up to handle corporate training for Arthur D. Little (ADL), but rather to service the training and development needs of ADL clients at locations around the world, such as those in Pakistan, Nigeria, and Egypt. Now it is setting off on one of its most challenging assignments as one of the first corporate universities to seek full national management accreditation. The hurdles it faces and its ideas about partnering with traditional schools are instructive to others who may wish to seek similar accreditation in the future.

Thomas E. Moore, the founding dean of the ADL School of Management and currently the dean of the School of Executive Education at Babson College, says that when ADL was handling major World Bank projects in far-flung locations, part of its contracts usually called for the training of managers in these locations. This training began as in-country training, but ADL soon discovered that it was not cost-effective. Eventually, all training was handled at ADL's corporate headquarters in Cambridge, Massachusetts.

The Arthur D. Little School of Management, until recently known as the Management Education Institute, offers a one-year master of science in management, as well as a series of shorter executive education programs. The goal of these programs is to develop state-of-the-art executive education for current and prospective ADL clients around the world.

Since 1964, more than 3,200 professionals from over 115 countries have participated in the School of Management's programs. After about ten years of existence, the program evolved into an 11-month schedule centered around general management topics. By 1973, it looked very much like a master's degree program. At that point, ADL went to the Commonwealth of Massachusetts and applied for and was granted permission to award the master's of science management degree. ADL then sought and received regional accreditation from the New England Association of Schools and Colleges. The school is also a member of the AACSB—The International Association for Management Education.

Says Moore, "At that point, ADL started offering an accredited master's of science in management to a class of between 45 to 60 students each year. These participants are from around the world. In most classes, we have 25 to 27 countries represented—usually half the students are sponsored by corporations and the other half come on their own."

In the early 1980s, ADL sought to expand the school's activities to include open enrollment for public management educational programs and custom designed executive programs for corporations, which continues to the present time.

ADL School of Management participants study with senior management consultants and Boston-area university professors in Arthur D. Little's corporate headquarters, which includes a library, health services, and dining areas. They may also attend special programs Arthur D. Little offers, including lectures by visiting consultants from the company's offices around the world.

The School of Management participants learn the latest management theory and "cutting edge" management practices from these ADL consultants. They are exposed to the real challenges confronting managers in diverse economies and they have first-hand access to the experts who are meeting those challenges.

"One of the concerns was that the school had drifted away from its core business of ADL consulting activities," says Moore. "Many of their clients were coming from parts of the world where ADL didn't do much consulting and our linkage between the consulting business and our school had gotten a bit fragile. One of my challenges was to re-establish that link and make sure the school was building upon ADL's strengths and competencies and at the same time bringing in the latest educational theory from sister business schools."

To achieve the school's goals, ADL decided it was critical to seek national accreditation from AACSB—The International Association for Management Education, the primary service organization and accreditation body for business schools in North America. Although ADL has been regionally accredited since 1973, receiving national accreditation is a major hurdle, according to Moore. "One of the most dramatic challenges of national accreditation concerns faculty," he says, "Right now, national accreditation requires that at the master's level about 80 percent of teaching be done by full-time Ph.Ds. The term 'full-time' has caused us some issues; we proposed to AACSB that we redefine the term to mean 80 percent of course work is taught by "dedicated" Ph.Ds. That way, these full-time faculty can have joint appointments between ADL School of Management and a traditional business school in the Boston area or in some other part of the world. We started experimenting with this arrangement in 1995. Now, we have joint appointments with a faculty member from Babson College and with our ADL Brussels office. In these cases, we actually pay for half of the salary and benefits for these faculty members and in turn they spend half the year with us."

This arrangement is no different than a traditional university professor who has a joint appointment between departments or between colleges. These faculty members count as full-time faculty. This is just one of several issues that need to be resolved when a corporate university seeks national accreditation.

While accreditation brings a stamp of approval within the academic community and validates the corporate university, managers must know that the accreditation process is arduous and expensive. Accreditation standards affect course structure, competency measures, mission, planning, governance, research, student services, financial resources, faculty qualification, program content, and admission criteria. These requirements may be at odds with the corporation's strategic goals, but to meet accreditation standards, the corporate university must be able to document its independence from the corporation. Finally, the cost of compliance, the cost of periodic self-study and peer review, and the opportunity cost (to say nothing of finding instructors properly certified to teach the courses) is an enormous expense.

While several corporate universities are exploring whether they should be offering some kind of portable accredited degree to their employees, they should be aware that the degree must meet outside requirements in terms of curriculum, faculty qualifications, and outside review. Corporate universities must understand that to receive accreditation they have to be less focused on just meeting company goals and much more aware and willing to meet the requirements of colleges and universities as set forth by an accreditation organization like the AACSB—The International Association for Management Education.

ADL's strategic alliance with Boston College's Carroll School of Management is indicative of ADL's commitment to partner with a nationally recognized university to take advantage of the economies of scale and the resources of a traditional research university. ADL students take their courses alongside Boston College business school students and have access to the same library, faculty, and building resources as well as to a curriculum strong in financial services, accounting, and organizational design. Under the agreement, the schools retain their distinctive identities and continue to grant their own degrees. At the same time, they work together to develop joint curricular and research initiatives.

## TRAINING THE VALUE CHAIN BECOMES A STRATEGIC GOAL FOR CORPORATE UNIVERSITIES

Forging and sustaining partnerships is quickly becoming a critical competency for progressive companies in the 1990s and beyond. This chapter surveyed some of the more innovative partnerships now underway between companies and their suppliers, customers, and institutions of higher education. The type and nature of these partnerships will fundamentally alter the way business is conducted now and in the future. Increasingly, organizations are committing to educate their entire "food chain"—the suppliers, customers, dealers, wholesalers, and future employees in a community. This emphasis on training all the members of their chain allows organizations an opportunity to gain a competitive edge in the marketplace by instilling a continuous learning culture throughout their system.

The corporate university is serving as the focal point for building these partnerships with institutions of higher education. Initially, these partnerships may start out as training programs or customized executive education seminars, but over time they grow and deepen into long-term alliances serving the needs of both the corporation, the individual participant, and the university. The most innovative examples of corporate/college alliances illustrate just how proactive corporations are becoming in their relationship with academia. Rather than passively funding tuition reimbursement programs, the corporations such as T. Eaton Company and Megatech Engineering are taking determined steps to actually create new customized degree programs to ensure their employees are trained in the skills that are essential to the strategic needs of the business. The best of the corporate/college alliances are becoming true customer/supplier partnerships anchored in a shared vision of the future needs of the work force.

*Chapter Seven*

# Corporate Universities: Opportunity or Threat to Higher Education?

*In an era of life-long learning, universities in the industrialized world will be marginalized unless they are efficient and flexible enough to meet today's myriad educational and training needs.*

—Sir John Daniel, vice chancellor, Open University

## THE METAMORPHOSIS OF THE EDUCATION MARKET

Education in the United States is undergoing a seismic shift. The traditional 18 to 24-year-old full-time undergraduate and graduate student, long the primary focus of four-year colleges and universities, no longer represents an overwhelming majority of the education market. Twenty years ago this population accounted for 80 percent of the market. Today, however, traditional full- and part-time students represent only 56 percent of the population pursuing higher education (see Figure 7–1). The future belongs to the non-traditional working adult student now estimated to be 44 percent of the education market, but expected to be the fastest growing segment of the post-secondary market through the twenty-first century.[1]

Behind the scenes of this educational metamorphosis, there are several powerful trends at work, as shown in Figure 7–2: the rise of the non-traditional student as a consumer of education; the rapid advancement of technology; the need for life-long learning; and increasing experimentation with distance learning. Together

**FIGURE 7-1**

---

### Changing Education Market

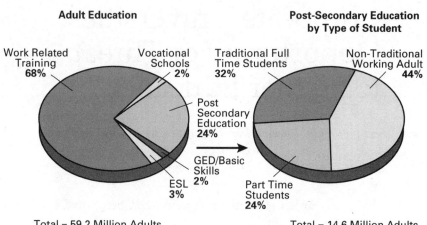

Adult Education

Work Related Training 68%

Vocational Schools 2%

Post Secondary Education 24%

GED/Basic Skills 2%

ESL 3%

Total = 59.2 Million Adults

Post-Secondary Education by Type of Student

Traditional Full Time Students 32%

Non-Traditional Working Adult 44%

Part Time Students 24%

Total = 14.6 Million Adults

Courtesy of Lehman Brothers

these trends are causing an earthquake of change and putting enormous pressure on the traditional educational system to forever alter the way it does business. A new landscape of higher education is emerging—one where the private sector will eclipse the public sector as the educator of choice for the non-traditional working adult student.

Just as the American healthcare system has moved from an inefficiently managed cottage industry dominated by the public sector to a market driven system, the American educational system must now transform itself to meet consumer demands for convenient and high quality on-demand education.

### Emergence of the Non-Traditional Student as a Consumer of Education

Today's well-informed consumers are demanding huge changes in industries as diverse as retailing and financial services. Consider for a moment the retailing industry where merchandise that was

FIGURE 7–2

## The Emergence of a Market-Driven Education Model

**Traditional Education Model**

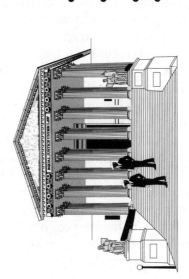

- 2 and 4 year colleges and universities
- 18-24 year old fulltime students
- Capital intensive campuses

**Forces of Change**

- Non-Traditional Students (Working Adults)
- Rapid Advancement of Technology
- Need for Continuous Learning
- The Internet/Distance Education

**New Education Model**

Virtual University

Consortia

Externally Focused Corporate Universities

For Profit Educational Firms

© 1997 Corporate University Xchange, Inc.

once available only in a store is now available at home, through mail order catalogs, the computer, and television. While retail sales levels in shopping centers fell between 1988 and 1992, consumer purchases from the home, paid for by check or credit card, grew by 30 percent.[2]

Successful retailers understand the importance of convenience and consistency of service and have made heavy investments in training front-line employees. Consider McDonald's Hamburger University. Developed in 1963, it claims to be the nation's number one trainer, larger even than the United States Army for the size and scope of its classes. In fact, Hamburger University now trains employees in 65 countries around the world and has hardwired simultaneous translation facilities for 18 languages into its campus outside Chicago.[3] McDonald's has been joined by Target Stores, which launched Target University in 1990, and Sears, where as part of a major corporate overhaul, CEO Arthur Martinez created Sears University in 1994. In each case, the corporate university has become the focal point for extensive, innovative learning programs as well as on-demand learning support services to ensure well-trained front-line employees serve the customer and keep the business on a one-to-one basis.

Charles Schwab, founder of the discount brokerage firm that bears his name, caught this wave of consumerism early on and introduced to their regular customers twenty-four hour, seven days a week order entry for stock trades. To capture the "do-it-yourself" consumer, Schwab went even further by offering a 10 percent discount to customers who enter their orders directly on a telephone keypad. They now account for 20 to 25 percent of the firm's trades. Today, Schwab University ensures that the customer is king by providing Schwab employees with state-of-the-art training in customer service, leadership development, and sales/marketing. This boom of corporate universities in the service sector is the clearest evidence that corporations in the retailing and financial services sector are taking consumer demands for convenience and quality seriously. Corporations as diverse as McDonald's, Target, Sears, and Charles Schwab recognize that consumers "want it their way," and have created a learning infrastructure to train front-line employees in how to deliver fast, flawless, and convenient service.

Now these consumers are seeking the same level of customer service from their educational providers that they have become accustomed to from their retailers and financial service providers. Consumers of educational services are saying, "I want convenience, I want self-service and I want quality products that help me advance in my career." Will the educational system change and meet these consumer demands? The current educational system still focuses primarily on the needs of the on-campus 18 to 24-year-old student. More often than not, college and university curricula are built around what the faculty believe is needed in the marketplace, rather than what industry requires for success. What's more, courses are usually designed to be of the same duration, taught mostly in daylight hours, and at times convenient to the faculty.

Increasingly, non-traditional working adult students, the fastest growing segment of the post-secondary education market, are demanding the education system provide them with services to fit their overbooked personal and professional lives. According to a national survey of 1,124 adults conducted by the Social and Economic Sciences Research Center of Washington State University, working adults identified busy lives, inflexible course schedules, and the lack of available courses offered nearby as the major barriers to obtaining education and training. What these non-traditional students want is "just-in-time" education they can use on the job.[4]

### Rapid Advancement of Technology

It took 38 years for the telephone industry to reach 10 million customers, but only two years for the Internet to reach the same number of customers. The Internet is evolving exponentially, with the citizens of cyberspace outnumbering all but the largest nations. The Internet is now on pace to reach 50 million households a scant eight years after its official birth in 1994 as a consumer medium.[5]

This rapid advancement of technology is having an enormous impact on the individual worker. Consider for a moment the job of a telecommunications technical associate as defined by Bell Atlantic Corporation. The introduction of new technologies such as wireless and open systems interconnections requires the telecommunications technician to not only be conversant with these new technologies, but also possess broad business skills that go beyond technical knowledge. Rather than knowing just one narrowly defined job, these technicians must know how to navigate a complex workplace where they must demonstrate an extensive knowledge of new technologies as well as an understanding of how various products and services fit emerging customer needs.

The Bell Atlantic NEXT STEP program has responded to this challenge by designing a new degree program—an associate degree in applied science with a focus in telecommunications technology. What is particularly unique, though, is how Bell Atlantic is using new technologies in the degree program to build team skills and collaboration among its employees. For example, all candidates for this new degree program are provided with a computer and access to the Internet so they can collaborate on projects with co-workers from other sites and begin to build networking and team problem-solving skills. The advancement of new technologies in the telecommunications industry has created an opportunity for Bell Atlantic to use the Internet and on-line discussion forums to train its workers.

## Need for Life-long Learning

The term "life-long learning" is now part of our vocabulary. It describes the need for workers to continue their education and development throughout their lives as they face multiple careers in changing economic circumstances.

Increasingly, employees are recognizing that work and learning are becoming the same thing, with learning occurring in the workplace rather than in a university classroom. This need for life-long learning is best captured by Richard Soderberg of the National Technological University when he says, "People mistakenly think that once they've graduated from college they are good for the next decade—when in fact they're really good for the next ten seconds."[6]

In industries as diverse as computers, healthcare, utilities, telecommunications, and even training and development, our knowledge and skills are only adequate for a period as short as 12 to 18 months. This emphasis on life-long learning does not stop with our jobs. Think of yourself as a consumer. In the past year, you probably have learned how to set up Windows 95 on your home computer, programmed your home security system, shopped for products on the Internet, and helped your son or daughter load a CD-ROM onto your home computer. Life-long learning is becoming necessary for survival in both our professional and our personal lives.

This demand for life-long learning brings with it a new set of consumer requirements. Non-traditional working adult students aged 25 and up are constrained by where they live, what they can afford, as well as job and family responsibilities. Most universities have responded to this demand for life-long learning by adding new programs and services for part-time working adult students, but the core activity of the university—teaching to full-time 18 to 24-year-old students—has changed little. Semester-long courses taught on-campus continue in lockstep sequence during the hours of 8:00 a.m. to 5:00 p.m. Working adult students are demanding something more—namely flexibility, convenience, and the option to pursue education at a distance in order to fulfill their continuous learning needs.

Because life-long learning has become so crucial, corporations are increasingly shouldering the responsibility for servicing the educational needs of working adults. Education, once the purview of the church, then the government, is now rapidly falling to corporations. The rapid growth of corporate universities, from 400 in 1988 to over 1,000 today, underscores the fact that the private sector is entering the business of education in order to remain competitive in the global marketplace. Consider just one corporate university—Motorola University—to understand the scope of this commitment to educating the work force. In 1995 alone, 128,000 Motorola employees participated in 633,000 days of training under the umbrella of Motorola University.

## Introduction of Distance Education

As corporate America encourages the work force to become life-long learners, the traditional model of the university campus-bound classroom is being supplemented by the virtual classroom where lectures, notes, and class assignments can be accessed at any time of the day or night. In fact, researchers from the Social and Economic Sciences Research Center of Washington State University found that 29 percent of the 1,124 working adults surveyed actually prefer distance education as a means of accessing work-related continuing education.[7]

With the introduction of distance learning, the paradigm of learning is shifting from faculty-centered to learner-centered. Jack Wilson, the creator of the acclaimed studio course at Rensselaer Polytechnic University, expresses the challenge created by this paradigm shift: "The current teaching/learning paradigm is one where the faculty is expected to work very hard (preparing for class and lecturing to students) while the student sits back and passively listens. I want to reverse this dynamic."[8]

In order for Wilson's vision to become a reality, students must first have access to the right equipment in order to communicate and collaborate with other students, as well as faculty. This is gradually happening as a growing base of well-equipped personal computers with CD-ROM players, modems, and on-line software enters the marketplace. Lehman Brothers Technology Group estimates that the installed base for 486 or better modem-equipped multimedia personal computers will reach 51 million in 1998, up from 12 million in 1995.[9]

The other important variable here is the motivation of the learner. Students must want the traditional dynamic of passive learning reversed. Increasingly, we have evidence that the non-traditional segment of the student population—the working adult—does in fact want greater control and access to continuous learning. Why? Primarily because working adults are beginning to see a correlation between continued education and their employability. According to the Bureau of Labor Statistics, 58 percent of the jobs created by the year 2005 will require some college. In fact, 45 percent of all jobs created between the years 1983 and 1993 required some education beyond high school, compared to 30 percent in 1983. Hence, the individual worker is beginning to see the payoff in the marketplace of increased education and training.[10]

With technological advances and student motivation for distance learning, the non-traditional student segment will begin to see greater access to life-long learning. The only question appears to be: who will emerge as the principle supplier of on-demand education—corporate universities, for-profit education firms, or institutions of higher education?

## HIGHER EDUCATION'S DILEMMA

The challenge for universities to move from a teacher-centered on-campus model of education to a learner-centered one where the emphasis is on providing students with the tools and resources to be responsible for their own learning is not an easy shift. Even as colleges and universities continue to face enormous pressures to acquire new students, lower costs, and become more efficient in their operations, many continue to offer more of the same—additional classes aimed at the full-time on-campus student.

Making traditional university education truly learner-centered presents a huge challenge for campus institutions. The demand for life-long learning suggests a fundamental question about what business educators are in and who their customers are. McDonalds, Target, Sears, and Charles Schwab are just four institutions that have been faced with this question in their respective industries and have re-created their businesses to better serve customer demands for quality, convenience, and personal service. Higher education is rapidly facing the same question and must examine whether it will continue to focus on the traditional student or reconceive the academic model to address the need for life-long learning.

## NEW ENTRANTS TO THE EDUCATION MARKET

Corporate universities, consortiums, virtual universities, and for-profit education firms have sprung up and proliferated to serve the non-traditional working adult market segment. They have taken on the challenge of meeting the consumer demands of this market by proactively designing learning experiences, tools, and support services that are convenient, accessible, and offered on demand. As a group, these new entrants represent both an opportunity for partnering (as demonstrated in Chapter 6) but also direct competition to the traditional educational system. They will force change and experimentation in how and where education is offered to the growing segment of working adult students.

## Externally Focused Corporate Universities

The growth of corporate universities is signaling a demand for a new model of higher education—one that is offered "just-in-time" and focused on the skills, knowledge, and competencies needed for success in the fast changing global marketplace. Time has become a "four-letter word" in meeting the life-long learning needs of working adults. The 50 corporations profiled in this book have created more than "dressed up training departments." Many have experimented heavily with new technologies to provide learner-centered training to the desktop, home, and hotel room of working adults. They are now doing something more: they are taking their innovative spirit and knowledge of the education and training market and offering training to outsiders for a fee.

Motorola University has a 179 page catalogue listing over 200 courses, many available to non-Motorolans. In fact, Motorola University has been selling select training programs to suppliers and customers for almost a decade. Disney Institute, since its profile in the book, *In Search Of Excellence,* has opened up its programs in customer service and people management to outsiders. Recently, a host of other organizations have entered the open enrollment arena such as: Saturn Outside Services, the consulting arm of Saturn Corporation that markets consulting and customer enthusiasm programs to outsiders, as well as Bell Atlantic Learning Center, the Baltimore, Maryland based company that actively sells training programs and courseware in the open market. The goal for these externally focused corporate universities is to market their state-of-the-art training programs and courseware as a source of revenue for the corporation.

Now, Southern California Water Company's Employee Development University (EDU) has joined this group of externally focused corporate universities with a mandate to become a world-class educational provider to the water industry.

**Southern California Water Company Employee Development University: Certified water education for an industry.** Southern California Water Company (SCWC), a $152 million utility company located in San Dimas, California, boasts a corporate university—Employee Development University (EDU)—that has its sights on marketing its programs and services to other companies.

After a lengthy application and evaluation process, the International Association for Continuing Education and Training (IACET), a national approval body, recently (July 1997) granted certified provider status to EDU. This means that courses offered by EDU must meet the IACET criteria for quality and consistency in continuing education and training.

EDU seeks to position itself as more than just an internal training unit at SCWC, but as a statewide learning facility that could potentially become the educational arm of other utility companies. "One of the main reasons we went through the IACET certification," says Diane Rentfrow, corporate dean of EDU, "is because the courses submitted for Continuing Education Units (CEUs) are portable and can be marketed to other companies."

EDU also embarked on the process of establishing portable credentials because they wanted to be known not as a training department, but as an employee development program that reaches out to anyone—in addition to its more than 450 employees—interested in life-long learning. In other words, having the authorization to grant CEUs means EDU can now offer its innovative programs to outsiders. According to Rentfrow, "our certified provider status adds value to our educational programs; it's not just training; the intent is to help people to become more employable."

Presently, most water industry training is provided by a patchwork of consulting firms, community colleges, and technical courses offered by other organizations, but EDU hopes to change that. EDU's newly created courses or "Program Tracks," developed from strict IACET criteria to meet all requirements for CEUs, include such critical business areas as: Water Quality, Water Supply, Customer Service, Water Distribution, Regulatory and Financial Management, and General Enhancement.

Rentfrow says another reason EDU sought continuing education accreditation was to hedge against future regulations: "I foresee industries requiring continuing education units for many jobs.

The water industry and the utilities as a whole will be saying that in order to maintain competencies in water quality or other areas, you must maintain a certain amount of CEU credits. I anticipate that this is coming."

EDU has been approached by other companies to partner with them because of their certified provider status. These companies are interested in EDU's programs and services and would like EDU to deliver value-added learning so that their employees can receive CEUs.

To help achieve certified provider status and better live up to its motto—"empowering people to learn, change, and grow"—EDU has greatly expanded its learning facilities. It is all part of EDU's preparations for the marketplace. Rentfrow details EDU's plans: "Following IACET facilities and learning support standards, we have designed a new, state-of-the-art facility for learning and we are ready to roll out our training to outsiders." Rentfrow recognizes that marketing EDU externally does require a major commitment, starting with obtaining the necessary copyright on all their training materials and programs to developing a marketing strategy for entering the open enrollment training business.

The EDU team is currently working on developing a strategic business plan to identify key initiatives in order to sell their programs and services to the rest of the industry. "Our goal is to position EDU as a profit center," says Rentfrow, "and we want to start marketing our programs to other water company professionals, and ultimately to consumers." Says Rentfrow, "within the next decade, we envision a learning academy on weekends so consumers can learn about water and how much we take this precious commodity for granted in our lives." Just as Disney Institute has reached out to the consumer market, corporate universities such as Employee Development University are setting their sights on not just offering learning programs to professionals at other companies in their industry but one day opening their doors as a community-based life-long learning institution.

### Consortiums

While externally focused corporate universities present one alternative to traditional education, yet specialized within an industry and geography, another alternative springing up is the consortium, a group of companies who come together to pool their training resources and together offer these to working adults. Consortiums act as training brokers, acquiring content from traditional institutions of higher education or even corporate universities, and then offer this back to the open market. In this scenario, corporate universities as well as traditional universities become both customers and suppliers to the consortium.

**Global Wireless Education Consortium: Educating a new industry.** The Global Wireless Education Consortium (GWEC), based in Mankato, Minnesota, is an example of how the consortium concept brings together companies with common interests to create an educational solution for an entire industry. The founding members of GWEC are Ericsson, AT&T Wireless Services, Lucent Technologies, AirTouch Communication, and Motorola, along with Mankato State University, South Central Technical College (in North Mankato, Minnesota), and the University of Texas at Dallas.

GWEC was formed in late 1996 in response to an overwhelming need for skilled employees in an industry that is growing exponentially. It is estimated that the number of worldwide wireless device users has quadrupled to over 250 million in the last five years. That number is expected to almost triple by 2001. This means that the demand for wireless technicians and engineers will drastically increase over the next two decades, maybe as much as ten-fold.

Misty Baker, executive director of GWEC, describes the situation that spawned her organization: "There is obviously a huge and growing need for wireless technicians and engineers. Industry people have had a great deal of problems not only in recruiting, but also in retention. They're spending a lot of time getting these people trained and often they're taken away by another company at maybe a 25 percent bonus."

"A network of astute industry people have come together proactively and said, 'this is a people problem and we can either sue each other, like the software industry is doing, or we can collaborate to solve the problem.' They realized they didn't have to talk about products or salaries or share other proprietary information, but they could talk about how to mutually solve the problem of educating a pool of wireless technicians and engineers."

GWEC presents yet another model of education where corporations and academia come together as partners to solve a common problem. A lot of past alliances have been built from an education standpoint: "you give us funds, you give us equipment, and we'll do our part as educators." This time, the corporations who have formed GWEC are working with educators to develop the curriculum to fit their specific needs.

Radio Frequency Training (RFT), the basis of wireless technology, was once a standard component of engineering schools and electronics courses and flourished during the heyday of radio, but the advent of computers all but dissolved this curriculum. Now RFT has come full circle and is more necessary than ever. This technological lapse is a large part of the problem the GWEC must address. In some cases, the curriculum must be built from the ground up.

The shortage of skilled wireless employees provides a near textbook example of how rapid technological innovation combined with inadequate communication between industry and education can create glaring discrepancies between the skills of graduates and the requirements of industry. According to Baker, "The wireless industry began to realize that there was a huge shortage and everybody was talking about how they couldn't find the people and even if they found them, they had to embark upon 6 to 12 months of basic training. The industry people said 'we're developing basic RF courses, why don't you in higher education partner with us to develop a wireless concentration.'"

Forming a consortium may seem like an incredibly difficult undertaking, due in large part to the cultural disparities between industry and education, to say nothing of the varying interests of industry competitors being asked to partner with one another, but the advantages of a consortium soon become obvious.

"If these companies tried to do individually what the consortium is doing," says Baker, "they would each be spending resources to do the same things over and over but only be zeroing in on one geographic area, with one school. With the consortium they can pool their resources and go nationwide, even worldwide, more quickly and build wireless programs in many schools. This effort will attract more attention to the educational program and therefore get more engineers and technicians into the wireless field. GWEC is designed to eliminate duplication of funds and effort. It's much more efficient as a means of educating additional engineers and technicians; it's exponentially increasing the pool available."

A key advantage to this collaboration is that it allows the participating companies to take advantage of the latest in training at a far more reasonable cost and makes the latest in training techniques and materials available quickly to all the members. The industry members of GWEC, for example, share the latest multimedia courseware (CD-ROM, CBT, etc.) licensing this material to GWEC, who in turn licenses it to the GWEC schools for use in their curriculum. This makes the curriculum development process much shorter, which is absolutely crucial in such a rapidly moving industry where traditional materials, such as textbooks—which take about two years to develop—are wholly inadequate to keep pace with new developments.

With an estimated 300,000 new wireless technicians needed in the next decade, the goal of GWEC is to have a total of 100 participating schools. GWEC is growing mainly because it has established itself as a means of effectively creating a pool of trained technicians. GWEC is a prime example of the type of corporate/academic partnerships we will see more of in the future.

### Virtual Universities

Another variation on the traditional education model is the virtual university. A virtual university is essentially a distance-teaching institution offering degree level courses. Although many universities offer both distance and classroom teaching, virtual universities are those institutions where distance education is clearly the primary avenue to learning. In addition, many virtual universities are "mega universities," defined by Sir John Daniel as having over 100,000 active students and thus having attained certain economies of scale in their operation.[11]

Figure 7–3 lists 11 of these virtual mega universities around the globe. As a group, these 11 virtual universities enroll 2.8 million students for an aggregate budget of around $900 million, or about

FIGURE 7-3

## Eleven Mega-Universities

| Country | Name of Institution | Established |
|---------|---------------------|-------------|
| China | China TV University System | 1979 |
| France | Centre National d' Enseignement a Distance | 1939 |
| India | Indira Gandhi National Open University | 1985 |
| Indonesia | University of Terbuka | 1984 |
| Iran | Payame Noor University | 1987 |
| Korea | Korean National Open University | 1982 |
| South Africa | Unviersity of South Africa | 1873 |
| Spain | Universidad Nacional de Educacion a Distancia | 1972 |
| Thailand | Sukhothai Thammathirat Open University | 1978 |
| Turkey | Anadolu University | 1982 |
| United Kingdom | The Open University | 1969 |

Courtesy of *Mega-Universities and Knowledge Media,* Sir John Daniel, 1996 (London: Kogan Page Limited)

$320 per student. Compare this to the traditional higher educational system in the United States with over 3,500 degree granting institutions serving 14 million students in capital intensive campuses, and spending $199 billion. This represents an average cost of $14,200 per student. The differences in economies of scale are quite startling and present a powerful new model of higher education, one that is cost effective, not constrained by ivy walls, and serves the needs of working adults. Open University, having trained over 2 million students since its inception in 1969, illustrates the challenges and opportunities in educating at a distance. Think of Open University as a model for corporate universities and traditional educators who want to meet consumer demands for life-long learning delivered at a distance.

**Open University: A model of market-driven learning.** The Open University (OU), based in the United Kingdom, is essentially a virtual university with a total student "body" of over 200,000 in both degree and non-degree programs. Kitty Chisholm, OU's director of development, points out the major difference between OU and the traditional campus-based university: "It isn't a physical place for its students—it is an experience, a learning community."

Open University is aptly named because there are no entry qualifications (except for higher degrees) and none of the obstacles encountered in a more traditional setting. Of OU's current enrollment, 120,000 students are working towards an undergraduate degree, while another 10,000 are registered for post-graduate degrees. The median age for OU students is in the mid-thirties and about 70 percent of its students remain in full-time employment throughout their studies.

Open University has concentrated on providing open learning to all residents of the European Union and Asia. As of 1998, Open University will move into the United States and deliver courses via the Internet. OU teaches its students through supported distance learning, primarily using custom designed paper-based study materials as well as video, audio, and CD-ROM. Some courses also include television and radio programs on the national BBC networks. Also, a tutor is assigned to each student to guide him or her through the coursework.

The Internet, however, in addition to its role as provider of general university information, such as class schedules and course catalogs, is the key to OU curriculum delivery. Students communicate with their tutors and fellow "classmates" via e-mail and teleconferencing while also submitting assignments electronically. In addition, OU relies on conventional on-site delivery systems using regular mail and telephone to communicate with students and meet with them at live local study centers as needed. It is this combination of delivery mediums that sets OU apart from institutions of higher education that also offer distance learning.

OU represents a very interesting model in its cost-effectiveness and economies of scale (OU courses cost 40 to 60 percent less than the equivalent face-to-face courses). OU's appeal as an educational solution is evident by the fact that 4000 companies, including

American Express, AT&T, Ford, and IBM, among other multi-national giants, sponsor their employees in OU business courses.

Monterey Tech is another institution outside the United States where distance learning has become the principle means of delivering education to graduate students and working adults. Monterey Tech, like Open University, is also characterized by a large, far-flung student body and a multi-campus structure.

**Monterey Tech: Delivering learner-centered education.** Monterey Tech (MT), like Open University, relies on distance learning to service over 70,000 graduate and continuing education students at 26 campuses throughout Mexico, as well as outposts in Central and South America (undergraduate students receive instruction mostly through classroom-based learning). Satellite TV and the Internet are the principle vehicles through which students receive instruction at MT. At MT, distance learning has evolved from what was initially just a more technological method of teaching students the same old way, to a highly flexible, learning-centered model.

Initiated seven years ago, the MT distance learning program—officially known as the Virtual University—offers three major programs: business administration, engineering and information technology, and education. Business administration courses account for 65 percent of the total capacity.

MT's Virtual University started as a way to broadcast the courses in ethics and values and entrepreneurship. Subsequently, MT started using satellite-based communications to facilitate coordination among the 26 campuses across Mexico. MT then leveraged their satellite network and began offering courses to other countries in the region. Now they serve over 25,000 executives annually in South and Central America. Satellite TV has proven to be the most effective means of delivering distance learning, primarily because phone lines in the region are not particularly dependable.

MT's Virtual University has undergone a major change in recent years and approaches the whole idea of distance learning differently than it used to. According to Dr. Jaime Alonso Gomez, dean and professor, Graduate School of Business and Leadership at Monterey Tech, "In the initial years we put our professors on TV and they taught the courses as they normally would. Now the educational paradigm has changed and we are no longer in the business of teaching, but learning—particularly focusing on developing self-learning capabilities among our students."

At MT, each course is designed a semester in advance according to the learning paradigm. ("It's much more a pull system than a push system," says Gomez.) Before the course starts, students from the MT system can download supporting materials from the course's own web page. During this time they can also begin interacting among themselves and building a learning community.

During the course, professors make changes based on feedback from local facilitators. A facilitator might, for example, supply contextual information regarding markets or demographics. These changes continue during the courses. After the semester is over, the professor and the instructional design staff meet to discuss feedback and implement course improvements suggested from students.

"Inherent to our success is the ability to adjust for variable time, space, and learning rhythm," adds Gomez. "Technology can always be obtained, but what we need are professors with tremendous capacity to improvise, be flexible, and be able to deal with issues such as servers being overloaded, or other technical malfunctions."

In addition to their satellite and Internet delivered courses, MT also has a program called Pay Per Learn that uses cable television to offer courses. This program, developed in conjunction with a cable company, allows MT to go into homes and other companies to deliver customized education. Pay Per Learn has fostered a number of alliances with banks, mining companies, manufacturing companies, and others who use this system to train their executives.

Monterey Tech is another innovative example of an institution of higher education that not only uses technology to accelerate learning, but importantly adheres to a central guiding philosophy that embraces advanced methods of delivery. Monterey Tech is more than an extension of the current education model; it is an attempt to change the nature of how people learn.

## For-Profit Education Firms

For-profit education firms have entered the higher education arena with a business model focusing on the delivery of degree-oriented higher education for working adults. What these for-profit education firms understand is the need to be customer-driven, meaning they offer full-time working adult students the opportunity to pursue their education in a responsible amount of time while continuing to meet their personal and professional responsibilities. As a testament to the market niche these for-profit education firms are filling, the Apollo Group—which includes the University of Phoenix and its distance education operation—is now, on a consolidated basis, one of the largest accredited institutions of higher education in the United States. With 40,000 students, University of Phoenix has grown into the largest private university in the United States, surpassing both University of Michigan and University of Southern California.

**University of Phoenix: The for-profit education alternative.** Just as the Ivy League model was developed two centuries ago to accommodate aspiring clerics, so the University of Phoenix has been shaped by the needs of working adults to have fast, flexible and convenient continuing education.[12] The University of Phoenix (UOP), a subsidiary of the publicly-traded Apollo Group, is a for-profit university that focuses on providing business education to the non-traditional student market. Perhaps the most extensive example of how UOP operates is its recent learning alliance with the AT&T School of Business and Technology (ASBT) to provide graduate and undergraduate degree programs to a potential pool of 200,000 AT&T employees worldwide. This is possibly the largest and most comprehensive alliance between private industry and an accredited, degree-granting university to date and examining how this alliance operates provides some insight into the evolution of a market-driven education model.

UOP, founded in 1974, has 51 campuses and learning centers in the United States as well as multiple distance learning programs that allow students to receive training anywhere, anytime. Since its inception, the university has serviced over 350,000 students in forty-seven sites across the United States. All registrants are required to be a minimum of 23 years of age, have several years of work experience, and be currently employed. The average age of the UOP student is 34-years-old, which is indicative of the university's original mission to address the needs of the working adult. Classes at UOP are held at night, from six to ten. Courses consist of five to six weekly sessions, taken one right after another. Each degree program is identical from one campus to the next. Think of UOP as the educational equivalent of Southwest Airlines. Tenure doesn't exist and one is not likely to find the frills of football stadiums or swimming pools. What UOP does provide is a uniform educational product delivered in a consistent way by experienced working professionals at an affordable price.

John Sears, UOP's vice president of Institutional Development says, "We focus strictly on the education itself, that's what people come to us for." In nearly every respect UOP breaks the mold of the traditional university, primarily in the fact that it is run as a business, whose product happens to be education, and geared towards business people and business organizations.

"We serve two customers," says Sears. "Our primary customer is the student. We have to provide a quality learning experience in every course in order to satisfy a sophisticated and demanding customer. But we also recognize that there is a shadow consumer—the employer of the student, who may be contributing tuition assistance and providing the environment where much of the student's research and project activity is conducted."

UOP's orientation toward the non-traditional student, its practitioner faculty, and business operating model were obviously attributes that influenced AT&T School of Business and Technology's decision to choose UOP as a learning partner. Dr. June Maul, director of Customer and Multimedia Solutions at ASBT, discusses a key factor in their decision to partner with UOP: "When we started talking to them we learned that, particularly in the area of quality, they had pretty much the same orientation we did. They're an organization that bases their business on a number of quality principles, such as focusing on the customer, and measuring the quality of learning they provide to the institution."

One of the more unique and valuable aspects of the UOP/ASBT alliance is the course mapping process whereby UOP certifies that specific combinations of ASBT courses meet a carefully defined standard. Students are then awarded academic credit for the ASBT training they have completed that may be applied toward a degree. This is the all-important portability benefit that makes this alliance a win-win situation for the student, the corporation, and the university. Essentially course mapping works in the following way: UOP evaluates each course that ASBT provides and the learning outcomes of ASBT courses are correlated to similar learning outcomes throughout UOP's standard curriculum. The resulting articulation enables the university to award academic credit to students who complete a defined series of courses from ASBT. This credit may be used to waive a required course in a degree program or may be applied as elective credit. This course mapping process is a way to leverage training dollars: employees get the skills they need while the corporation saves tuition reimbursement dollars.

"There are significant benefits for every stakeholder involved," says Sears. For the student, this alliance makes the educational process more efficient by eliminating the need to duplicate course content. Awarding academic credit for relevant training that AT&T requires of employees results in significant savings of money and time for both the student and ASBT. ASBT students wishing to capitalize on the convenience and portability of University of Phoenix programs contribute positively to the university's enrollment growth.

The alliance between the University of Phoenix and the AT&T School of Business and Technology may presage a future where the corporate university melds with the for-profit firm and each contribute something to the alliance and each gains something very important from it. This mindset will become increasingly important over the coming years as the partnership model grows in importance for both corporations, institutions of higher education and for-profit education firms.

**Academic response: University of Warwick corporate/ college model.**   With the rise of externally-focused corporate universities, consortiums, virtual universities, and for-profit education firms, traditional educators face significant strategic challenges. The model of how to prosper and grow amid competition from new entrants can be found across the Atlantic in Coventry,

England, at the University of Warwick. The slogan of the Warwick Manufacturing Group (WMG), a separate entity within the engineering department of the university, says it all: "Academic excellence with industrial relevance." This is an accurate assessment of both their philosophy and their practice because, like few other universities in the world, they have embraced the synergy of corporate learning and academia.

WMG, which was founded in 1980 by Kumar Bhattacharyya, has become a model of how best to weave practical business learning into the fabric of an institute of higher learning through extensive partnerships with major global corporations and an international learning network that is the quintessence of portability.

In addition to an engineering doctorate program, WMG offers two other main programs: the Integrated Graduate Development Scheme (IGDS), which is designed for prospective senior managers who already possess a degree and several years of managerial experience; and the Integrated Manager Development Scheme (IMDS), geared toward supervisors and middle managers who don't necessarily have a formal degree, but have 10 or more years of managerial experience and require exposure to broad business ideas and strategic imperatives. Both programs require their participants to be employed and sponsored by the company for which they work (*integrated* refers to the integration of personal career development and the vocational aspirations of the sponsoring company).

The programs comprise a series of courses, called modules, that last for either a whole week—in the case of IGDS participants— or a half-week for those in the IMDS. Participants take one module at a time, then, most importantly, go back to their jobs to apply their learning. They return six to eight weeks later to do another module. According to Professor John Hearn, director of Program Development at WMG, "One of our prime criteria here is that learning must be quickly transferred to the workplace. We don't have formal examinations, we have what are called post-module assessments, which give the participants tasks which seek to relate the work of the module to the workplace."

The modules are split into four main categories: 1) Business, 2) Operations, 3) Technology, and 4) People Management. Some of the modules within these areas include: 1) Business Strategy,

Strategic Marketing, Business Environment and Economics; 2) Quality Systems, Logistics and Operations Management, Project Planning, Management and Control; 3) Emerging Technologies, Environmental Impact, New Materials; and 4) Human Factors in Industry, Improving Manager Performance, Improving Personal Performance, and Management of Change.

WMG's programs are international in scope and the whole system—with slight variations in the mode of delivery—has been transported to such countries as China (including Hong Kong), Malaysia, Thailand, India, and South Africa. Essential to WMG's operation is its system of alliances with numerous companies. Rover, part of Germany's BMW (and originally known as British Leyland) is a founding partner and presently WMG's largest partner firm. The alliances are defined by the fact that both Warwick and the firms have a joint responsibility to define, develop, deliver, and monitor the programs. For example, Warwick staff typically deliver half of a module and senior managers from partner companies or other external agencies help to deliver the other half. Hearn says of this arrangement, "The partners keep it up-to-date, they bring in case studies which are relevant to present day industry and so it's a very tight partnership that we have covering both design and delivery. Most of the work in the UK is done here at Warwick, but sometimes we run programs on-site for big companies. Overseas we generally work with a partner university to deliver the programs and take special care to suitably localize the material delivered to the needs of the environment for that country."

The WMG vision, as reflected in their integrated system, is to provide its partners and participants with the most up-to-date and applicable learning curriculum possible based on international best practice—the optimum business education. Hearn adds, "Industry has told us that they need a flexible system which is responsive rapidly to the changing needs of industry and responsive to global competitive pressures. Of course these days technology is advancing at a terrific pace. Business policies and practices are expanding equally fast, so they need an educational system which can be agile on its feet in the same way manufacturing needs to be agile."

WMG, in addition to its corporate partnerships and international network, is also a member of a consortium called TEAM.

Through TEAM, individuals can take modules at any participating university in England; however, the WMG network per se is particularly appealing because of its centralized quality control procedure. This means that all assessments are carried out at Warwick, and the same examination board administers modules for WMG's overseas components. This allows students from the UK to readily take modules at its overseas centers, and in turn allows foreign students to take modules at Warwick. This translates into portability on an international scale, which seems highly relevant in an increasingly interdependent global economy.

WMG represents a model of seamless integration of business training with academic education. Importantly, this model incorporates many of the features of a market-driven education system: it is learner-centered, flexible, relevant to the workplace, and cognizant of the learner's global education needs.

## THE FUTURE: A MARKET-DRIVEN EDUCATION SYSTEM

With the steady expansion of the adult education population, along with the changing dynamics of how the entire world conducts business, it is inevitable that employee training would undergo a sea change. The facts are indisputable: the rise of the working adult student, the need of life-long learning, the emphasis on portable credentials, and a heavy experimentation with distance learning. Consequently, the relationship between the private sector and academia is, and continues to be, permanently altered.

The business marketplace has now enveloped higher education and encroached upon its sacred terrain. Continuous learning in the workplace is more necessary than ever. Yet, corporate training budgets, owing to downsizing, rapid technological advancement, and the need for a sustained competitive advantage, are tighter than ever. This tension drives the emergence of a new learning model where corporations become both the customers and suppliers of education. The market-driven educational model is emerging with its focus on convenience, self-service and uniformity.

In this market-driven educational model, the learning providers will work with customers to serve their needs for cost-effective, strategically relevant learning delivered in a combination of modalities—classroom, desktop, and satellite. If institutes of higher education wish to remain viable forces in the private sector of America they will no doubt be forced to rethink their relationship to business and overhaul their methodologies, products, services, and delivery vehicles. Essentially this means they will have to behave more like businesses and treat their "consumers," that is, adult students and their sponsoring companies, as valued customers.

If academia is to adopt this consumer mindset, they will have to offer their customers a broader range of products, services, and delivery options and be more responsive to corporate strategic needs. Because companies are demanding more focused, strategically-aligned education for their employees, academia will have to redefine their business and even consider operating as franchises within the facilities of their corporate partners. Think of how banking has evolved in the last 10 years to meet consumer demands for accessible on-demand financial services. ATMs are now in most corporate sites. The newest financial service now includes roving bank branches that operate out of a truck, similar to the Good Humor Truck. In fact, more than 50 financial service firms including NationsBank, Wells Fargo, and First Chicago are expanding their self-service banking operations. Will universities follow suit and offer self-service, on-demand education?

Academic institutions, as they become more comfortable with their role as business partners, might find it especially useful to embrace an expanding palette of market-driven strategies that range from having an on-site presence in a corporation to licensing/merchandising and packaging curriculum to be transferred back and forth between companies and their learning partners.

This new learning paradigm that includes many new entrants to the education market may not be the only threat to higher education. Perhaps, as some of the educators in this chapter suggest, the real threat to higher education comes from within higher education itself; a complacency mindset that fails to deliver a full range of products and services to the educational market. As the forces of change gain ground, the education market will be changed forever and move into the era of consumerism.

## Chapter Eight

# Twelve Lessons in Building a World-Class Work Force

*The success of virtually all Americans in the new economy now depends on their ability to gain new knowledge and learn new skills.*

—Vice President Al Gore, Life-long Learning Conference

A global marketplace, technological innovations in higher education, and a continuing reorganization of the workplace are the new realities facing today's organizations and their employees. To compete, nothing short of world-class performance will do. The limited demands on workers to know only one narrow repetitive job no longer apply. Now, workers from the factory floor to the customer service hotline and ultimately to the executive suite must think and act at higher levels. For more and more companies, the choice is growing increasingly stark: go for world-class performance or be left behind.

Corporate universities represent an attempt to meet this challenge. As a group, the companies profiled here are taking determined steps to forge a work force excellence that will promote their own future survival. As this book has shown, the companies who have established corporate universities have fundamentally altered their thinking about who should participate in education and development and what they should be focusing on. Continuous learning, a heightened focus on broad, yet deep business literacy skills and, importantly, building partnerships with suppliers, customers, and educators are emerging as dimensions of best practices in corporate education and development.

The innovative and highly developed model for training represented by corporate universities provides a valuable blueprint for companies of all types and sizes interested in enhancing their own corporate education programs. As we enter the 21st century, the skills of the work force will be fundamental to each company's competitiveness. All companies, regardless of whether they are public or private institutions, will need to develop strategies for promoting continuous learning in the workplace in order to successfully compete in the global marketplace. The lessons learned from the companies profiled here, if acted upon, can enhance any corporate education program, whether grand or modest in scale. This chapter looks at twelve specific lessons for improving work force competitiveness by implementing best practice education and development programs.

These twelve lessons reflect a central belief: a company's work force is its primary resource for creating a sustainable differentiation in the marketplace. Work force-based competitive advantage is proving more enduring than technology-based competitiveness, which quickly slips away as new technologies become equally accessible to companies on a global basis. Work force excellence, however, is the unique result of a company's hiring and training practices; it creates an advantage that cannot easily be duplicated and can always be renewed and improved upon.

This book has examined how the corporate university has been put to use by scores of organizations to provide continuous life-long learning. In essence, this heightened focus on continuous learning has shifted the paradigm of corporate education. The focus of organizations with best practice corporate universities is moving from a training orientation to a life-long learning orientation where the emphasis is on self-management, individual and team accomplishments, and an identification with improving one's portfolio of skills. What's more, as corporate universities offer an alternative to the traditional education system, the target audience for employee education is expanding from internal employees and even value chain participants to outside companies on a fee-for-services basis.

The goal of the world-class organizations represented here is to create the benchmark for best practice corporate education and development programs within their industry. By focusing on continuous learning rather than conducting one-time training events, these companies are essentially forging a new contract with employees, one driven by building technical and leadership skills rather than having employees participate in a smorgasbord of single solution training programs. This focus on learning to improve on-the-job performance is best illustrated in the National Semiconductor University Learning Philosophy, depicted in Figure 8–1. This learning philosophy, standardized under the National Semiconductor University (NSU) umbrella, is designed to address the strategic imperatives of National Semiconductor. NSU has become the vehicle for disseminating the corporate learning philosophy and ensuring strategic alignment to business unit goals.

## FIGURE 8–1

### National Semiconductor Learning Philosophy

| Past Focus:<br>Training As An Event | Current Focus:<br>Learning To Improve Performance |
|---|---|
| ● Widespread Focus | ● Directed Focus |
| ● Intellectual Partner | ● Business Partner |
| ● Classes and Programs Designed to Address NSC Corporate Level Programs | ● Classes and Programs Designed to Address NSC Business Unit's Achievement of the Strategic Imperatives |
| ● Global Interaction | ● Global Collaboration |
| ● Driven by Broad Corporate Initiatives | ● Driven by Corporate and Business Unit Needs |
| ● Serve as the Implementation Vehicle for NSC's Vision | ● Technical & Leadership Emphasis as well as an Agent of Change |

Courtesy of National Semiconductor University

## TWELVE LESSONS IN BUILDING A WORLD-CLASS WORK FORCE

### 1. Tie the Goals of Education and Development to the Strategic Needs of the Organization

As we have seen, learning at best practice corporate universities link the results of learning to the organization's strategic business requirements. In an article in *Fortune* magazine, Thomas Stewart described core competencies as the sum of everything everybody in the company knows that gives the company a competitive edge in the marketplace.[1]

The core curricula at such corporate universities as Motorola University, Fidelity Investments Service Delivery University, and Bank of Montreal Institute for Learning do just this. The formal and informal learning programs under the corporate university umbrella zero in on the skills, knowledge, and competencies that define the uniqueness of each company. For example, Motorola University has been instrumental in the development of global business leadership skills in China in order to transform Chinese nationals into Motorola business leaders. Similarly, Fidelity Service Delivery University (SDU) ties employee contributions to business results. Under the SDU framework for employee development, Fidelity employees learn a common vocabulary that includes an understanding of Fidelity's hierarchy of customer needs and specifically how meeting these customer needs translates into delivering exceptional levels of customer service. Finally, the Bank of Montreal Institute for Learning focuses on linking the bank's key business goals with each individual employee's learning objectives.

Having successfully aligned learning with their core competence, the organizations profiled here ensure that education and development stays on track by establishing a governance structure. This structure comprises line business managers from various disciplines (sales, manufacturing, engineering) who function in a manner similar to the organization's board of directors. Essentially, these board members advise, counsel, review, and manage the overall learning function and ensure that it is linked to the company's strategic vision. While the governance structure at each corporate university differs in its composition, the goals remain similar: to lend an informed, objective perspective and create a standardized business-driven focus to all education and development.

## 2. Involve Leaders as Learners and Faculty

Top management at companies with corporate universities are becoming increasingly involved in and committed to the learning process. The CEO, in particular, is spending a significant amount of time facilitating learning. In fact, a committed and involved CEO is the single most important factor in the success of a corporate university. CEOs ranging from Jack Welch and Andy Grove to Richard Teerlink and Jack Smith are facilitating executive development programs. In fact, in the case of Harley-Davidson, CEO Teerlink participates in new employee orientation programs to the point of becoming a certified trainer for Harley-Davidson's course on corporate values.

Andy Grove, in his book *High Output Management*, devotes an entire chapter to "Why Training Is The Boss's Job." Here Grove describes his training repertoire as including facilitating three-hour sessions on 'What Makes Intel, Intel,' which focuses on the history, objectives, organization, and management practices of the highly successful chip maker. As Grove points out, "Some 2 percent to 4 percent of our employees' time is spent in classroom learning and we believe much of this instruction should be given by our own managerial staff."[2]

In announcing GM University, Chairman, CEO, and President Jack Smith and the seven members of the General Motors President's Council each selected one of the five General Motors core values (e.g. customer enthusiasm, integrity, continuous improvement, teamwork, and innovation) and shared their perspective at a General Motors Global Automotive Leadership Conference. It's this type of public demonstration of teaching and role modeling that communicates a commitment to learning.

It is not just the CEO that is involved in learning programs at the corporate universities profiled here. These learning sessions led by senior business managers communicate the importance of stepping back, listening to employees, and learning from them.

For example, the Faculty Club at National Semiconductor University gives employees an opportunity to participate in a dialogue and exchange of ideas with senior management on a variety of topics, including: leadership, product development, and new ventures. Each Faculty Club session consists of an informal presentation by a senior manager, followed by a discussion period. The value of these sessions is to promote a culture of continuous learning within the National Semiconductor organization under the umbrella of the corporate university. You learn and are recognized by teaching has become the battle cry among these best practice organizations.

The Tennessee Valley Authority (TVA) University has fully embraced the idea of manager-as-faculty. Seven hundred TVA middle and senior managers participate in a rigorous certification program to become instructors, with a goal of delivering 150 hours of classroom instruction within a 12-month period. Instruction by senior management carries a high degree of credibility by virtue of their proximity to actual corporate operations. Managers develop group management skills along with a deeper knowledge about TVA's business and participants benefit from the real-world knowledge of seasoned managers, who also serve as role models.

This type of active involvement of senior managers as faculty at best practice corporate universities sends a powerful message throughout the organization. What these organizations are doing is raising the bar for everyone else by becoming actively involved in the education and development of their work force. Managers from senior line leaders to the CEO participate in workout sessions, orient new hires to the vision and values of the organization, and even facilitate leadership development programs where they pass along the war stories about what has made the organization successful.

### 3. Select a Chief Learning Officer to Set the Strategic Direction for Corporate Education

Corporate universities have emerged as the strategic umbrella for all corporate education—including employees, value chain members, and even outsiders. Presiding over this strategic direction of corporate education is the chief learning officer, who has joined the chief information officer and chief financial officer at the strategic planning table to work with senior executives and build a vision for how learning can make a competitive difference to business performance.

Research conducted by Corporate University Xchange, Inc. has identified several key roles the chief learning officer should possess in order to lead a high performing corporate education department. These key roles span those of a visonary for the education function, to an alliance builder working with business managers both inside and outside the organization to manage a vast array of learning partnerships. The trend toward partnering with external vendors to produce a greater share of learning programs means the chief learning officer must be astute in selecting and managing vendors who will include traditional universities, consulting firms, virtual universities, and for-profit education firms. Some of these learning partnerships will be with small start-up firms and others will be with well-known and brand name universities. This increased complexity of the job of managing the education function points to the need for organizations to select a senior business manager to lead the education department.

As evidence of the increased importance placed on corporate education, a growing number of chief learning officers are now reporting to the chief executive officer in order to provide overall strategic direction for the education function and act as the primary link for aligning education to the goals of the business.

### 4. Consider Employee Orientation an Ongoing Strategic Process, Rather Than a One-Time Event

Orientation programs were once the job of junior human resources managers who covered such topics as vacation schedules, insurance, health benefits, and often a departmental organization chart—all within a couple of hours. Today, orientation is increasingly viewed as a strategic process and a vehicle for having employees develop a firm foundation in the organization's values, culture, traditions, and philosophy of customer service. Interestingly, nearly all of the corporate universities profiled in this book have included a formal, ongoing process to instill in employees the organization's core values and how to live out these values in one's day-to-day job.

Delivery of these programs has gone through a paradigm shift. In the past, these programs were delivered in a traditional lecture format, often as a discrete event. Now, the emphasis is on action learning, often involving senior managers as instructors to engage in dialogue with employees and share their lessons and commitment to core company values. Many of these programs are also adding a high tech component. Oracle University's CD-ROM orientation for new hires, known as *Inside Track*, uses the metaphor of automobile racing to provide a media rich approach, combining graphics, movies, and a rock n' roll/jazz soundtrack to deliver an orientation that is engaging as well as entertaining. Some orientation programs, such as Dell University's, are on the company intranet and are updated frequently to include the latest information on the company products, services, and personnel.

Regardless of a company's specific orientation program, the growing trend among those profiled in the book has been to view orientation as the foundation for employee empowerment rather than an overview of policies and procedures.

### 5. Design a Core Curriculum to Stress the Three Cs: Corporate Citizenship, Contextual Framework, and Core Competencies

The common themes that run through the curricula at corporate universities are a direct result of what's happening in the workplace. As noted throughout this book, to be successful in the workplace, one needs broad yet deep business skills. Jobs today require employees to solve problems, think creatively, listen to co-workers and customers, negotiate, and, above all, assume responsibility for their own learning.

Now, as companies drive decision making down the organization, more and more employees must think and act like managers. This has led corporate universities to develop broad curricula stressing the three Cs: building corporate citizens, providing a contextual reference, and developing core competencies.

**Building corporate citizens.** As outlined in Chapter 4, an increasing number of world-class companies are developing learning programs to ensure the work force is knowledgeable about the vision, history, culture, traditions, and values of the company in order to promote a sense and spirit of corporate citizenship. The goal here is to engender a strong feeling of attachment and connectedness to the company similar to what citizens feel for their city or country. Companies want employees to identify with the firm and to live out the corporate mission in their day-to-day jobs.

**Providing contextual reference.** The second C is contextual reference, which refers to providing learning opportunities about the company's products, services, and industry dynamics in the context of what competitors are offering in the marketplace and the best practices of the industry as a whole. Numerous programs and initiatives are cropping up at corporate universities to train employees in the features and benefits of their own company's products, as well as how they stack up against competitors, products, and services. The goal is for all employees to be able to clearly communicate the company's strategic intent to both current and prospective employees. In addition, advances in learning technologies are providing a rich opportunity for companies to use multimedia as the medium to provide contextual training. Oracle's *Inside Track,* highlighted in Chapter 4, is an innovative and entertaining tool to learn about Oracle's products, services, and position within the industry. What's more, it presents an opportunity for Oracle employees to see and hear CEO Larry Ellison and President Ray Lane talk about the company's strategies. This type of interactive and entertaining medium is far more memorable and impactful than simply reading about the strategy in the company's annual report.

**Developing workplace competencies.** The final C refers to building the company's core competencies. This involves training employees in the specific competencies the corporation has deemed critical to its long-term success. A number of companies intent upon building a world-class work force are distinctive for having spent extensive time, money, and resources conducting research and benchmarking studies to target and define the set of core competencies required of employees to maintain overall competitiveness.

Several core workplace competencies have emerged from the research conducted at the various companies profiled in this book.

They are outlined and defined in detail in Chapter 4, but they are worth mentioning again to stress the types of competencies the workplace of the future will demand from its employees. As you look down this list, you will recognize the emergence of technological literacy as a key competency needed for success. Technological innovations—such as 56.6 modems and non-PC Internet appliances—will explode in the coming decade, requiring us to spend more of our professional and personal lives "on-line." Specifically, the core workplace competencies profiled in this book include:

1. *Learning to learn.* Being responsible for one's continuous learning and understanding the optimal way one learns new skills.

2. *Communication and collaboration.* Communicating effectively with co-workers, knowing how to work in groups, and collaborating with team members to share best practices across the organization.

3. *Creative thinking and problem-solving.* Knowing how to identify problems and see the connections between the solution discovered and possible approaches to the next problem.

4. *Technological literacy.* Using the latest technologies to connect your team members around the globe.

5. *Global business literacy.* Understanding the "global big picture" of how the business operates through a core set of business skills such as finance, strategic planning, and marketing.

6. *Leadership and visioning.* Having a vision for one's work team or department that fits into the corporate mission and goals.

7. *Career self-management.* Having the ability to manage one's own career by identifying the skills and knowledge one needs to be valuable in the workplace and then working to acquire them.

While these competencies were once associated with managers, they are quickly becoming part of an empowered worker's toolkit in the twenty-first century. Because 80 percent of the people who will be working in the year 2000 are already on the job, the responsibility for providing life-long learning opportunities is increasingly falling to the private sector. Businesses that thrive in the twenty-first century will be those that organize themselves for learning and then capitalize on what they have learned.

### 6. Link What Employees Earn to What They Learn

One of the important contributions of many corporate universities has been to encourage the creation of an annual individual learning and development plan as a vehicle for employees to be accountable for learning new skills. These plans are quite specific. They lead each employee to higher and higher levels of both professional and team performance. They are reviewed regularly to respond to the evolving needs of the workplace and the marketplace and ensure that the *right* employees participate in the *right* training and learning activities at the *right* time.

The pace of change requires that employees take a proactive stance toward education and training. This means that each and every employee should have a clearly articulated education and development plan outlining the combination of formal and informal learning activities he or she will complete and a timetable for completing them.

The Individual Development Plan serves a number of purposes. First, as its name implies, there are many ways for employees to develop themselves. Hence, these plans define the formal and informal learning opportunities, which can range from taking a course either in a classroom, on-line, or via satellite; completing a CD-ROM; requesting a developmental assignment; or even being an instructor in a training class. In addition, these plans instill in each employee a commitment to self-development. Because the workplace is changing so fast, employees cannot rely on their supervisors or their human resources managers to manage their careers; instead, they must be responsible for their own self-development. Based on the principle that what gets measured gets done, these plans have become an important tool to help employees examine their needs, plan their professional and personal development, and track their performance against the goals laid out in the plan.

Finally, these development plans ultimately hold each employee accountable for achieving his or her learning goals. As the example from Saturn Corporation illustrates in Chapter 4, achievement of one's development goals can be closely tied to compensation at both the individual and team level. In fact, as the Saturn at-risk compensation percentage increased from 5 to 12 percent so did the total compensation of each Saturn employee. Gary High, director of Human Resources Development of Saturn Corporation, believes that as employees learn specifically what is required of them, they will be increasingly motivated to achieve their goal and, in the process, improve their overall performance.

A corollary to the earning-learning rule is that security no longer comes from sticking to a single company for 25 years, but from maintaining a portfolio of flexible skills. This link of accountability to learning ultimately benefits both the individual employee and the corporation: the employee adds to his or her skill level while the corporation develops the highly skilled work force that is a sustainable competitive advantage in the marketplace.

### 7. Experiment with Technology to Measure, Track, and Accelerate Learning

The corporate university has become a testing ground for experimenting with new ways for employees to learn new skills and new roles within the organization. The traditional classroom format in which the trainer does most of the talking is being supplemented with many more innovative delivery modes. Corporate universities are experimenting with ways to encourage employees to learn at the desktop. Here, trainees may be at their desktop working but with the push of a button, they can be hyperlinked to web sites of interest, conduct research on-line, enter a corporate repository of white papers and speeches, or listen to the "corporate stories" of experts delivered during a computer simulation.

Chapter 5 presents a number of examples of these experimental learning vehicles. The idea behind creating learner-centered education and development is that instead of passively memorizing a set of instructions for how to perform a certain task, employees can use a variety of delivery modalities to actively learn new skills on-the-job.

Combining intranet technology and classroom instruction, Oracle University (OU) represents a best practice example of learner-centered education where OU becomes an integrated learning solution that functions as a single point of entry for all training and development at Oracle. The OU virtual campus, conceived as a modular desktop network, provides a wide range of product knowledge, industry knowledge, technical skills, sales methodologies, and Oracle-specific processes, such as how to use the Oracle sales automation system.

In addition to OU's desktop learning feature, a global network of regional classrooms—in the United States, Europe, the Middle East, and Asia—provides employees with the opportunity to practice hands-on skill building and motivational exercises. Oracle Interactive Business TV, a component of this regionally-based training, brings experts into the classroom—via satellite TV—sometimes on a mass global scale to share success stories and expertise.

The key to the learning solutions offered by Oracle University is that they are prescriptive—meaning users identify their job role and then go through a skills assessment specific to that job. The result of this assessment determines which learning interventions are recommended for the user. Corporate universities such as Oracle University will provide the learning infrastructure to support just-in-time learning, but what is also coming to the forefront is the need to have a vast cataloguing ability so that the appropriate resources for just-in-time learning can be accessed immediately.

### 8. Extend The Corporate University Beyond Internal Employees to Key Members of the Customer/Supply Chain

The companies profiled here, such as Motorola, Harley-Davidson, and Anheuser-Busch, all make heavy investments in training their work forces (most invest between 3 and 5 percent of their payroll on training), but they do something else as well. They extend their training throughout their entire customer and supply chains. It is no longer enough to just have well-trained employees. To succeed, companies are realizing their success is dependent to a large extent upon the success of a select group of suppliers and customers. The companies profiled in this book are shouldering the responsibility of improving their total human capital by providing training to the company's entire business network, that is, their employees, customers, suppliers, and, importantly, the universities whose graduates will someday enter their work forces. This emphasis on training all the members of a company's value chain is redefining the nature and scope of training. Companies no longer simply train customers in how to use their products or services. Instead, today's customer training programs are more closely geared to helping customers run their businesses more profitably.

Consider the example of Harley-Davidson University. Training Harley-Davidson's large network of dealers (900 in the United States and Europe) has become more important than ever now that Harley-Davidson has greatly expanded their merchandising and product line beyond motorcycles to include such items as clothing and collectibles. This immediately created a learning gap that Harley-Davidson University was responsible for closing. Harley-Davidson University, through their use of technology and a heightened awareness of the importance of connecting to dealers, has developed an integrated curriculum that offers hard business literacy skills such as financial analysis, inventory control, and smart buying practices, as well as skills in customer service and negotiation. What's more, Harley-Davidson University also developed a toolkit for dealers to create their own web sites. Dealer web sites are designed to link to the main Harley-Davidson web site, which in turn provides links to the dealers' sites. This interlinking of electronic marketing serves as a metaphor for Harley-Davidson's concerted effort to include dealers in the training process.

Harley-Davidson is also expanding their intranet to become a communications link between the company and its dealers, providing information on warranties, product updates, etc. For Harley-Davidson University, dealers are not peripheral elements of the whole training process, but crucial links whose education needs have to be addressed continually and through a variety of different approaches in order to maintain a fully integrated dealer-manufacturer partnership.

Anheuser-Busch is another company taking major steps to build an alliance with its dealers. The Busch Learning Center (BLC) is their answer to training their sales network of 34,000 wholesale employees and a field sales force of 500. As part of Anheuser-Busch's training approach, BLC not only imports knowledge and training to the wholesalers, but also goes one step further by accessing information and best practices from the wholesalers and sharing it with the entire sales network. This previously untapped source of valuable information was made available through a diligent effort by Anheuser-

Busch to align all training with business strategies in what An-heuser-Busch calls "training for performance."

Another twist on customer and supplier training is that smaller companies are doing it too. Customer training used to be the domain of such giants as IBM and Xerox. Now, firms such as Lord Corporation, the $336 million maker of products for motion control, is using the educational infrastructure of a corporate university to forge closer links with its customers and suppliers. In 1994 it created the Lord Institute for Technical and Management Training to provide training to both employees and suppliers. Lord and other smaller companies are discovering that being able to offer this kind of benefit helps differentiate them from competitors.

Perhaps the most innovative efforts in extending this passion for training throughout the company's customer supply chain are those that involve reaching out to colleges and universities as customers of education. No longer are companies content to pay their employees' tuition. Instead, they want to talk jointly about their needs and requirements for a well-trained work force, just like a true customer/supplier relationship. Innovations such as developing customized degree programs for an industry are becoming more commonplace as corporations partner with institutions of higher education to ensure their learning programs are aligned to their business strategies.

### 9. Operate the Corporate University as a Line of Business Within the Organization

One of the most interesting discoveries in our continuing research into best practice corporate universities is the fact that most have a similar mission statement, regardless of size, specific industry, or the country in which they operate. With varying refinements of language, the mission of most corporate universities is to: "serve as a partner so employees can achieve exceptional performance and the organization meets its business goals and is recognized as a leader in the industry."

The commonality of this mission does not detract from its value; simply put, world-class corporate universities must satisfy the goals of service, satisfaction, and value to survive within their respective organizations. Successful management of a corporate university requires a delicate balancing act between meeting the demands of the internal clients, acknowledging the realities of the staff, and understanding the organization's strategic goals.

Hence, the model for tomorrow's corporate university is today's premier professional service firm. As the Bank of Montreal Institute for Learning (IFL) charter says, "We choose to be judged by our contribution to performance." In the case of the Bank of Montreal, Southwestern Bell, and Petróleos de Venezuela this means designing a funding model where customers pay for services on a tuition basis. This funding model necessitates the importance of creating a professional service mindset where delivering outstanding customer service is critical to success.

In implementing this funding model, corporate universities can learn from premier professional service firms how to meet client expectations 100 percent of the time. At the heart of a premier professional service firm is the ability to deliver exceptional service levels to clients. Some of us may mistakenly associate client service as "schmoozing," "stroking," or "hand holding" clients. Instead, the key to providing quality client service revolves around utilizing superior account management skills.

David Maister, a consultant to professional service firms such as Arthur Andersen, Ketchum Communications, and Towers Perrin, stresses the importance of using quantitative feedback tools such as client questionnaires to rate the level of service an organization provides its clients. A sample of typical questions included in a client feedback questionnaire follows. As you read these, think about the value in having a system in place within your corporate university to probe for the following data regarding the relationship between the corporate university and your clients:

- Do corporate university professionals understand the business of their clients?
- Do they show creativity in proposing solutions?
- Can they redefine the current view of the problem?
- Is their communications free of training jargon?
- Do they speak the language of the business?
- Do they show an interest in the client beyond the specifics of the task at hand?
- Have their solutions improved the performance of the business unit?[3]

In creating this type of feedback system, it is important to devise a system so you can fully understand how clients perceive the level of service provided by the corporate university and what changes can be made to improve it. This type of analysis will go a long way toward building a professional service mentality within a corporate learning function.

### 10. Develop a Range of Innovative Alliances with Higher Education

The job of continuously updating an employee's knowledge and skills is huge, and corporate universities are joining forces with conventional universities and merging the goals of all the participating parties—students, corporation, university—into one mutually beneficial partnership. Rather than simply giving a list of requirements to higher education, businesses are now spelling out the specific skills, knowledge, and competencies needed for success in an industry.

Those thinking of forming a corporate/college partnership must consider the future of their business and then select the best learning partner to help achieve business results. In other words, rather than engage in a series of disconnected programs and initiatives, businesses are using a methodical process to link an organization's strategic objectives to those of its learning partners.

Whirlpool Corporation provides an example of a growing company that needed to greatly expand its training initiative. After purchasing the appliance division of an international company with far-flung business interests, Whirlpool launched Brandywine Creek Performance Centre (BCPC) to fulfill its mandate to communicate the company's strategic vision, cultivate leaders, and develop core business competencies. To help fulfill these goals BCPC created a learning consortium, forming alliances with Indiana University, University of Michigan, and INSEAD in France. The university partners were chosen as much for their ability to develop and deliver world-class training programs as their willingness to develop a shared vision with Whirlpool. Working with multiple universities presents a challenge for any corporate university. BCPC's approach was to take the best of what each university had to offer, link this to the needs of Whirlpool, and create an integrated learning system.

Ultimately, the objective of a corporate/college alliance, such as the one involving Whirlpool and its academic partners, is to integrate business practice and business education. The Warwick Manufacturing Group (WMG), a division of Warwick University in England, is an academic institution that has successfully achieved this objective on an international scale. Their whole curriculum, intended primarily for middle and upper-level managers, is closely aligned with and customized to suit the business objectives of its many corporate partners. In these alliances, both WMG and the partnering firms have a joint responsibility to define, develop, deliver, and monitor the programs. WMG's goal, as reflected in their slogan, "Academic excellence with industrial relevance," is to deliver optimal business education in partnership with corporations.

Warwick University students take a series of modules each lasting 40 to 80 hours, then return to their jobs to apply that learning. WMG fields a practitioner faculty, relies heavily on practical fieldwork and real-life case studies, and links its modules to the specific needs of the sponsoring organizations. The goal for Warwick and other best practice corporate/college alliances is to integrate employee career development with business goals of partner firms.

## 11. Demonstrate the Value of the Corporate University Learning Infrastructure

Corporate learning initiatives are finding it increasingly critical to develop measurements for assessing the contribution an investment in human capital has on achieving business strategy. A number of corporate universities are developing innovative "report cards" to top management on the value their learning investment has made to the corporation.

The most cutting edge measurement systems are holistic, meaning they determine what impact the corporate university has on overall achievement of business strategies, as well as the specific impact on customer retention, customer satisfaction, and the level of employee innovation.

This interest in demonstrating the value of the corporate university is becoming increasingly critical. As corporate universities increase in scope, stature, and budget within their respective organizations, they are being charged to operate as a business; meaning delivering exceptional service to their customers and creating business-driven measurements. As part of this move to operate as a business, corporate university directors will want to explore how to cost-effectively capture the economies of scale in the centralization of the corporate education function. A host of holistic measurements will be developed to assist the corporate university to better operate as a business. These range from customer satisfaction surveys, employee satisfaction/retention surveys, and design cycle time standards, to the ability of the corporate university to assist the organization in entering emerging markets. As organizations require their corporate education functions to prove their value, a holistic model of measurement is increasingly necessary to assess this outcome.

Skandia, a Swedish insurance firm, has gone the farthest in actually developing a supplementary report to the firm's annual report summarizing its contribution. This level of analysis is indicative of the importance senior management is placing on communicating the value of an investment in intellectual capital. The measurement tool—known as the "Skandia Navigator," is intended to provide a balanced, comprehensive overview of the company's financial *and* intellectual capital, measuring such indicators as Customer Focus, Process Focus, Employee Focus, and Renewal and Development Focus. This holistic measurement model reflects the company's belief that value growth is dependent on their ability to create, sustain, and benefit from intellectual capital.

### 12. Develop the Corporate University as a Branded Competitive Advantage and Profit Center

To develop a well-trained work force committed to life-long learning is reason enough to establish a corporate university, but the advantages go beyond these immediate benefits. Best practice corporate university actually adds value to a company in a variety of ways.

First, a world class corporate university functions as an ongoing advertisement for an organization's "best in the business" work force. Accordingly, if the corporate university has in fact developed a highly skilled, technologically sophisticated work force, the benefits of this should be evident in market share, profitability, employee satisfaction/retention, and customer development/ retention. In other words, organizations with corporate universities will measure these indicators and tout the corporate university as a major asset and distinguishing feature within an industry.

A corporate university can also increase competitive advantage by leveraging its organization's "brand name," and operating as a branded competitive advantage to the customers and partners of the organization. By branding and marketing their expertise, facilities, and training products to outsiders, corporate universities are beginning to defray their own operating expenses and generate positive revenue for their parent organization.

The corporate universities of Motorola, Disney, and Saturn have all capitalized on their parent company's household names and have begun selling themselves to outsiders as branded learning products. Internally developed training tools at Bell Atlantic's corporate university, including courseware, electronic performance support systems, and multimedia development software have found their way to the open market. Smaller companies are also getting into the act, like Southern California Water Company's Employee Development University, which had their courses certified by a national accrediting board and is now marketing them to other water companies.

Many organizations that have decided to outsource large segments of their training function will look to established corporate universities to design and deliver both customized and general learning solutions. This will expand an already growing training market and, increasingly, corporate universities that have proved to be major providers of world-class education to their own employees will evolve into profit centers.

Any company, of any size, can benefit from these twelve lessons, whether or not they organize their corporate learning function around the structure of a corporate university. The group of trend-setting companies profiled in this book who are investing heavily in training their workers serves as a useful model for organizations who aspire to world-class performance. Clearly, a challenging road lies ahead for corporations, and an array of innovative efforts to redefine corporate learning are emerging. The ability of the companies profiled here to create a world-class work force lies in their realization that learning and development constitute continuous life-long endeavors for the corporation, the individual employees within it, as well as key members of the corporation's customer/supply chain. Increasingly, these corporations are becoming a major force in post-secondary higher education. The 50 organizations profiled here are challenging institutions of higher education to experiment with new tools, practices, and technologies to best serve the needs of a growing consumer segment of working adult students.

# *Appendix*

## YOUR NETWORKING GUIDE TO FIFTY CORPORATE UNIVERSITIES

Your company may be interested in benchmarking the best practices of companies who are committed to building a world-class work force. The following is a list of 50 companies who share a common goal: they all look at training as a process of life-long learning rather than a place to "go get trained." This list of 50 companies is not meant to be a comprehensive one encompassing every organization with a corporate university processing this philosophy of life-long learning. It is, however, a list of companies providing exemplary ongoing learning opportunities for internal employees and, in many cases, key members of the company's customer/supply chain. Increasingly, these companies will be studied by scores of others as training becomes *the* critical tool to building a world-class work force.

**Air University**
United States Airforce
55 Lamay Playa South
Maxwell Air Force Base
Montgomery, Alabama 36112-6424

**Arthur Anderson Center for Professional Development**
Arthur Anderson & Co.
1405 North Fifth Avenue
St. Charles, Illinois 60174-1264

**Arthur D. Little School of Management**
Arthur D. Little
35 Acorn Park
Cambridge, Massachusetts 02140

**AT&T School of Business and Technology (ASBT)**
AT&T
19 School House Road
Somerset, New Jersey 08875

**Bank of Montreal Institute for Learning**
Bank of Montreal
3550 Pharmacy Avenue
Scarborough, Ontario M1W 3Z3 Canada

**Bell Atlantic Training, Education and Development**
Bell Atlantic Corporation
1095 Avenue of the Americas
New York, New York 10036

**The Busch Learning Center**
Anheuser-Busch, Inc.
701 Market
St. Louis, Missouri 63101

**Cable & Wireless College**
Cable & Wireless plc
320 Westwood Heath Road
Coventry, West Midlands CV4 8GP, UK

**Centro Internacional de Educación y Desarrollo**
Petróleos de Venezuela
Av. Intercomunal La Trinidad-El Hatillo Con Calle El Angel De La
Tahona Urb.
Las Esmeraldas, Caracas 1083
Venezuela

**Charles Schwab University**
Charles Schwab
101 Montgomery Street
San Francisco, California 94104

**Dell University**
Dell Computer Corporation
2214 West Braker Lane
Austin, Texas 78758-4053

**Disney Institute**
The Walt Disney Company
P.O. Box 10,000
Lake Buena Vista, Florida 32830-1000

**The Eaton School of Retailing**
The T. Eaton Company Ltd.
250 Young Street
Toronto, Ontario M5B 1O8 Canada

**Employee Development University**
Southern California Water Company
630 East Foothill Boulevard
San Dimas, California 91773-1207

**First University**
First Union Corporation
301 South College Street
Charlotte, North Carolina 28288-0957

**FORDSTAR**
Ford Motor Company
330 Towne Center Drive
Dearborn, Michigan 48126

**General Electric Management Development Institute**
General Electric
Old Albany Post Road
Ossining, New York 10562

**General Motors University**
General Motors Corporation
General Motors Building
Detroit, Michigan 48202

**Hamburger University**
McDonald's Corporation
Ronald Lane
Oak Brook, Illinois 60521

**Harley-Davidson University**
Harley-Davidson, Inc.
3700 W. Juneau Avenue
Milwaukee, Wisconsin 53208

**Iams University**
The Iams Company
7250 Poe Avenue
Dayton, Ohio 45414

**Intel University**
Intel Corporation
2565 Walsh Avenue
Santa Clara, California 95051

**Lord Institute**
Lord Corporation
1635 West 12th Street
Erie, Pennsylvania 16514

**MasterCard University**
MasterCard International
2000 Purchase Street
Purchase, New York 10577

**MBNA Customer College (MBNA America)**
MBNA America Bank N.A.
400 Christiana Road
Newark, Delaware 19713

**McDonnell Douglas Learning Center**
McDonnell Douglas Corporation
P.O. Box 516
St. Louis, Missouri 63166

**Megatech Academy**
Megatech Engineering, Inc.
1950 Concept Drive
Warren, Michigan 48091

**Mercantile Stores University**
Mercantile Stores Company, Inc.
9450 Seward Road
Fairfield, Ohio 45014-2230

**Motorola University**
Motorola, Inc.
1303 East Algonquin Road
Schaumburg, Illinois 60196-1097

**National Semiconductor University**
National Semiconductor
P.O. Box 58090
Santa Clara, California 95052-8090

**Oracle University**
Oracle Corporation
500 Oracle Parkway
Redwood Shores, California 94065

**Presbyterian Healthcare Educational Services**
Presbyterian Healthcare System
5750 Pineland, Suite 140
Dallas, Texas 75231-4425

**Quality Academy**
Northern States Power Company
414 Nicollet Mall
Minneapolis, Minnesota 55401

**Raychem University**
Raychem Corporation
300 Constitution Drive
Menlo Park, California 94025-1164

**Rover Business Learning**
Rover Group Ltd.
P.O. Box 41, Longbridge
Birmingham B31 2TB, UK

**Saturn Training Center**
Saturn Corporation
100 Saturn Parkway
Spring Hill, Tennessee 37174

**SBC Center for Learning**
Southwestern Bell Corporation
6301 Colwell Drive
Irving, Texas 75039

**Sears University**
Sears Roebuck & Company
3333 Beverly Road
Hoffman Estates, Illinois 60179

**Service Delivery University**
Fidelity Investments
82 Devonshire Street
Boston, Massachusetts 02109

**Southern Company College**
The Southern Company
64 Perimeter Center East
Atlanta, Georgia 30346

**Sprint University of Excellence[SM]**
Sprint Corporation
2330 Shawnee Mission Parkway
Westwood, Kansas 66205

**SunU**
Sun Microsystems
2550 Garcia Avenue
Mountain View, California 94043

**Target Stores University**
Target Stores (Division of Dayton Hudson Stores)
33 South 6th Street
Minneapolis, Minnesota 55402

**TVA University**
Tennessee Valley Authority
400 West Summit Hill Drive
Knoxville, Tennessee 37902

**UCH Academy**
University of Chicago Hospitals
5841 S. Maryland Avenue
Chicago, Illinois 60637

**United HealthCare Learning Institute**
United HealthCare
450 Columbus Boulevard
Hartford, Connecticut 06115

**The University**
Van Kampen American Capital
2800 Post Oak Boulevard
Houston, Texas 77056

**Verifone University**
Verifone
One Northwinds Center
2475 Northwinds Parkway, Suite 600
Alpharetta, GA 30201

**Whirlpool Brandywine Performance Centre**
Whirlpool Corporation
78300 C.R. 378
Covert, Michigan 49043

**Xerox Management Institute**
Xerox Corporation
Box 2000
Leesburg, Virginia 20177

# BENCHMARKING BEST PRACTICES AMONG CORPORATE UNIVERSITIES

## *Corporate University Xchange, Inc.: Assisting Organizations Build World-Class Learning Infrastructures*

### *Our Mission*

To provide best demonstrated practice research in the design and development of world-class corporate universities.

### *Our Capabilities*

We fulfill our mission by offering:

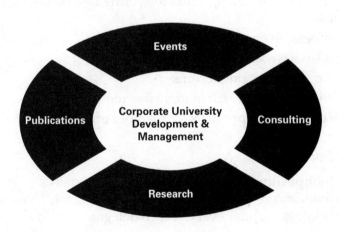

© 1997 Corporate University Xchange, Inc.

### *Consulting Services*

**Consulting on Launching and Enhancing a Corporate University**—Consulting engagements include all aspects of launching a corporate university or enhancing an existing corporate university.

**Framework for Building Corporate/Academic Partnerships**—Consulting for both corporate universities and institutions of higher education on how to create a strategic learning alliance.

## Research

***Annual Survey of Corporate University Future Directions***—detailed research report of best demonstrated practices among 100 corporate universities, segmented by industry and size of organization, including over 70 charts and graphs.

**Chief Learning Officer Xchange™**—a member-driven research and benchmarking forum for deans of corporate universities.
*Membership benefits include:*

- On-site benchmarking visits to world-class corporate universities
- Member-driven research
- Exclusive website
- Best practice sharing forums
- Publication of research in exclusive reports
- Development of products for member organizations

## Events

**Symposium Series**—*Corporate Universities Enter the Twenty-first Century* and *Designing a Virtual Corporate University* are the conferences we offer every year to delegates worldwide.

A host of respected international practitioners share insights and offer guidelines on successful corporate university management. Discover new tools and preview the latest technologies from our business partners, understand how to market your corporate university inside and outside your organization, and learn how to form a successful corporate/college partnership.

## Publications

***Corporate Universities International***—a bimonthly newsletter covering the latest corporate university developments:

- Results from our *Annual Survey of Corporate University Future Directions*
- "How to" advice from practitioners of international corporate universities
- Trends in corporate university funding, management, and marketing
- Strategies for using the latest learning technology
- Profiles of leading vendors, for-profit education firms, and universities

If you're interested in any of our products or services or would like to share your best practices for our newsletter, *Corporate Universities International* or the next edition of *Corporate Universities: Lessons in Building a World-Class Work Force,* please contact us at:

Corporate University Xchange, Inc.
381 Park Ave. South, Suite 713
New York, NY 10016
Phone: (212) 213-2828
Fax: (212) 213-8621
e-mail: info@corpu.com
www.corpu.com

# FIFTEEN FREQUENTLY ASKED QUESTIONS ABOUT CORPORATE UNIVERSITIES

As you embark on the journey of planning, designing and implementing a corporate university, it is likely you will encounter many of the following questions—probably by a senior manager in your firm. This list of frequently asked questions was compiled and developed over the past five years by participants in our workshops on "Designing a Corporate University." Read over the list and add to it via our website at www.corpu.com.

1. What is a corporate university?
   A corporate university is the strategic umbrella for developing and educating employees, customers, and suppliers in order to meet an organization's business strategies.

2. How is a corporate university different from a training department?
   A corporate university differs from a training department in a number of ways. A training department tends to be reactive, decentralized, and serves a wide audience with an array of open enrollment programs. A corporate university, on the other hand, is the centralized umbrella for strategically relevant learning solutions for each job family within the corporation.

3. Who delivers the learning programs in the corporate university?
   A wide array of learning partners serve as the delivery arm for the corporate university. These range from trainers, business unit managers, university faculty, consultants, and oftentimes the senior most management including the CEO.

4. Why call this learning initiative a "university," why not just an enhanced training department?
   A growing number of corporations are opting to call their education function a university because the message is clear: Learning is important and by using the metaphor of a university the intent is grand. In addition, corporations are using the university model to brand their educational programs, courseware, and processes. Just as a successful

consumer packaged goods firm brands its products, corporations are realizing that while they may be spending millions of dollars in training their work force, they are not branding the initiative and hence effectively managing the investment.

5. What industries have demonstrated a high degree of interest in launching a corporate university and why? The industries with the greatest interest in creating a corporate university tend to be in high technology, manufacturing, financial services, telecommunications, healthcare, and utilities. The reasons range from the high degree of consolidation typically evident in these industries to the advent of new technologies and the shortened shelf life of knowledge required to operate successfully in these industries.

6. How many corporate universities exist today and how many Fortune 500 companies have corporate universities? There are over 1000 organizations with something called a corporate university, college, academy, or institute of learning. This is up from 400 in 1988. Furthermore, our *Annual Survey of Corporate University Future Directions* found nearly 40% of Fortune 500 firms have a corporate university.

7. What are the barriers to launching a corporate university? According to our *Annual Survey of Corporate University Future Directions*, key obstacles to launching a corporate university include:

*Lack of sustained top management commitment to the corporate university model.* This is a case where the corporate university is the dream of one CEO, but when that CEO leaves, the corporate university is not institutionalized. The CEO may have had the grand vision for the corporate university but he did not become actively involved as a learner.

*Lack of consensus among middle managers on the need for a corporate university.* Middle managers may publicly state the need but may not provide adequate time for rank and file employees to participate in learning programs.

*Inability to develop a link between the corporate university and the company's business goals.* Without a network of senior business managers to act as ambassadors and advisers, the corporate university flounders.

*Lack of visibility of the corporation's emphasis on learning.* Employees do not understand what the corporate university provides to them and how to utilize the learning resources.

*Inability to prove the value of the corporate university.* This continues to be the biggest concern of chief learning officers — how to measure the impact the corporate university has on the overall performance of the corporation.

8. What are the drivers within a corporation to create a corporate university?

Over the years in workshops and consulting engagements with organizations who are considering launching a corporate university, we have found there are essentially four key drivers to launch a corporate university. They include:

Desire to link learning and development to key business goals

Create a systematic approach for learning and development

Spread a common culture and values across the organization

Develop the employability of workers

9. How important is brick and mortar to the university model?

Of the 50 corporate universities listed in the *Appendix* of this book, roughly half do in fact have separate buildings for their corporate university. However, the decision on whether or not to dedicate a formal building to learning is a complex one. Some attribute the need for brick and mortar to the importance the company gives to education and hence the need for a symbol for learning. Others insist that as more of a corporation's employees reside outside the United States, there is a greater need to have a common place to gather and share best practices.

10. Is there an example of a corporate university that had a
    building and then closed the building to focus on
    distributed learning?
    Often the decision on whether or not to build a separate
    facility for learning involves the strategies and needs of the
    organization. Consider, for example, Holiday Inn
    University, established in Memphis, Tennessee in the 1970s
    as a separate facility for learning. This was closed in 1990
    because the model of "sending employees off to go get
    trained," was no longer a model that made economic sense
    to the company. The advent of technology replaced the
    bricks and mortar with a mobile van known as the Road
    Scholars, composed of several teams of trainers. Each team
    was equipped with a van, laptop computers and state-of-
    the-art training materials ready to use in on-site training
    sessions. But when Holiday Inn led an expansion into
    China, the company decided a separate facility for learning
    was important, given the respect the Chinese hold for
    higher education.

11. What are the critical success factors in launching a
    corporate university?
    There are several key factors that determine the success of a
    corporate university. While these factors differ significantly,
    the major themes of success include:
        Involve top management in the corporate university.
        This means more than simply having a CEO who
        publicly states the corporate university is his/her vision.
        It means having a CEO who actually gets involved as a
        teacher, role model learner, and "salesman" for the
        corporate university effort.
        Involve senior and mid-level business unit managers in
        developing a shared vision for the corporate university.
        This usually translates into creating a governance
        structure where line business managers share their key
        business challenges and, specifically, how the corporate
        university can help them achieve their business goals.
        Create a funding model that moves toward a "pay-
        for-services" basis. While an organization will still fund

major corporate-wide educational initiatives, the primary source of funding for the corporate university is from its customers—the business managers and also external customers, suppliers and outsiders. This ensures active involvement and linkage to business unit goals.

Experiment with technology to deliver learning and development to employees. This means creating both learner-centered training programs as well as embedding more learning into the workplace, so employees learn as they work.

Proactively develop partnerships with institutions of higher education to offer portable credentials to working adults. This can range from evaluating current training programs for their eligibility for college credit to actually working with a university to create a customized degree program for an entire industry.

Build holistic measurements to evaluate the impact the corporate university has on overall achievement of business strategies as well as specifically on customer and employee retention/satisfaction and innovation in the workplace.

Constantly communicate to employees, business unit managers, and other key stakeholders the value of the corporate university.

12. What is the typical operating budget for a corporate university?

According to our *Annual Survey of Corporate University Future Directions*, where we interviewed 100 corporate university deans, we found the average corporate university budget to be $10.7 million dollars. This represents 2.2 percent of an organization's payroll.

13. Where does the corporate university usually report within an organization?

The vast majority of corporate universities report through to the Human Resources department. However, a growing number are reporting to chief financial officers, chief information officers and the CEO.

14. Do corporate universities offer accredited degree programs?
    Our *Annual Survey of Corporate University Future Directions*
    found that almost 40 percent of corporate universities are
    interested in granting an accredited degree. Usually this is
    in partnership with an institution of higher education such
    as the T. Eaton Company/Ryerson Polytechnic University
    degree in retail management.
    Corporate University Deans state that their reason for
    wanting to offer accredited degrees is to offer their
    employees portable credentials.

15. Are corporate universities an opportunity or a threat to
    institutions of higher education?
    Corporate universities as well as virtual universities and
    for-profit education firms have sprung up to serve the
    needs of working adults. These new entrants to the
    educational system have emerged and proliferated because
    they offer a market-driven model of education with a focus
    on convenience, self-service and uniformity of product. As a
    group these entrants represent both an opportunity for
    partnering as well as direct competition to the traditional
    educational system.

# Notes

## CHAPTER 1

1. Zuckerman, Mortimer B., "Where Have The Good Jobs Gone?" *U.S. News & World Report*, July 31, 1995, page 68.
2. Markels, Alex, "Restructuring Alters Middle-Manager Role But Leaves It Robust," *Wall Street Journal*, September 25, 1995, page 1.
3. Ibid., page 12.
4. Baker, Stephen and Larry Armstrong, "The New Factory Worker," *Business Week*, September 30, 1996, page 56.
5. Sullivan, Robert, "Making Money The Old Fashioned Way," *Rolling Stone*, February 23, 1995, page 54.
6. Knecht, Bruce, "Banks Profit By Sweet-Talking Overdue Payers," *Wall Street Journal*, June 27, 1994, page B1.

## CHAPTER 2

1. Ulrich, Dave, *Human Resource Champions: The Next Agenda For Adding Value And Delivering Results* (Boston: Harvard Business School Press, 1997), p. 13.
2. Peak, Martha, "Go Corporate U," *Management Review*, February, 1997, p. 25.
3. Thornburg, Linda, "Growing Trend: CEO Becomes Chief Learning Officer," *Corporate University Xchange*, July/August, 1995 p. 6.
4. Miles, Robert, "Corporate Universities," Unpublished paper, Emory University (Atlanta: 1993) December, 1993, p. 18.
5. Annual Report of Whirlpool Corporation, 1995 (Benton Harbor, Michigan: 1996) p. 3.

6. Sprint's University of Excellence SM Business Case Analysis, November 20, 1991, Executive Summary, p. 12.

7. "Southern Company College Redefines Its Mission," *Southern Highlights,* October 2, 1995, p. 6.

8. Southern Company Leadership Profile, 1995, p. 1.

9. Dobyns, Lloyd and Clare Mason-Crawford, *Quality Or Else: The Revolution In The World Of Business* (Boston: Houghton Mifflin, 1991), p. 144.

10. Smart, Tim, "Jack Welch's Encore," *Business Week,* October 28, 1996, p. 157.

11. Ibid., p. 155.

12. Senge, Peter M., *The Fifth Discipline: The Art and Practice Of The Learning Organization* (New York: Doubleday Currency, 1990), p. 14.

## CHAPTER 3

1. University Of Chicago Hospital Academy Personnel Policy Guidelines, September 1, 1993, p. 2.

2. Blair, Diane, "Bank Of Montreal Institute For Learning: Why An Institute For Learning," Unpublished paper, January, 1996, p. 2.

3. Ibid., p. 3.

4. Vierling, Jackie, Program Manager, General Electric Management Development Institute, Presentation delivered to Corporate University Conference, May, 1995, New York City.

5. Welch, Jack, "A Boundary-less Company in a Decade of Change," Speech presented at the General Electric Annual Meeting of Shareowners, Erie, Pennsylvania, April 25, 1990, p. 1.

6. Blair, Diane, "Bank Of Montreal Institute For Learning: Why An Institute For Learning?" Unpublished paper, p. 8.

7. Tapscott, Don, *The Digital Economy: Promise and Peril In The Age Of Networked Intelligence* (New York: McGraw-Hill, 1995) p. 17.

8. Stevens, John, Director of Professional Policy Institute Of Personnel and Development, United Kingdom and Ireland, Pa-

per delivered to CIBIT Knowledge Management Conference, May, 1997, Netherlands.
9. Kerr, Steven, "GE's Collective Genius," *Leader to Leader*, Premier Issue, p. 30.

## CHAPTER 4

1. Dillman, Don, Christenson, James A., Salant, Priscilla and Warner, Paul D. *What The Public Wants From Higher Education, Workforce Implications From A National Survey* (Washington State University: Social and Economic Sciences Research Center, November 1995), p. 9.
2. Leibowitz, Zandy B., Nancy K. Schlossberg, and Jane E. Shore, "Stopping the Revolving Door," *Training & Development*, February, 1991, p. 43.
3. Ibid., p. 44.
4. Heskett, James L. and Lawrence Schlesinger, "Putting The Service-Profit Chain To Work," *Harvard Business Review*, March/April, 1994, p. 103.
5. McColgan, Ellyn A., "How Fidelity Invests in Service Professionals," *Harvard Business Review*, January/February, 1997, p. 137.
6. Ibid., p. 139.
7. "SDU Already Changing For The Better," *SDU Journal*, Spring, 1996, p. 5.
8. Heiman, Marcia and Joshua Slomianko, *Learning to Learn On The Job* (Alexandria, VA: American Society for Training and Development, 1989), p. 2.
9. First Union, Leadership Success Series, "Meeting Today's Challenges through Self-Directed Learning," February 27, 1997, produced by First University, First Union Corporation.
10. Carnevale, Anthony P., Leila J. Gainer, and Ann S. Meltzer, *Workplace Basics: The Essential Skills Employers Want* (San Francisco: Jossey-Bass, 1991), p. 11.
11. Stamps, David, "Communities of Practice, Learning Is Social, Training Is Irrelevant," *TRAINING*, February, 1997, p. 40.

12.  Greco, Jo Ann, "Corporate Home Schooling," *Journal of Business Strategy*, May/June, 1997, p. 51.
13.  Williamson, Mickey, "High-Tech Training," *BYTE*, December, 1994, p. 24.
14.  Schank, Roger, *Virtual Learning* (New York: McGraw-Hill, 1997), p. 27.
15.  Gates, Bill, "Linked Up for Learning: Using Technology On The Campus," *Educational Record*, Volume 77, Number 4, Fall, 1996, p. 35.
16.  Vicere, Albert A. and Robert M. Fulmer, *Crafting Competitiveness* (United Kingdom, Capstone Publishing Limited, 1996), p. 248.
17.  *Motorola Opportunities*, Third Quarter, 1995, Volume 12, Issue 2, p. 3.
18.  Burke, Leo, CAMP, Unpublished paper, presented at Worldwide Learning, Training and Education Research Conference, Kuala Lumpur, Malaysia, March 15, 1995.
19.  Avishai, Bernard, "In China, It's The Year Of the Manager," *Fast Company*, September/October, 1996, p. 62.
20.  Ibid., p. 64.
21.  Rifkin, Glenn, "The Loneliness of the Lay-Off Survivor," *New York Times*, January 3, 1993, Business Section, p. 1.
22.  Champy, James, *Reengineering Management* (New York: Harper Business, 1995), p. 162.
23.  Waterman, Robert H., Waterman, Judith A. and Collard, Betsy A., "Toward a Career-Resilient Workforce," *Harvard Business Review*, July/August, 1994, p. 89.
24.  High, Gary, "Lifelong Learning," speech given at the American Society for Training & Development, International Conference and Exposition, May 31, 1992.

## CHAPTER 5

1.  Flisi, Claudia, "Distance Learning," *Newsweek*, October 9, 1995, page 10.
2.  The following was adapted from "Learning Technology Selection Guidelines: An Introduction and Workshop Notes,"

BBN Corporation, Cambridge, MA and SunU Sun Microsystems Selection of Media Options For Training Delivery.

3. "The Virtual Classroom: A Reality at the Southern Company," *Electrical World*, March, 1995, p. 52.
4. Webber, Alan, "What's So New About The New Economy," *Harvard Business Review*, January/February, 1993, p. 8.
5. Stewart, Thomas, *Intellectual Capital: The New Wealth Of Organizations* (New York: Doubleday Currency, 1997), p. 111.
6. Barret, Randy, "Coopers & Lybrand's Network Grows by Plan," *Interactive Week*, January 13, 1997, p. 22.
7. Ghazi, Kian, *The Adult Education Market: A Comprehensive Guide*, (New York: Lehman Brothers, 1997), p. 84.
8. Stewart, Thomas, *Intellectual Capital: The New Wealth Of Organizations*, p. 40.
9. Tapscott, Don, *Digital Economy, Promise and Peril In The Age Of Networked Intelligence* (New York: McGraw-Hill, 1996), p. 203.

## CHAPTER 6

1. Barr, Stephen, "Off The Shelf, Off The Mark," *CFO*, April, 1997, p. 45.
2. Harris, Roy, "A School Of Your Own," *CFO*, April, 1997, p. 50.

## CHAPTER 7

1. Ghazi, Kian, *The Adult Education Market: A Comprehensive Guide* (New York: Lehman Brothers, 1997), p. 14.
2. Herzlinger, Regina, *Market Driven Health Care* (Reading, MA: Addison Wesley Publishing Company, Inc., 1997), p. 8.
3. Davis, Stan and Jim Botkin, *Monster Under The Bed* (New York: Simon & Schuster, 1994), p. 129.

## CHAPTER 8

1. Stewart, Thomas A., "Brainpower," *Fortune,* June 3, 1991, p. 44.
2. Grove, Andrew S. *High Output Management* (New York: Random House, Inc. 1983), p. 225.
3. Maister, David, *Managing The Professional Service Firm* (New York: Simon & Schuster, 1993), p. 83.

# Bibliography

Armstrong, David. *Managing By Storying Around: A New Method of Leadership.* New York: Doubleday Currency, 1992.

Avishai, Bernard. "In China, It's the Year of the Manager," *Fast Company,* September/October 1996.

Baker, Stephen and Larry Armstrong. "The New Factory Worker," *Business Week,* September 30, 1996.

Barr, Stephen. "Off the Shelf, Off the Mark," *CFO,* April 1997.

Barret, Randy. "Coopers & Lybrand's Network Grows By Plan," *Interactive Week,* January 13, 1997.

Blair, Diane. "Bank of Montreal Institute for Learning: Why an Institute for Learning?" Unpublished paper, January 1996.

Burke, Leo. CAMP, unpublished paper, Director of Center for Management and Organizational Learning, given at Worldwide Learning, Training, and Education Research Conference, Kuala Lumpur, Malaysia, March 15, 1995.

Byrne, John A. "Paradigms for Postmodern Managers," *Business Week Special Issue: Reinventing America,* January 19, 1993.

Carnevale, Anthony P., Leila J. Gainer, and Ann S. Meltzer. *Workplace Basics: The Essential Skills Employers Want.* San Francisco: Jossey-Bass, 1991.

Carr, Clay. *Smart Training: The Manager's Guide to Training for Improved Performance.* New York: McGraw-Hill, 1992.

Champy, James. *Reengineering Management.* New York: HarperBusiness, 1995.

Cooper, Helene. "The New Educators: Carpet Firm Sets Up an In-House School to Stay Competitive," *The Wall Street Journal,* October 5, 1992.

Daniel, John, Sir. *Mega-Universities and Knowledge Media.* United Kingdom: Kogan Page Limited, 1996.

Danilov, Victor J. *Corporate Museums, Galleries, and Visitor Centers: A Directory.* New York: Greenwood Press, 1991.

Davis, Stan and Jim Botkin. *Monster Under the Bed.* New York: Simon & Schuster, 1994.

DeCarlo, Charles R. and Ormsbee W. Robinson. *Education In Business and Industry.* New York: Center for Applied Research in Education, 1966.

DePree, Max. *Leadership Is An Art.* New York: Dell Publishing, 1989.

Dertouzos, Michael L., Richard K. Lester, and Robert M. Solow. *Made in America: The MIT Commission On Industrial Productivity.* New York: Harper Collins, 1989.

DeYoung, Garrett. "Reward Your Suppliers and They'll Reward You," *Electronic Business,* June 25, 1990.

Dillman, Don, James A. Christenson, Priscilla Salant, and Paul D. Warner. *What the Public Wants from Higher Education, Work Force Implications from a National Survey.* Washington State University, Social and Economic Sciences Research Center, November 1995.

Dobyns, Lloyd and Clare Mason-Crawford. *Quality or Else: The Revolution in World Business.* Boston: Houghton Mifflin, 1991.

Drucker, Peter. "Management in the Information Age," *The Wall Street Journal,* July 8, 1987.

Edvinsson, Leif and Michael S. Malone. *Intellectual Capital.* New York: HarperBusiness, 1997.

Eurich, Nell. *Corporate Classrooms.* The Carnegie Foundation for the Advancement of Teaching. Princeton: Princeton University Press, 1985.

Feder, Barnaby. "At Motorola, Quality Is a Team Sport," *New York Times,* January 21, 1993.

Filipczak, Bob. "CEO's Who Train," *TRAINING,* June 1996.

Flisi, Claudia. "Distance Learning," *Newsweek,* October 9, 1995.

Gates, Bill. "Linked Up for Learning: Using Technology on the Campus," *Educational Record,* Vol. 77, No. 4, Fall 1996.

Geber, Beverly. "Saturn's Grand Experiment," *TRAINING,* June 1992.

Gery, Gloria. *Electronic Performance Support Systems.* Boston: Weingarten, 1991.

Ghazi, Kian. *The Adult Education Market: A Comprehensive Guide.* New York: Lehman Brothers, 1997.

Graham, Ellen. "Digging for Knowledge," *The Wall Street Journal,* September 11, 1992.

Greco, Jo Ann. "Corporate Home Schooling," *Journal of Business Strategy,* May/June 1997.

Harris, Roy. "A School of Your Own," *CFO,* April 1997.

Heiman, Marcia and Joshua Slomianko. *Learning to Learn on the Job.* Alexandria, Va.: American Society for Training and Development, 1989.

Herzlinger, Regina. *Market Driven Health Care.* Reading, Mass.: Addison Wesley Publishing Company, Inc., 1997.

Heskett, James L. and Lawrence Schlesinger. "Putting the Service-Profit Chain to Work," *Harvard Business Review,* March/April 1994.

High, Gary. "Lifelong Learning," speech given at the American Society for Training and Development, International Conference and Exposition, May 31, 1992.

Jones, Robert T. "The New Workplace and Lifelong Learning," *CAEL Forum and News,* Spring/Summer, 1997.

Kanter, Rosabeth Moss. "Change: Where to Begin," *Harvard Business Review,* July/August 1991.

Kerr, Steven. "GE's Collective Genius," *Leader to Leader,* Premier Issue.

Knecht, Bruce. "Banks Profit by Sweet-Talking Overdue Payers," *The Wall Street Journal,* June 27, 1994.

Leibowitz, Zandy B., Nancy K. Schlossberg, and Jane E. Shore. "Stopping the Revolving Door," *Training & Development Journal,* February 1991.

Lemonick, Michael. "Tomorrow's Lesson: Learn or Perish," *Time Special Issue Beyond the Year 2000,* Fall 1992.

Magnet, Myron. "The Truth about the American Worker," *Fortune,* May 4, 1992.

Maister, David. *Managing the Professional Service Firm.* New York: Simon & Schuster, 1993.

Markels, Alex. "Restructuring Alters Middle-Manager Role but Leaves it Robust," *The Wall Street Journal,* September 25, 1995.

Marshall, Ray and Marc Tucker. *Thinking for a Living.* New York: Basic Books, 1992.

McColgan, Ellyn A. "How Fidelity Invests in Service Professionals," *Harvard Business Review,* January/February, 1997.

Meister, Jeanne C. "Retail U," *TRAINING,* March 1992.

Meister, Jeanne C. *Corporate Quality Universities: Lessons In Building A World-Class Work Force.* Burr Ridge: Irwin Professional Publishing, 1994.

Miles, Robert. "Corporate Universities, "unpublished paper, Emory University (Atlanta: 1993), December 1993.

Neufeld, Evan. "Where are Audiences Going?" Internet Advertising Bureau, 1996.

Peak, Martha. "Go Corporate U," *Management Review,* February 1997.

Peters, Tom. *Thriving on Chaos: Handbook for a Management Revolution.* New York: Knopf, 1986.

Prahalad, C. K. and Gary Hamel. "The Core Competence of the Corporation." *Harvard Business Review,* May/June 1990.

Reich, Robert. *The Work of Nations.* New York: Knopf, 1991.

Reich, Robert. "Hire Education," *Rolling Stone,* October 20, 1994.

Rifkin, Glenn. "The Loneliness of the Layoff Survivor," *New York Times,* January 3, 1993.

Rothschild, Michael. *Bionomics: The Inevitability of Capitalism.* New York: Henry Holt, 1990.

Schank, Roger. *Virtual Learning.* New York: McGraw-Hill, 1997.

Schor, Juliet B. *The Overworked American.* New York: Harper Collins, 1991.

Senge, Peter M. *The Fifth Discipline: The Art and Practice of the Learning Organization.* New York: Doubleday Currency, 1990.

Senge, Peter M. "The Leader's New Work: Building Learning Organizations," *Sloan Management Review,* Fall 1990.

Sherman, Stratford. "A Brave New Darwinian Workplace," *Fortune,* January 25, 1993.

Slater, Robert. *The New GE: How Jack Welch Revived an American Institution.* Homewood, Ill.: Business One Irwin, 1992.

Smart, Tim. "Jack Welch's Encore, " *Business Week,* October 28, 1996.

Stamps, David. "Communities of Practice, Learning Is Social, Training Is Irrelevant," *TRAINING,* February 1997.

Stevens, John, director of Professional Policy Institute of Personnel and Development, United Kingdom and Ireland, paper delivered to CIBIT Knowledge Management Conference, May 1997, Netherlands.

Stewart, Thomas A. "Brainpower," *Fortune,* June 3, 1991.

Stewart, Thomas A. "GE Keeps Those Ideas Coming," *Fortune,* August 12, 1991.

Stewart, Thomas A. *Intellectual Capital, The New Wealth of Organizations.* New York: Doubleday Currency, 1997.

Sullivan, Robert. "Making Money the Old Fashioned Way," *Rolling Stone,* February 23, 1995.

Tapscott, Don. *The Digital Economy: Promise and Peril in the Age of Networked Intelligence.* New York: McGraw-Hill, 1995.

Thornburg, Linda. "Growing Trend: CEO Becomes Chief Learning Officer," *Corporate University Xchange,* July/August 1995.

Thurow, Lester, speech, "The State of American Competitiveness and How it Can Be Improved," A Report of the procedures from the Xerox Quality Forum II, sponsored by Xerox Corporation July 31–August 2, 1990, Leesburg, Virginia.

Tichy, Noel and Stratford Sherman. *Control Your Destiny or Someone Else Will.* New York: Doubleday, 1993.

Ulrich, Dave. *Human Resource Champions: The Next Agenda for Adding Value and Delivering Results.* Boston: Harvard Business School Press, 1997.

Ulrich, Dave and Hope Greenfield. "The Transformation of Training and Development to Development and Learning," *American Journal of Management Development*, Vol 1, No. 2, 1995.

Vicere, Albert A. and Robert M. Fulmer. *Crafting Competitiveness.* United Kingdom: Capstone Publishing Limited, 1996.

Waterman, Robert H., Judith A. Waterman, and Betsy A. Collard. "Toward A Career-Resilient Workforce," *Harvard Business Review*, July/August 1994.

Webber, Alan. "What's So New About the New Economy," *Harvard Business Review*, January/February 1993.

Welch, Jack. "A Boundary-less Company in a Decade of Change," speech presented at the General Electric Annual Meeting of Shareowners, Erie, Pennsylvania, April 25, 1990.

Wiggenhorn, William. "Motorola U: When Training Becomes an Education," *Harvard Business Review*, July/August 1990.

Williamson, Mickey. "High-Tech Training," *BYTE*, December 1994.

Yuzo, Yasuda. *40 Years, 20 Million Ideas: The Toyota Suggestion System.* Cambridge, Mass.: Productivity Press, 1991.

Zuckerman, Mortimer B. "Where Have All The Good Jobs Gone?" *U.S. News & World Report*, July 11, 1995.

# Index

## A

Accelerating learning, 242–43
Accreditation, 250
  corporate universities, 201–5
  learning milestone, 32, 33
Acculturation training, 93–94
Action learning, 110–11
Adult student, 207–9, 211
AirTouch Communication, 219
Air University, 135–36, 166
Alliance builder, 87
Alliances. See Higher education
    partnerships; Partnerships
Allied Signal, 50–51
Allocation, self-funding vs., 51–53
Andersen Consulting, 111–12
Anheuser-Busch. See Busch Learning
    Center
Annual survey, of corporate
    universities future directions,
    24–28
  corporate universities as business
    in, 26–28
  learning alliances in, 25–26
  management commitment in,
    24–25
  virtual corporate universities in, 26
Apollo Group, 226
Arthur Andersen Corporate
    University, 69–70
Arthur D. Little School of
    Management accreditation,
    202–5

AT&T School of Business/University
    of Phoenix partnership, 76
AT&T Universal Card University
    (UCU)
  communications vehicles of,
    82–83
  orientation programs of, 95–
    96
AT&T Wireless Services, 219

## B

Bank of Montreal Institute for
    Learning, 22–23
  core curriculum of, 236
  impetus for, 64–65
  Learning Maps of, 48–49
  linking skills to business goals in,
    31–33
  marketing success of, 83
  measurement systems of, 78–
    79
  mission of, 246
  process vs. place, 33–34
  products and services of, 74–75
Bell Canada, 35
Big picture, company, 98–104
Boston College/Arthur D. Little
    partnership, 205
Brand name, corporate university as,
    250–51
Building blocks, design, 65–85. See
    also Designing corporate
    universities

Building world-class work force, 233–51. *See also* Work force, building world-class
Bureau of Engraving and Printing, 8
Busch Learning Center, 44–45
  customer-driven curriculum at, 179–80
  dealer training at, 245
  origins of, 179
  retailer training at, 181
  virtual university at, 180–81
  wholesaler training at, 178–81
Busch Satellite Network, 44–45, 180
Business, university as, 245–47
Business Analysis course, 111
Business-driven measurements, 248–49
Business goals, learning in support of, 31–33
Business literacy, global, 13–14, 92, 114–19, 240
Business partner, 86
Business Practices Course, 111–12
Business Practices School, 111
Business skill building, 116–19

C

3 Cs core curriculum, 38–42, 89–93, 238–41
Canada, retail sector training in, 34–35
Career resilient work force, 10
Career self-management, 16, 92–93, 122–26, 241
Carroll School of Management/Arthur D. Little partnership, 205
CD-ROM training, 142–44
Center for Research in Lifelong Learning, 194
Centralization, 72
Central Michigan University/ Megatech Engineering partnership, 196–97

Centro Internacional de Educación y Desarrollo (CIED), 116–19
Certification, professional, 192–94
Chase Manhattan Bank, 5–6
Chief executive officer, in launching university, 61–65
Chief learning officer, 85–86
China Accelerated Management Program, 119–22
China Management Training Program, 54–55
Chrysler, 4–5
Citizenship, corporate, 90, 93–98, 239
  development of, 41
  metaphors in, 94–98
  organization values, vision, and culture in, 93–94
Client feedback questionnaires, 246–47
Client Relationship Manager, 75
Collaboration skills, 13, 91, 108–10, 240
Collaborative learning technologies, 144–48
College credit, 201–202
College partnerships. *See* Higher education partnerships; Partnerships
Columbia/HCA Healthcare value chain training, 46
Communication
  board members, 82
  bold communications vehicles, 83
  branded communications vehicles, 82
  design of university, 80–85
  investors, 84–85
  marketing university success in, 83–84
  work skill, 108
Communication skills, 13, 91, 108–10, 240
Communities of practice, 109–10
Company–supplier relationship, 43

Compensation, employee self-
    development and, 126–28,
    241–42
Competencies, workplace, 104–5
    core, 12–19, 105–26, 236
        career self-management, 16,
            92–93, 122–26
        communication and
            collaboration skills, 13, 91,
            108–10
        creative thinking and problem
            solving, 14, 91, 110–12
        global business literacy, 14–15,
            92, 114–19
        leadership development, 15, 92,
            119–22
        learning to learn skills, 12–13,
            91, 105–8
        technological literacy, 14, 91–92,
            112–14
    development of, 240–41
Competency-based model, 31
Competitive advantage, 57–58
    partnerships, 168–71
    university as, 250–51
Computer-based training (CBT)
    151–54. See also Virtual
    universities
Computers, laptop, 166
Consortiums, 197–201, 218–21
    Global Wireless Education
        Consortium (GWEC), 219–21
    Southern Company/Emory
        University, 198–99
    TEAM, 230–31
    United Healthcare/Rensselaer
        Learning Institute, 199–200
    Whirlpool Brandywine Creek
        Performance Centre, 247–48
Contextual framework, 41, 90–91,
    98–105, 239
    company's big picture in, 98–104
    core workplace competencies in,
        104–5
Convenience, 210–11

Convergence, product, 168
Conversation, 145. See also
    Communication
Coopers & Lybrand
    KnowledgeCurve, 148–49
Core competencies, 105–26. See also
    Competencies, workplace
Core curriculum, 38–42, 89–93,
    238–41
Corporate universities, 19, 29
    accreditation of, 201–5
    annual survey of, 24–28
        corporate universities as
            business in, 26–28
        learning alliances in, 25–26
        management commitment in,
            24–25
        virtual corporate universities in,
            26
    as businesses, 26–28, 245–47
    consortiums of, 197–201. See also
        Consortiums
    corporate mindset in, 34
    design of, 59–87. See also
        Designing corporate
        universities
    emergence of, 19
    externally focused, 216–21
    goals and principles of, 30–31
    higher education vs., 207–32. See
        also Higher education vs.
        corporate universities
    learning laboratories in, 130–67.
        See also Learning laboratories
    learning programs in, 88–129. See
        also Learning programs
    metaphor of, 34–35
    models of, 29–58. See also Model
    networking guide to, 252–59
    origin of, 59–60
    paradigm shift in, 21–22
    as shared internal services, 27
    training departments, 22–23
    virtual, 26, 221–25. See also Virtual
        universities

Corporate University Xchange, 24
Corporations
    as educators, 10–13
    in transition, 3
Creative thinking, 13, 91, 110–12,
    240
Credit, college, 201–202. *See also*
    Accreditation
Crotonville Management
        Development Institute. *See*
        General Electric Crotonville
        Management Development
        Institute
Culture, corporate, 93–94
Curriculum, 88–93
    core, 236
    customer-driven, 179–80
    themes of, 128–29
Customer Fulfillment Center, 77
Customer training, 243–45
    dealers and wholesalers, 175–81
        Busch Learning Center, 178–81
        Harley-Davidson University,
            175–78
Customized education, 186–91

**D**

Dealers
    partnerships with, 174–81
        Busch Learning Center, 178–81
        Harley-Davidson, 175–78
    training of, 175–78
        Anheuser-Busch, 245
        Harley-Davidson University,
            244–45
Decentralization, 72
Deep Woods Technology, 148
Degree programs, 190–97, 201
Dell University, 113–14, 154–56
Designing corporate universities,
    59–87
    building blocks in, 65–85
        communication, 80–85
        governance system, 65–68
        learning partners, 75–76

Designing corporate universities
    *(continued)*
        measurement system, 77–80
        organization, 71–73
        products and services, 74–75
        scope and funding strategy,
            69–71
        stakeholders, 73–74
        technology strategy, 76–77
        vision, 68–69
    chief learning officer in, 85–87
    top management in, 61–65
Development goals, *vs.* strategic
        needs, 236–37
Dilemma, higher education, 215
Disney University, 250
Distance learning, 213–15. *See also*
        Virtual universities
Distributor Executive Development
        Institute (DEDI), 45

**E**

Earning-learning linkage, 126–28,
    241–42
Eastman Kodak Company, action
        learning in, 110–11
Eaton School of Retailing, 34–35,
    191–95
Economic value-added (EVA)
        training, 190
Education. *See also* Learning
    customized, 186–91
    goals *vs.* strategic needs in, 236–37
    learner-centered, 243
    market-driven, 231–32
    passive *vs.* active, 214
    student-centered, 214–15
    teacher-centered, 214–15
Educational Development
        University (EDU), 250
Education firms, for-profit, 226–31
    University of Phoenix, 226–28
    University of Warwick, 228–31
Education market
    corporate universities in, 10–12

Education market *(continued)*
  metamorphosis of, 207–15
    distance education in, 213–15
    life-long learning and, 212–13
    non-traditional student in, 208–11
    technological advancements in, 211–12
  new entrants to, 215–31
    consortiums, 218–21
    externally focused corporate universities, 216–18
    for-profit education firms, 226–31
    virtual universities, 221–25
  total U.S., 10–11
Educators. *See also* Faculty
  corporations as, 10–12
  K-12, 36–37
Electric Utility Game, 103–4
Electronic learning storefront, 151–54
Electronic Performance Support System (EPSS), 155
Embedded learning, 154–56
Emory University/Southern Company consortium, 198–99
Employability, lifetime, 9–10
Employee Development University (EDU), 217–18
Employees
  compensation and self-development of, 126–28, 241–42
  curriculum input from, 238
Epsilon, 6–7
Ericsson, 219
Executive education, customized, 186–90
Externally focused corporate universities, 216–18

F
Facilities, physical, 37–38
Faculty
  managers as, 237–38
  sea gull, 50

Faculty Clubs, 109–10
Feedback questionnaires, 246–47
Fidelity Institutional Retirement Services Company, 98–102
Fidelity Service Delivery University (SDU), 236
First Union College for Commercial Bankers, 143
First Union Corporation orientation program, 106–8
First Union National Bank, multimedia-based learning in, 142–44
First University, 142–44
Flat, flexible organization, 1–7
FORDSTAR, 137–39
For-profit education firms, 226–31
  University of Phoenix, 226–28
  University of Warwick, 228–31
Funding
  allocation *vs.* self-, 51–53
  strategy for, 69–71

G
General Electric
  Business Manager course at, 21
  value chain training in, 46
General Electric Crotonville Management Development Institute, 51
  China Management Training Program of, 54–55
  global learning focus of, 53–55
  new market entry and, 58
  origin of, 54
  scope of, 70–71
  top management in, 65
Global business literacy, 13–14, 92, 114–19, 240
Global focus, 53–55
Global Wireless Education Consortium (GWEC), 219–21
GM University, 237
Governance system, 65–68

## H

Hamburger University, 210
Harley-Davidson University,
        175–78, 244–45
HDNet, 175, 177
Higher education partnerships,
        181–205, 247–48. *See also*
        Partnerships
  accreditation in, 201–5
  consortiums in, 197–201
  criteria for, 184–85
  customized executive education
        in, 186–90
  degree programs in, new, 190–
        97
Higher education *vs.* corporate
        universities, 207–32
  dilemma of higher education and,
        215
  education market metamorphosis
        and, 207–15
    distance education in, 213–15
    life-long learning in, 212–13
    non-traditional student in,
        208–11
    technological advancements in,
        211–12
  market-driven education and,
        231–32
  new entrants to education market
        in, 215–31
    consortiums, 218–21
    externally focused corporate
        universities, 216–18
    for-profit education firms,
        226–31
    virtual universities, 221–25
Higher learning partnerships,
        182–205. *See also* Partnerships
Human capital, as value, 2–3

## I

Iams University, 45
Indiana University, 187–89, 248

Individual Development Plan,
        241–42
Individual training plans (ITPs), 127
INSEAD, 187–89, 248
*Inside Track*, 96–97
Insourcing, 27
Integrated Graduate Development
        Scheme, 229
Integrated Manager Development
        Scheme, 229
Intel, 237
Intellectual Capital (IC) model, 56–57
Intellectual job component, 8
Interactive Distance Learning (IDL),
        140–42
International Association for
        Continuing Education and
        Training (IACET), 217–18
Internet, 150–62. *See also* Web-based
        learning
  customer base for, 211
  planned future use of, 150, 151
Intranet-based learning, 150–62. *See
        also* Web-based learning
  Dell University, 154–56
  Harley-Davidson University,
        244–45
  SunU, 151–54
  Verifone University, 156–58
  Xerox Management Institute,
        158–62
Intranet knowledge databases,
        148–50
Introduction to the Learning
        Organization, 105–6
IT&T School of Business and
        Technology/University of
        Phoenix partnership, 226–28
Ivy League Factor, 184

## J

Java, 153
Job security, learning *vs.*, 9–10
Just-In-Time Learning, 157

**K**

*Keiretsu,* 46, 169
KnowledgeCurve, 148–49
Knowledge databases, Intranet,
    148–50
Knowledge economy, 7–9
Knowledge shelf life, 9
Knowledge workers, 8

**L**

Laptop computers, 166
Leaders
    as learners and faculty, 237–38
    learning facilitation by, 49–51
Leadership, 241
Leadership development, 15, 92,
    119–22
Leadership skill building, 116–19
Leadership Success Series, 106–8
Leading the Enterprise (LTE),
    158–62
Learner-centered education, 243
Learning. *See also* Education
    accelerating, 242–43
    business goals and, 31–33
    commitment and accessibility to,
        34
    continuous, 37
    delivery formats for, 47–49
    distance, 213–15
    electronic storefront for, 151–54
    embedded, 154–56
    globally focused, 53–55
    interactive, 111–12
    Interactive Distance (IDL), 140–42
    intranet-based, 150–62. *See also*
        Intranet-based learning
    job transfer of, 49
    Just-In-Time, 157
    life-long, 131–32, 212–13
    management support of, 95
    measuring, 242–43
    mission, scope, and nature of,
        19–23

Learning *(continued)*
    multimedia-based, 142–44
    performance-based, 32–33
    satellite-based, 136–42. *See also*
        Satellite-based learning
    self-paced, 77
    technology assisted, 165–67
    tracking, 242–43
    *vs.* job security, 9–10
    web-based, 150–62. *See also* Web-
        based learning
Learning alliances, 25–26. *See also*
        Higher education
        partnerships; Partnerships
Learning-earning linkage, 126–28,
    241–42
Learning environment, new. *See*
        Learning laboratories
Learning for Success, 31–33
Learning infrastructure value,
    248–49
Learning laboratories, 130–67
    criteria for media selection in,
        134–65
    collaborative learning
        technologies, 144–48
    intranet knowledge databases,
        148–50
    multimedia-based learning,
        142–44
    satellite-based learning, 136–42
    virtual campus, 162–65
    web-based learning, 150–62
    technology-assisted learning in,
        165–67
Learning Manager, 75
Learning Maps, 48–49, 144, 146–48
Learning officer, chief, 85–87
Learning partners, 75–76. *See also*
        Higher education
        partnerships; Partnerships
Learning programs, 88–129
    contextual framework in, 98–105
    company's big picture in,
        98–104

Learning programs *(continued)*
    core workplace competencies in,
        104–5
    core workplace competencies in,
        105–26
    career self-management, 122–26
    communication and
        collaboration skills, 108–10
    creative thinking and problem-
        solving, 110–12
    global business literacy, 114–19
    leadership development,
        119–22
    learning to learn skills, 105–8
    technological literacy, 112–14
    corporate citizenship in, 93–98
    metaphors in, 94–98
    organization values, vision, and
        culture in, 93–94
    corporate university curriculum
        in, 88–93
    globally focused, 53–55. *See also*
        Global business literacy
    self-development–compensation
        linkage in, 126–28
    themes of, 128–29
Learning pyramid, 36–37
Learning solutions, prescriptive, 164
Learning systems, performance-
    based, 32–33
Learning to learn skills, 12, 91,
    105–8, 240
Life-long learning, 131–32, 212–13
Lifetime, of industrial firms, 58
Lifetime employability, 9–10
Lord Corporation, 172–74, 245
Lucent Technologies, 219


**M**

Management
    commitment of, 24–25
    launching university, 61–65
    support of learning by, 195
    top, 61–65

Management Development Institute,
    CIED, 117–19
Manager-as-faculty, 237–38
Managers On-line Success Tool (The
    MOST), 155
Mankato State University, 219
Market-driven education, 231–32
Markets, entry into new, 58
MBA programs, U.S., 186–87
McDonald's Hamburger University,
    210
Measurement systems
    business-driven, 248–49
    design of university, 77–80
    Kirkpatrick, 55
    learning, 242–43
    outputs plus inputs, 55–57
Media selection criteria, 134–65. *See
    also under* Learning
    laboratories
Megatech Academy, 196
Mindset
    corporate, 34
    shared, 40–41
Model, corporate university, 29–
    58
    3 Cs core curriculum in, 38–42
    business goals in, 31–33
    competitive advantage from,
        57–58
    globally focused learning
        programs in, 53–55
    leaders facilitating learning in,
        49–51
    learning delivery formats in,
        47–49
    new markets entry and, 58
    output measurement in, 55–57
    process *vs.* place, 33–38
    self-funding *vs.* corporate
        allocation in, 51–53
    value chain training in, 42–47
Monterey Tech, 224–25
Motorola, in Global Wireless
        Education Consortium, 219

Motorola Customer and Supplier
    Institute, 70
Motorola University
    branded product, 250
    China Accelerated Management
        Program of, 119–22
    competitive advantage from,
        57–58
    core curriculum in, 236
    educational alliances of, 35–36,
        46–47
    funding of, 52–53, 171
    global learning focus of, 53–54
    physical facility in, 37
    scope of, 69–70
    student population in, 213
    supplier dialogues in, 43
Multimedia-based learning, 142–44

**N**

National Semiconductor University
    (NSU)
    communications vehicles of, 82
    communities of practice in,
        109–10
    employee input in, 238
    governance structure of, 66–68
    learning philosophy of, 235
National Technological University,
    212
Networking guide, 252–59
Next Step, 71, 195
Non-traditional student, 208–11
Northwest Pennsylvania Technical
    Institute (NPTI), 172–74
NYNEX University, 211–12
    alliance of, 26
    Next Step program of, 71

**O**

One Company Initiatives, 187
Open University, 223–24
Oracle Interactive Business TV-
    Oracle Channel, 165

Oracle University
    contextual reference at, 239
    learner-centered education at, 243
    orientation program of, 96–97
    virtual campus of, 162–65
Organization, 71–73
Orientation programs
    AT&T Universal Card University
        (UCU), 95–96
    First Union Corporation, 106–8
    Oracle University, 96–97
    Saturn Corporation, 105–6
Output measurement, 55–57
Outreach, 168–206. See also
    Partnerships
Outsourcing training, 250–51. See
    also Higher education
    partnerships; Partnerships

**P**

Partnerships, 168–206
    business, 44
    competitiveness with, 168–71
    dealers and wholesalers, 174–81
        Busch Learning Center, 178–81
        Harley-Davidson, 175–78
    higher education institutions,
        181–82, 247–48 (See also
        Higher education
        partnerships)
        Megatech Engineering/Central
            Michigan University, 196–97
        T. Eaton Company/Ryerson
            Polytechnic University,
            191–96
        Whirlpool Brandywine Creek
            Performance Center, 187–90
    higher education institutions,
        framework for, 182–205
        accreditation in, 201–5
        consortiums in, 197–201
        criteria for, 184–85
        customized executive education
            in, 186–90

Partnerships *(continued)*
  new accredited degree
    programs in, 190–97
  impetus for, 170
  Motorola University, 35–36
  need for, 168–69
  suppliers, 172–74
  value chain training in, 205–6
Passport to Excellence, 95–96
Pay Per Learn, 225
People Development Strategic Plan,
    124–26
Performance-based learning
    systems, 32–33
Petroleos de Venezuela, S.A., 116–19
Problem solving, 13, 91, 110–12, 240
Process *vs.* place, 33–38
Product convergence, 168
Products and services, 74–75
Psychological contract, new, 9–10

**Q**

Questionnaires, client feedback,
    246–47

**R**

Radio Frequency Training (RFT), 220
Raychem, 124–25
Rensselaer Learning Institute
    consortiums, 199–200
Respects Shareholder Value, 40
Retailer training, at Busch Learning
    Center, 181
Retail management certificates, 193
Retail sector training, in Canada,
    34–35
Return on investment (ROI)
  models of, 53
  Xerox Management Institute,
    161–62
Robert Morris Associates (RMA), 143
Roles and skills, broader, 1–12. *See
    also* Workplace changes
Root Learning Maps, 48

Rover Group Open Learning
    Centres, 49
Ryerson Polytechnic University, 35
Ryerson Polytechnic University/T.
    Eaton Company partnership,
    191–96

**S**

Satellite-based learning, 136–42
  FORDSTAR as, 137–39
  Southern Company College,
    140–42
Saturn Corporation
  Individual Development Plans at,
    242
  learning culture at, 126–28
  orientation program of, 105–6
Saturn University, 250
SBC Center for Learning, 83–84
Schwab University, 210
Scope, 69–71
Sea gull faculty, 50
Sears, restructuring of, 145–46
Sears Total Performance Indicators,
    146–47
Sears University, 146–48, 210
Self-development, compensation
    and, 126–28
Self-funding *vs.*corporate allocation,
    51–53
Self-management, career, 16–19,
    92–93, 122–26, 241
Self-paced learning, 77
Self-service, 211
Senior education officer, 87
Service Delivery University (SDU),
    98–102
Services, 74–75
Six Sigma, 43
Skandia Navigator, 56–57, 249
Skills
  broader, 1–12. *See also* Workplace
    changes
  business, building, 116–19

Skills *(continued)*
  collaboration and communication, 12, 91, 108–10, 240
  leadership, building, 116–19
  learning to learn, 12, 13, 91, 105–8, 240
  linking to business goals, 31–33
  z-shaped, 17–18
Soft technologies, 144
South Central Technical College, 219
Southern California Water Company Employee Development University, 217–18, 250
Southern Company College
  best practice university processes in, 116
  contextual training in, 102–4
  core curriculum of, 39–42
  corporate strategic education focus in, 115
  Electric Utility Game in, 103–4
  Emory University consortium of, 198–99
  global business literacy training in, 114–16
  performance review system in, 40
  satellite-based learning in, 140–42
  stakeholders in, 73
  values training in, 39–40
  vision statement of, 69
Southern Company Television Network, 140
Sprint University of Excellence, 38
Stakeholders, 73–74
Storefront, electronic learning, 151–54
Strategic needs, *vs.* education/development goals, 236–37
Student-centered education, 214–15
Student of the Business program, 102–4

Students
  motivation of, 214
  Motorola University, 213
  non-traditional, 208–11
  working adult, 207–9, 211
Subject Matter Expert, 75
SunU, 27
  funding of, 52–53
  web-based learning at, 151–54
Suppliers
  partnerships with, 172–74
  relationship with, 43
  training of, 243–45
Systems thinker, 86–87
System-wide innovation, 36–37
System-wide training, 42

T

T. Eaton Company, 191. *See also* Eaton School of Retailing
Target University, 210
Teacher-centered education, 214–15
TEAM consortium, 230–31
Technological advancements, 211–12
Technological literacy, 13, 91–92, 112–14, 240
Technology assisted learning, 165–67
Technology-based training, 132–34
Technology build mode, 140–41
Technology strategy, 76–77
Themes, 128–29
The Next Steps, 195
Thinking, creative, 13, 91, 110–12, 240
Top management, 61–65
Tracking learning, 242–43
Training departments, 22–23
Transition, corporation, 3
TVA performance management system, 50
TVA University, 21
  impetus for, 62–63
  instructors in, 50

TVA University (continued)
  manager-as-faculty in, 238
  values training in, 41

**U**

United Healthcare, 184
United Healthcare/Rensselaer
  Learning Institute
  Consortium, 199–200
United Technologies, 200
University of Chicago Hospital
  Academy, 63–64
  corporate citizenship training in,
    93
  measurement systems of, 79–80
  vision statement of, 69
University of Michigan, 187–89,
  248
University of Phoenix/ AT&T School
  of Business partnership, 76
University of Texas at Dallas, 219
University of Warwick, 228–31
University partnerships. See Higher
  education partnerships;
  Partnerships
Upskilling work forces, 128
U.S. Airforce. See Air University

**V**

Value, of learning infrastructure,
  248–49
Value chain training, 42–47, 170–71,
  205–6
Values, corporate, 93–94
Values training
  Southern Company College,
    39–40
  TVA University, 41
Van Kampen American Capital
  University, 77
Verifone University, 156–58
Virtual campuses, 162–65
Virtual classroom, 213–14

Virtual universities, 26, 221–25
  Busch Learning Center, 180–81
  integrated learning and
    performance support at, 165
  mega-universities, 221–22
  Monterey Tech, 224–25
  Open University, 223–24
  Oracle University, 162–65
  Verifone University, 156–58
Vision, 68–69, 93–94
Vision 2000, 64–65
Visioning, 241

**W**

Warwick Manufacturing Group,
  229–31, 248
Warwick University, 248
Web-based learning, 150–62. See also
  Internet and Intranet
  Dell University, 154–56
  Harley-Davidson University,
    244–45
  SunU, 151–54
  Verifone University, 156–58
  Xerox Management Institute,
    158–62
Whirlpool Brandywine Creek
  Performance Centre
  Business Analysis course in, 111
  business school partnerships of,
    187–90
  consortium of, 247–48
  physical facility in, 37–38
Wholesalers
  partnerships with, 174–81
  training of, 178–81
Workers
  better-educated, 4–5
  knowledge, 8
Work force
  building world-class, 233–51
    3 Cs core curriculum in, 238–41
    alliances with higher education
      in, 247–48

Work force (continued)
  education/development goals
    vs. strategic needs in, 236–37
  employee learning vs. earning
    in, 241–42
  leaders as learners and faculty
    in, 237–38
  measuring, tracking, and
    accelerating learning in,
    242–43
  National Semiconductor
    learning philosophy and, 235
  training customer/supply chain
    in, 243–45
  university as branded
    competitive advantage in,
    250–51
  university as organizational
    business line in, 245–47
  value of learning infrastructure
    in, 248–49
  career resilient, 10
Workplace changes, 1–28
  broader roles and skills, 1–12
    corporations as educators in,
      10–12
    flat, flexible organization in, 1–7
    knowledge economy in, 7–9
    knowledge shelf life in, 9
    lifetime employability in, 9–10
  corporate universities annual
    survey, 24–28
    corporate universities as
      business in, 26–28
    learning alliances in, 25–26
    management commitment in,
      24–25

Workplace changes (continued)
    virtual corporate universities in,
      26
    corporate university emergence,
      19
    mission, scope, nature of corporate
      learning, 19–23
  workplace competencies, new,
    12–19
    career self-management in, 16
    collaboration and
      communications skills in,
      12
    creative thinking problem
      solving in, 13
    global business literacy in,
      13–14
    leadership development in, 15
    learning to learn skills in, 12
    technological literacy in, 13
Workplace competencies, 12–19,
    104–26, 236, 240–41. See also
    Competencies, workplace
World-class work force, 233–51. See
    also Work force, building
    world-class

X

Xerox, 3–4
Xerox Management Institute
  laptops in, 166
  web-based learning at, 158–62

Z

Z-shaped skills, 17–18, 90, 92